TAKE THE LEAD

TAKE

— THE —

LEAD

HANGING ON, LETTING GO, AND
CONQUERING LIFE'S HARDEST CLIMBS

SASHA DIGIULIAN

ST. MARTIN'S PRESS
NEW YORK

First published in the United States by St. Martin's Press, an imprint of St. Martin's Publishing Group

www.stmartins.com

The Library of Congress Cataloging-in-Publication Data
is available upon request.

ISBN 978-1-250-28070-1 (hardcover)
ISBN 978-1-250-28071-8 (ebook)

Our books may be purchased in bulk for promotional, educational, or business use. Please contact your local bookseller or the Macmillan Corporate and Premium Sales Department at 1-800-221-7945, extension 5442, or by email at MacmillanSpecialMarkets@macmillan.com.

First Edition: 2023

10   9   8   7   6   5   4   3   2   1

To my family for always supporting me.

And to Mother Nature for her inspiration.
May we protect her for generations to come.

A GLOSSARY FOR CLIMBING

ANCHOR—A point on a climb where the rope is attached to the rock—usually at the top of the route, but it can also be mid-route or at the bottom of the route—to secure the belayer. Anchors may be chains, traditional gear, bolts, or slings.

ASCENDER—A mechanical device allowing a climber to use the rope to move upward or to haul gear. Used in aid climbing, mountaineering rescue, and caving.

BASE—An acronym that stands for four categories of fixed objects from which one can jump: buildings, antennas (radio masts), spans (bridges), and earth (cliffs).

BELAY—A technique used to hold a rope in order to arrest a falling climber. An anchor, as in "I'll set up a belay here." A **BELAYER** is the person who manages the rope so as to catch the climber on the other end in case of a fall or slip.

BIG WALL—An especially high cliff that requires multi-pitch climbing and usually takes days to ascend.

BOLT—Permanent protection drilled into the rock. Most commonly used as sport-climbing protection and for belay and rappel anchors.

BOULDERING—Climbing close to the ground without use of a rope. Can be done on boulders or at the base of a rock face.

CAMALOT (CAM)—A spring-loaded protection device that, when a trigger is pulled, retracts so that it can be inserted into cracks. When the trigger is released, the cams expand and lock into the crack, and can be easily removed.

CARABINER—An aluminum snap link used to connect the rope to the anchor.

CHALK—Magnesium carbonate powder for hands to keep them dry and improve grip.

CRIMPER—A small shallow edge just wide enough for one or two finger joints or one fingertip. Crimpers require strength from finger joints and tendons to leverage. One "crimps" on a crimper.

FREE CLIMB—A climb using only hands and feet on the rock. Rope is used only for safety and is not relied upon for upward progress. Opposite of an "aid climb," which makes use of rope, fixed bolts, pitons, or foot slings to ascend the face. Involving a rope, this type of climbing is typically the "safest" form of climbing, as opposed to free soloing.

FREE SOLO—A climb without a rope, which is usually very high-risk. Unlike bouldering, free soloing goes far above the ground on full-length routes.

HOLD—A rock-like grip attached to a climbing wall for climbers to grab or step on. Indoors, in artificial climbing, this "hold" is plastic. Outdoors, it is a natural break or protrusion on a rock face.

JUG—The easiest hold for climbers to grab, as they are typically deeply incut. Jugs provide room for a full hand.

LEADER—The climber who goes up first, clipping their side of the rope through protection using carabiners or quickdraws, which are two carabiners connected with a short sling, or runner. "Take the lead" is an expression used by the climber going first.

NUT—A metal wedge threaded on a wire and used for protection by wedging it into a crack in the rock.

ONSIGHT—Climbing a route without falling or resting on gear and without prior knowledge of the route or moves. Applies to difficult climbs.

ONSIGHT DIFFICULTY—The test, in a competition, of how far a climber can progress on a wall or on a natural rock climb, with no prior knowledge of the climb.

PINCH—A hold that typically has a loaf-like shape, with two faces to it. Pinches require a tight grip with one's hand muscles, as though squeezing a brick.

PITCH—The length of a climb that can be protected by one rope length. Multi-pitch climbs are found on cliffs taller than one rope length. A single-pitch route requires only one rope length.

PITON—An iron spike (aka "pin") that comes in various sizes and shapes and that can be hammered into cracks and clipped for protection. Now seldom used because of the damage to rocks.

POCKET—An opening on a rock that may be shallow or deep and range in size in the number of fingers it can accommodate—from one finger (mono) up to four fingers.

PORTALEDGE—A collapsible, hanging cot anchored to one main bolt for sleeping on cliff faces.

PROTECTION or "PRO"—Any equipment placed in the rock to catch a climber's fall.

QUICKDRAW—A piece of equipment that allows the climbing rope to run freely through bolt anchors or other protection while one is leading.

RACK—The collection of gear on a climb, usually composed of ropes, protection, quickdraws, carabiners, and other equipment for getting up and back down.

RAPPEL—To descend a height by lowering oneself on a fixed rope, with feet against the wall. Friction is placed on the rope, usually with a belay device, to keep the descent slow and controlled.

ROUTE—The path up a specific climb.

SEND—Climbing a route without falling or resting on gear. The term is synonymous with doing something to the utmost level of completion. "Sending it" also means being present, trying hard, and living fully.

SLOPER—A typically rounded hold without any edge to grip on to. Instead, a climber must use the friction of their skin to gain leverage.

SPORT CLIMBING—Climbing using pre-placed protection such as bolts or a top rope. Frequently involves difficult gymnastic moves.

TRADITIONAL or "TRAD" CLIMBING—Rock climbing using protection placed by the lead climber and removed by the second.

TAKE THE LEAD

PROLOGUE

From a distance, the sheer limestone wall rising into the clouds looks to be a smooth, gray monolith. Only up close are the cracks and bulges visible, as are the pockets, only wide enough for one finger, and the small steel bolts on which to attach my rope. Up here on the fourteenth pitch of this climb, a thousand feet from the ground, I feel completely alone. A hundred feet below me, my belayer hangs from an anchor, holding the end of the rope. My last piece of gear is twenty feet behind me. It runs through the center loop of my harness, neatly tied off in a figure-eight knot. At nine millimeters in diameter, it is not much thicker than a couple shoelaces tied together. Hard to believe it can withstand the tug of 2,646 pounds of force—but it can.

The coarse sandpaper rock has shaved my fingertips bloody. The pain is like a thousand tiny needles, but I welcome it—it reaffirms my grip, my connection to the wall. My toes burn— squeezed into the climbing shoes I wear a size too small so they can connect on the tiniest cracks and divots. Keeping my core tight, I maneuver my hips ever so slightly to the left in order to position my center of gravity above my left toe, which is balanced on a pebble-sized protrusion. I lift up my right foot, aiming toward a tiny edge the size of a quarter, and catch it with my big toe. I adjust my weight back over my right foot. It's as if my hands and toes are Velcroed to the wall, if only for a couple moments, while I scan the surface above, looking where to reach.

Reading the rock is second nature to me. I can spot a path between holds the size of peanuts, recognize which shadows suggest a crack in an otherwise smooth surface, and visualize my next moves. The wind whistles through my ponytail and cools my bare shoulders. I dip my left hand into the bag of chalky powder hanging from my waist, behind my back, in order to dry my sweaty palm. I shake off the excess. I'm ready to grab my next hold . . . a jump away.

I take a quick breath, and tell myself, *Go!* I pivot onto my right foot while launching off my left. I swing into my right hip, push off with my fingertips, and lunge upward, "seeing" myself grab the hold. In that same instant, I realize I've miscalculated. My hand brushes the rock and in less than a millisecond the wall recedes as my body falls backward into midair.

Gravity yanks me down—twenty feet, past where I clipped onto, and then another twenty feet until the rope cinches tightly, catching me in my harness. I swing from the mountain like a pendulum, my fall abruptly broken. I can feel my blood pumping through my forearms and into my hands. Droplets escape from my raw fingertips and seep through my cuticles. It feels sticky. I feel defeated, but I shout down to my belayer, "Good catch! I'm okay. I undershot it!"

She yells back, "So close!"

I steady myself in space, a thousand feet above the valley floor. *If I had just held on a little bit longer with my left hand . . . If I had eyed the hold with more accuracy . . . If, if . . .*

I shift in my harness and grab the rope in front of me. I

kick my feet up into the air and thrust my hips forward to get back onto the wall. I return to the place I fell from to fine-tune the sequence and better understand what I did wrong. Then I lower back down to the start of that pitch—the fourteenth out of twenty-eight pitches. I allow myself a twenty-minute rest. There's nothing I can do but try again, but my consolation prize is knowing now where that next little hold is hiding. I will not miss it.

Next time will be the send: I won't fall.

1

At the top of the climbing wall, forty feet off the ground, I looked down in time to join in singing "Happy Birthday to You!" to my brother, Charlie. I may have been only three-foot-six, but at that moment there was no one in the world taller than I was, and no one happier.

Mom had decided to throw Charlie's eighth birthday party at a climbing gym—though, back in 1999, those places were few and far between. Mostly they were converted warehouses on the outskirts of cities that could only be found with a GPS, but Sportrock, one of the first climbing gyms in the country, had recently opened its second gym in my hometown of Alexandria, Virginia. Neither Charlie, nor I, nor anyone else we knew, was a rock climber. Mom simply thought it would be an adventure. Charlie invited his entire hockey team and school friends—all boys—and me, the kid sister, younger by fourteen months, and just shy of my seventh birthday.

My mom has told me that I was climbing before I could crawl, and that once I could stand, all bets were off as to what I'd try to scale. She said I couldn't have been more than three or four by the time I was shimmying up every doorframe in the house, gripping the molding with my toes and fingertips, my arms barely long enough to reach both sides. I'd scale the exposed bricks on the back of our house, dangle off high branches and banisters, and swing upside down on monkey bars until I felt as if my head would explode. Climbing felt instinctive, in the same way that other athletes seem instinctively to know how to swing a tennis racket or palm a basketball the first time they try.

Stepping into Sportrock that first time was like stepping into a different climate. The air was still and warm and smelled of sweaty feet. I was transfixed by the huge gray wall spanning the length of the gym and covered with oddly shaped, multicolored knobs—the holds. It was like nothing I'd ever seen.

The instructors fitted us with harnesses, gave us chalk bags to hook around our waists, and then herded us to the beginner wall. At twenty-five feet high, it was smaller than the more advanced walls on the other sides of the gym, but to me it was towering. Charlie and his friends must have thought so, too, because for the first time since they'd arrived, they seemed almost subdued. Instead of the usual jockeying to be first in line, they all kind of shuffled together, with no one pushing to go first. *Are they nervous about climbing? How can they not see how exciting this is?* Even Charlie looked hesitant.

Charlie was the best athlete I knew—fastest runner in his class, a most valuable player in soccer and hockey. I always wanted to prove that I was as good an athlete as he was—especially to my dad, who went to all of Charlie's meets and games—so I turned everything into a competition. If Charlie was running, I had to run faster. A bike ride was like the Tour de France and I was the underdog. A walk to the bus stop became an Olympic sprint. I had to try and beat Charlie to the kitchen table for dinner and to the best seat on the living room sofa, the one directly in front of the TV. Charlie never felt the need to start the competition, but he also never let me beat him.

Climbing the wall seemed like something I could do—*why not?* It didn't occur to me that I couldn't. I just had to wait my turn. Charlie and one of his buddies were the first to be hooked onto the climbing lines—the ropes that allow a climber to safely scale the wall and be securely lowered to the ground after a fall.

And it didn't take long for them to do just that—fall. Two at a time, the boys easily grabbed onto their first couple holds and placed their feet. The problems started when they tried to pull themselves up to the next holds. Strength alone wasn't going to cut it. They wound up scrambling to find a foothold halfway through, or, lacking flexibility, failing to swing a leg high enough to reach the next grip.

When it was finally my turn, my small hands fit easily into the holds, while right away my feet found support. Knowing where to grab and push felt almost like second nature. Because I was flexible, I could reach my legs higher than the boys and pull my body up and over my hands to reach my next handhold, like a spider climbing a wall—smooth and swift. Climbing wasn't just about being strong; it was about using body and mind together to choreograph a dance on the wall.

Before I knew it, I was ringing the cowbell at the top. I pushed off and swung in the air, looking down for the first time. I'd been so focused on climbing that I hadn't realized that the farther I went, the farther away the floor became. I was the highest I'd ever climbed in my life. I felt as if I were floating, weightless, unafraid, and far away from everyone and completely on my own. Nothing had ever felt so exhilarating.

Over the next couple hours, we all tried the different routes up the beginner wall. When it was time for cake and ice cream, all I wanted to do was to keep climbing, so one of the instructors offered to belay me on the bigger wall. It was slanted so high over the floor I had to tilt my head all the way back to see the top. While Charlie and his friends turned in their harnesses and chalk bags, I tied into the top rope—the rope that passed through the anchor at the top of the climb and down to the belayer. I grabbed onto the first two holds and continued upward—each hold feeling like a little reward on the way. At the top, some forty feet off the ground, I looked down in time to yell "Look up, Charlie!" before being lowered to the ground.

My entire body was humming. I couldn't stop smiling. Charlie came over to me, a look of surprise over his face. I thought for sure he was going to say he had to try one more time so that he could show me that he couldn't be beat. Instead, he threw his hand in the air for a high five. "That was so cool, Punky!" he gushed. Charlie's nickname for me since I was three—pink for my favorite color, and monkey, because I was always climbing.

The instructor told my mom I was "a natural" and suggested I join the gym's junior team for beginner rock climbers. "Yes!" I yelled. "Mom, please, can I?"

I was already figure skating competitively—attending practice mornings before school. During the 1998 Winter Games, Mom and I were glued to the figure skating events, and I began to dream of being an Olympic skater. I loved the feeling of gliding across the ice, in control of my every move, but I hated falling on that cold, hard surface, and I grew bored of practicing the same moves over and over to the same beat of the same song. Competing was the best part—wearing bright, sparkly, beaded skating outfits and having Mom style my hair came a close second.

Sports meant a lot to my parents. My dad had played high school football, and he carried on his sturdy build the belly of a player twenty-five years removed from a gym, but he never lost his love of the game. He was a rabid armchair athlete and spent any free time he could watching sports—traditional sports, the kind he understood, the kind he grew up on: football, tennis, soccer, and ice hockey, his favorite. I'd be hard-pressed to imagine my dad as the athlete he once was, because I only knew him as a businessman—a workaholic at that—always in neat khaki trousers and a pressed shirt. He owned a rock and marble quarry, a marina, and boats, and his big dream was to build a development of town houses around that marina.

Mom had been on her high school track, volleyball, and gymnastics teams—though her trim, petite stature belied how many years had passed since then. Even after a successful career as a documentary producer, she was still proud of her time as a high school athlete and especially loved the sense of discipline and camaraderie it fostered. She and my dad believed that participating in sports was an important part of learning how to work hard, set goals, and commit to something one hundred percent, though neither of them were sure I needed one more activity on my plate.

When Mom realized how determined I was to climb, she convinced my dad to let me join the "team," which turned out to be just a ragtag group of kids climbing for the fun of it. No one ever mentioned competition. I had no idea there even was such a thing in climbing, but when Mom and I showed up at the gym a few months later, it was teeming with kids and closed for just that reason. Mom stopped a woman in a blue "JCCA Climbing" shirt who explained that it was the Capital Region Championships. I asked if I could compete.

I rented shoes, an extra-extra small harness, and a chalk bag, and joined a circle of kids doing warm-ups. I mirrored their moves as they stretched their arms out in front of themselves, opening and closing their hands like wizards working spells. At the rules meeting, we learned how each climber would compete on the three respective routes—the routes differing in difficulty based on the quality of the holds, the steepness of the wall, and the power and endurance required to reach the top *without falling.* My group's routes were marked with pink tape labeled "FU11"—Females Under Eleven.

In the U.S., climbs are graded on the Yosemite Decimal System (YDS), which was devised by the Sierra Club of Southern California in the 1950s. The number to the left of the decimal point refers to the class of terrain—1 and 2 refers to hiking and running trails, class 3 includes moderate climbing or "scrambling" (hiking steep terrain with the use of hands), class 4 is extreme scrambling, while class 5 generally requires climbing gear (protection). The second part of the number, from 2 to 15, refers to the difficulty of the moves and holds. The higher the number, the more difficult the climb. From 5.10 on, the ratings are then further subdivided by a, b, c, and d. A 5.13a would be much easier than a 5.13d. (To make it even more confusing, the French grading scale, used in most countries outside of the U.S., is based on a scale of 1 to 9, with letter grades a, a+, b, b+, c, and c+.)

The hardest climb I'd "sent"—climbed without falling—so far in practice was a 5.10. My category's climbs were two 5.10s and a 5.11, and I had one chance on each of them. I was psyched to try a new route. A newly taped climb was a whole new puzzle to solve. It also meant clean, brand-new holds instead of the usual ones, which were greasy and chalk-caked from weeks of climbers. Mom handed me a pink Vitamin Water to match my pink nail polish, pink shirt, and pink pigtail ties. "Good luck, Punky Pie."

Together, the other competitors and I were given an observation period, our one opportunity to look at the wall before climbing. The preview time gave us a chance to try to figure out the route—where we might place our hands and feet. We could even talk about the route among ourselves. Then we were led into our isolation area—a taped-off area with no view of our wall. The isolation area maintained fairness. No climber would have the advantage of watching the climber before her and benefiting from her mistakes or success.

I made it to the top of the first two climbs without any trouble, but the third was harder. The person who had "set" the route—the "route-setter"—had placed the holds much closer together than he would have for an adult, so to keep the route challenging, he made it more technically difficult. That meant making the holds smaller and sloping them down rather than inward, so that the climbers would have a tougher time curling their fingers into the space between the hold and the wall. A less solid grasp meant relying more on technique.

For me, technique would come to mean finding the way to balance my body weight between my hips and my foot placements while keeping my core engaged. It would mean finding a balance of motion and stillness at once, the ability to move upward, taking advantage of momentum while keeping my muscles taut and controlled, yet springy enough to move dynamically and efficiently. Pushing off with my feet, moving my hands to grasp the next hold, and then coming back to a taut, balanced position had to take less than three seconds to keep moving at a steady pace.

It would be a few years before I would truly appreciate the importance of technique, but at that time, on that wall, it felt as if my body already had an innate understanding. I had also already discovered that my flexibility came in handy. I swung my legs up high and made it to the top—the only one to do it without falling. I was aware of pushing off my feet and raising my hips while my hands let go of their holds—being suspended in the air for a moment before catching the next one.

I won my first medal at that JCCA competition, and with it, entered a whole new world: climbing not as a hobby, but as a *sport,* one that I totally loved and could excel at. I wanted to keep competing. I didn't know it, but the owner of Sportrock watched me climb that day. A week before the next local competition, he approached Mom and me. "There's an opening on our competitive team. The coach is new. He's a pro—Claudiu Vidulescu," he said.

Claudiu had been a champion international climber and head organizer for Romanian national competitions before his immigration to the States. He couldn't have been more than five-eight or -nine. With his short hair and angular features, and biceps bulging under a short-sleeved shirt that looked ironed onto his body, he looked more like a wrestler than one of the skinny climbers I was used to seeing at the gym.

Not surprisingly, his style of coaching turned out to be a lot like his appearance—tough and no-nonsense—which probably had something to do with his early climbing days in Communist Romania, where, as a kid, he would cut blocks from wood he'd scavenged and nail them to a tree to use as holds. He would wrap paper around the soles of his one pair of shoes and pretend they were climbing shoes. Despite his hardscrabble beginnings—or maybe because of them—he'd become one of his country's foremost rock climbers. "Rock climbing is a big deal in Europe. They have *national* teams," he told us.

At seven, I was the youngest and smallest member of the team. The others—Andrea Szekely and her brother Gabor, Paul and John Wallace, Zach Lerner, Tory Guido, and Eli and Isaac Levin—ranged in age from eight to thirteen. Climbing was our focus. All the other stuff that seemed to matter at school, like wearing the right clothes, saying the right things, and having the same interests as other kids, didn't matter at practice. At practice, my teammates and I shared one objective—to climb as well as we could. The fact that they were all older and more skilled than me only gave me the incentive to work hard and improve.

It's funny to look back and realize that I never worried about failing at that young age, because I failed all the time in comparison to them. I credit my parents with creating an environment for me to see struggle not as a barrier, but rather as a speed bump, a temporary obstacle. As the smallest kid on the team, I may have struggled to keep up with my teammates, but that only motivated me to figure out my own style of climbing.

My team became my family and my first heroes, especially Andrea and Gabor, who were a few years older. Their mom, Eva, had been a gymnast on the Hungarian team at the 1976 Olympics. She knew what it took to be a world champion, which may have explained why her kids were as driven and disciplined as they were. She also knew what I'd need to do to hold my own against the best of the best, the European climbers. She told my mom, "If Sasha wants to compete at the World Championship level, you must learn how to belay her."

There's no way to overstate the importance of good belayers—they're crucial to a climber's success. Good belayers anticipate the movement of their climber in order to understand the pace of feeding rope to her as she moves up the wall. If they give too little rope, they can hold back a climber; giving too much rope will make a fall that much longer and potentially more dangerous. Belayers hold their climber's safety in their hands.

I think understanding that safety issue was enough to spur my mom to take a belay authentication course—that and the fact that she enjoyed hanging out at my practice. After passing the test, she began the thousands of hours she would spend at the end of my rope in dark, drafty warehouses, often for two-plus hours a night, holding a rope and craning her neck to watch my every move. With her as belayer, I could spend every minute of practice climbing myself into a perfect exhaustion, because I never had to wait my turn to have someone belay me.

Mom was a five-foot-two firecracker, never afraid to speak her mind, especially where her kids were concerned—she would still be the one to call if I ever needed to get rid of a dead body. Nothing fazed her. She could talk Charlie and me through any dilemma on our adolescent plates: "Okay, what happened?"; "What can we do about that?"; "Why do you think you said what you did?" She had a cool confidence, as if she had everything under control, down to her personal style—nothing fancy, just neat and pulled together, a blazer and blouse tucked into trousers and a chunky necklace, even at the gym. She never cared what other people thought of her, even when she heard that other parents had dubbed her "Gucci Mom," only because she didn't feel the need to look the part of a gym rat or "yoga mom."

Seeing her at the bottom of my rope gave me a huge sense of safety and support. But although it brought us closer than we'd ever been, at times it did make her a target for my frustration: *You're not giving me enough rope! You gave me way too much. Weren't you paying attention?*

Usually, Mom was quietly understanding, but when she'd had enough, she let me know it: *If you don't like my belaying, find another belayer.* She'd walk away and I'd run after her and apologize—and during the next climbs I'd be extra appreciative. It was too easy to blame it on my mom's belaying if I wasn't climbing well. Fortunately, she knew that and wouldn't stand for it. If I was in a bad mood during practice, she would simply quit, which kept my attitude—and my ego—in check. And while I might have sassed her from time to time, I knew I could trust her, too.

During practice, Eva belayed Andrea and Gabor by our side. On the ground we urged each other on, but on the wall it was all business—no talking, and no complaining, just an implicitly shared goal. Climb, climb, and then climb better. During breaks, Eva would practice backward somersaults to a handstand. She had competed against Nadia Comăneci—the first gymnast ever to be awarded a perfect score at the Olympic Games—and she told us stories of how Nadia's coach would lock Nadia in the bathroom so that she couldn't snack between practicing her routines. *No snacks?* That was like a horror story to me. Second to climbing, snacks were my favorite thing about practice. (It never even occurred to me that the point of the story was how stressful and unpleasant Nadia's training may have been. I couldn't have imagined.)

Together, Andrea, Gabor, Paul, John, Zach, Tory, Eli, Isaac, and I were what Claudiu referred to as his dream team. Still, whatever we did, however well we climbed, we could always do better as far as he was concerned. During practice he'd walk around with a wooden stick and bark, "Why are you talking? Quiet, or I'll beat you! Shaddup and climb!" His motto: "Look at the rock, climb the rock, no bullshit!"

It didn't take us long to learn that Claudiu's "bark" was all show, but that didn't stop us from pushing harder. We lived to impress him, which wasn't easy, but when we did, he would flash one of his rare approving smiles, and we knew we'd earned it. Under his watchful eye, we trained three times a week—readying ourselves for competition against Junior National-level climbers all over the country.

Despite his gruffness, we knew he was proud of us. When it came time to decide on a slogan for our team's T-shirts, Mom jokingly suggested, SHUT UP AND CLIMB! Claudiu loved it, but the parents thought it might be better to keep it an "inside" joke, so the slogan was printed in Romanian.

We trained and traveled together as a team, but competed individually. A first place might be worth a hundred points, a second place ninety, et cetera. A "team" win was based on the total of each climber's results. Our climbers were winning, so our team was also winning. Within two years, I moved on from Regionals to Divisionals, and, finally, to Nationals—the stepping stone to competing at an international level. Making one of the top four individual spots at Youth Nationals would mean making the U.S. National Team, which I was dying to do—in part because they had very cool backpacks, jackets, and swag.

The qualifiers and semifinals at the 2001 Youth Nationals were the toughest climbs I'd competed in. It was my first time at such a high level of competition, against competitors from all over the country, but I tied for first with two other girls going into the finals. The three of us had reached top of the qualifying climbs, so we had the same number of points. The other girls had fallen off at different points (each hold up the wall was associated with a numerical point value), so they were ranked behind us.

After "reading the finals"—looking at the wall and deciding: *Where are the holds? What body position do I take? Where do I rest?*—I felt confident in what my sequences would be. I had an idea of which holds to grab and how best to position my body to set up for each move, although I knew it would be hard to know exactly what each hold would feel like until I'd grabbed it. I'd need to get into a flow without being overconfident, because the more flow a climber has, the greater the chance of over- or underestimating how good the hold is. Either way could mean a fall.

Despite my confidence, I was nervous. That climb felt like my everything, my ultimate moment. I was there to stake my claim as a legitimate climber. *Everyone cares about my performance—* and of course no one did except me. I was halfway through when I placed my foot on a hold without shifting my weight over it enough, so when I moved to the next handhold, my foot slipped. *No! No-no-no. What happened? How could I have done that, especially when I have so much more effort left in me, especially after I trained so hard?*

I ended up in tenth place. For the entire two-hour drive home, I cried in the backseat of the car as I replayed the slipup over and over in my head. Making the U.S. National Team had been my goal (the first of many that would take *at least* one attempt), and I'd blown it. I would have to wait a whole year before redeeming myself—what felt like a lifetime. I had no clue that falling (and failing) was one of the biggest parts of climbing. At nine, it seemed like the end of the world, but it was only the end of the season.

With time and distance, any mistake starts to feel manageable, so at some point I stopped reliving what I'd done wrong and started thinking about what I would do differently next time. School had ended for the year, which meant summertime at my parents' vacation home in Mont-Tremblant, Canada. By the time Mom and Charlie and I arrived (Dad would join us on weekends), my slipup felt as far away as Virginia.

My mother grew up in Canada, and her mother—my "Baba"— her sisters, and my cousins still lived there, so they spent school breaks with us in Mont-Tremblant. Our house was a magical place, a retreat and playground in one, nestled in a lush mountain forest, surrounded by lakes and trails. I could run wild in the woods, hike and swim and white-water raft on a river by our house with Charlie and my cousin Sadie, with little supervision.

One morning Mom had a surprise for me. "You said you

wanted to climb outdoors," she said. "So, there's someone we're going to meet." We drove to Val-David, a popular rock-climbing area forty minutes from our house, where we met François, a twenty-something guide certified in climbing by the town's mountain school. I liked him right away. He had a big, goofy smile and reddish-blond dreads peeking out from under a white turban.

We set out on a short hike through Val-David's lush old-growth forest to our first climbs. Boulders and tall vertical cliffs flanked our trail, some covered in thick moss, others cleared as a result of climber traffic, dotted with faint chalk marks. It wasn't my first time climbing outdoors—I'd been on outdoor climbing and camping trips with Claudiu and the team back in New River Gorge and Franklin in West Virginia—but Val-David was a chance to experience climbing one-on-one like a real pro. It was like being in a vast playground that I could explore without anyone else's agenda, and with my own guide and belayer.

The first two climbs we went to were a 5.11 and a 5.12. Both times I looked at the walls and envisioned my moves. Without too much trouble, I "sent" both—climbed from start to finish without falling—with François belaying me. He was genuinely impressed and completely surprised that I had handled both climbs so easily. He also seemed relieved that he hadn't been hired merely as a babysitter for a kid whose mom was trying to satisfy a whim. Now we were climbing *partners*. He asked if I wanted to try something more challenging. *For sure!*

We hiked a bit farther to a gleaming, blue-tinted wall with a slight overhang. Val-David is known for its awesome granite walls—ancient slabs that are beautiful shades of light blue, gray, green, and gold, but tended to tear hands and fingers like no other rock. This wall had mostly pockets up the face—in this case, ones that fit only two or three fingers. I squinted at it from top to bottom and then announced that I would climb up the sixty-foot middle route known as "Opium."

I tied onto the rope and François belayed me as I gave the route a few tries, but it was so much harder than I'd expected. I was just starting to realize the precision required in a tough climb. If my foot was even a centimeter off the strongest placing on a hold, I could slip. If I had my index finger instead of my middle finger aligned in a hold when I was trying to move off it, that could make a difference as well. The harder the climb, the more precise I needed to be in my every move.

I'd climb about twenty feet and then lose my footing and fall. Then I'd climb another ten to a different point on the wall, working out the sequences and finding all the little pockets and protrusions I'd need for my holds. I could manage most of the moves once I figured them out—usually after falling—so I couldn't imagine why I wouldn't succeed if I kept trying. I made progress, but I didn't make it to the top.

I went home with raw, shaved hands and fingers and begged Mom to let me climb with François the next day. That night I lay awake in bed, rubbing salve on my hands, thinking about the climb. I hadn't yet encountered a wall so difficult that it required more than two or three attempts. I thought about the feeling of the rock under my fingertips—coarse and sandy in some places, like the sharp bristles of a wire brush in others. I envisioned the sections of rock that had given me trouble and imagined where I'd place my hands next time and where I'd move my feet so that I'd be in position for the next move. I "saw" where I'd need to just trust my feet and will them to stay on the wall, and where to have faith in my fingertips.

The next day we hiked out to the same route. I warmed up before trying it again . . . and again and again, scraping open the blisters on my fingers until, finally, I sent it—my first 5.13a. I felt so happy I thought I would burst. I yelled down to François to lower me slowly so that I could hang on to that feeling of being suspended over the rock, over the forest. There was so much more mental and physical energy required in making my way up a wall outdoors, which made being lowered that much more delightful. I had earned that delight, earned my snacks and my rest, earned the feeling of putting my beleaguered feet into a pair of fluffy socks. I'd accomplished what I'd only *imagined,* and it made me feel as if anything was possible.

COMPETITIONS TOOK UP a lot of my weekends for the next few years. Mom drove me up and down the East Coast for local youth competitions, Regionals and Divisionals, which meant that she was usually the only member of my family to watch me compete. When I wasn't competing or training, Dad would take the family out on a boat—usually one that had been left as collateral for an unpaid slip at his marina. We'd water-ski, tube, or stop at crab shacks on the Chesapeake Bay, but by sixth grade I had less time for that. My sole focus had become climbing, and after two years of steady competitions, I was on a winning streak. All I wanted to do was keep up my momentum. And I wanted my dad to see me climb, but he seldom had time, blaming his busy work schedule.

Dad did, however, always find the time to watch Charlie's hockey practices and games. He'd watch quietly, but I could tell he was scrutinizing Charlie's every move. Afterward, he and Charlie would talk hockey the whole way home—Dad offering his analysis of everything that went right or wrong, and pointing out what he thought were bad calls by the referee. I craved that kind of bond, too, that attentiveness to what I was trying to do. I wanted more than "Good job" when I won, or "Oh, well" when I didn't. I wanted Dad to make the effort to understand, if not fall in love with, climbing, the way my mom had. It was as if I was in a serious relationship with someone my dad didn't have any interest in getting to know.

Even when Dad came to pick me up from practice, he never came early enough to watch me climb. My gym was only a fifteen-minute drive from our house, so sometimes I'd call him early, hoping he'd arrive in time to see me climb, but when he showed up, he'd ask why I wasn't ready to go. I don't think he related to climbing as a sport, because it wasn't like the sports he loved watching. Or maybe he had the same old skewed notion about rock climbers (left over from earlier decades, perhaps) as a lot of people, that they were hippies and dirtbags who lived vagabond lifestyles in vans around Yosemite Park—a notion I felt was uniquely American, since alpinists and climbers had been revered in Europe for decades. Either way, I felt as if he didn't care.

Dad was of a generation that understood success in terms of mainstream recognition and financial wealth. He liked to reference the renowned female athletes he watched on TV. If I wanted to grow a successful career, why not emulate them? *That* was the avenue to success for a female athlete. That was the way to make a living. He pointed to stars like Maria Sharapova, Venus Williams, and Anna Kournikova, telling me, "Sasha, maybe you should play tennis," or "Why don't you try tennis if you want to make a living as an athlete?"

Maybe that was part of my drive to be a success at climbing— to prove to Dad that I could not only make it to the top of the sport, but that I could make a living at it. I believed that if he saw my success, he'd be convinced. So, when I was invited to compete in the 2004 Junior Continental Championships in

Mexico City—after earning my coveted spot on the U.S. National Team—and Dad decided to come along, I was thrilled. I tried to explain the scoring system: *You have six minutes max on the wall and one chance to make it to the top without falling. You get a point per hold . . . the holds are what you climb on . . . the higher up you get the more points. "Control" is having your hand on a hold for more than three seconds, if you fall after control, you get a +, so maybe your score will be 32+ instead of just 32 because you secured the hold before falling. . . .*

He seemed impatient with it all, because it was confusing, and usually when something was confusing to him he'd declare it was a waste of time. But at least he was coming, because Mexico City wasn't just *any* indoor competition. It would be my first international appearance, and if I won, it could be the beginning of competing in other countries. If I won, Dad would see for himself how good I was at my sport and how much it meant to me.

The night before, as was our tradition before a competition, Mom braided my wet hair so I'd wake up with it all curly and frizzy. Then she put it in big, bushy pigtails I called my "fuzzy pigs." I imagined those fuzzy pigs as my superpower source. *I have my superpower. I'm ready. I got this.* On the wall, I thought of nothing except the climb in front of me, just as I had on "Opium." *Hands, hold, lift, pull, repeat.* I was the only one in my twelve-to-thirteen age category to complete all the climbs. I'd done my best. That's all I knew.

When I found out I'd won, I could barely keep from screaming for joy, and nor could my team. Cool, collected Claudiu even managed a nodding smile. As the judge placed the winning medal over my head I thought: *This is what it must feel like to be the star player on a team. I am the star player, not just some kid who likes to climb.* I'd not only won my first Continental

Championship, but my dad had seen me win. When I saw him after getting off the wall, he wrapped me in a bear hug. "You blew them away. No one stood a chance." He was beaming. *Now he would understand, because he understood winning.* His daughter was a champion. There could be nothing confusing about that.

After Mexico, a rep from a climbing shoe company called Mad Rock reached out to say that the company wanted to support me. *Support me?* That meant I was getting my first sponsor as an athlete. Only my climbing heroes and pro athletes had sponsors—pros like Maria Sharapova. I thought that by having a sponsor I could prove to Dad that climbing could be a career. I was twelve when I negotiated with the Mad Rock rep—without any help from my parents. The deal was that I would wear their shoes and they would give me a thousand dollars for coming in first and five hundred for placing on the podium.

A thousand dollars. That was a lot of money. Not only would Dad understand that I was a legit rock climber, he'd see that I could be in charge of my own business, just like him. I could be my own boss and contribute to my expenses. After signing with Mad Rock, I told my entire family, "I'm a professional climber now." I was so deadly serious that no one laughed. No one questioned me, and no one doubted me, but of course, as a professional female climber in the real world, that wouldn't always be the case.

2

"Earth, Wind & Fire," "American Pie," "No Tranquility," "Cadillac Thrills," and "Bumboy"—those were only some of the names of the truck-sized sandstone boulders in the Triple Crown, an outdoor climbing competition that took place in Alabama, North Carolina, and Tennessee.

Mom and I drove down to Boone, North Carolina, on Friday so we'd be close to the competition when it opened the following day. We knew that outdoor bouldering would be an entirely different thing than indoor sport-climbing competition, but the Triple Crown was unlike any climbing event we'd ever been to—more like a giant festival than a competition, with live bands, food and beer vendors, sponsor tents, and games for climbers and spectators alike. It seemed as if anyone and everyone who loved climbing was there, from amateurs to pros, from kids to "ancient hard persons" (referring to the thirty-five-and-older category) and "stone masters" (those forty-five and older). Participants and spectators alike had flown in or road-tripped from across the country and greeted each other like old friends.

Early Saturday morning, we pulled my "crash pad"—a portable foam mattress—out of the car and more dragged than carried it to the boulder field. I was nine years old and barely four-foot-six, so it felt twice my size. Still, I insisted on carrying it, because I wanted to look the part of a serious climber. I wanted to give the impression I knew what I was doing—even though it was my first bouldering competition.

In bouldering, climbers wait around the base of a boulder for what's called a "session"—kind of like when skateboarders wait around a bowl to take turns dropping in. Usually about fifteen feet high, boulders are the shortest climbs and don't require ropes. Instead, climbers place their crash pads on the ground to break their falls. The objective: Climb as many boulders as possible in a day—roughly from 8 A.M. until 4 P.M.—with the ten hardest climbs adding up to one's score.

The boulder "problem" refers to the route a climber takes. Reaching the top can take ten to twenty seconds or as little as five. The biggest difference, though, between sport climbing and bouldering is that in sport climbing, easier terrain separates the "cruxes"—the most difficult and dangerous sections of a route—but in bouldering, the entirety of the climb feels like the crux. There's no reprieve—it's powerlifting versus a cardio workout. To finish, a climber "tops out"—climbs over the top of the boulder and scrambles down the easiest side.

Mom and I figured we'd keep a low profile and try not to look like the newbies we were, but as soon as we arrived, not only did the other climbers make a point of welcoming us, they helped us haul my crash pad. They shared "beta"—the information on a climb, down to the moves and holds—and then gave me encouragement as I climbed. Mom was floored. "Wow, Sasha, there's so much camaraderie here. They're competitors, but they're cheering each other on. Definitely not like figure skating." *Definitely not*, I thought.

I felt as if I'd been accepted into a cool community of people who loved climbing as much as I did. In particular, they seemed almost fanatical in their love of outdoor climbing, as if it was the only kind of climbing that mattered. As much as I loved indoor competition, I could understand their way of thinking. Outdoors, climbing felt so much more freeing. With no set routes, people with different body types could climb in different ways. For me, that meant taking advantage of my flexible joints, very nearly dislocating my hips to hike my foot up high enough to make up for my shortened reach.

As usual for a competition, I was decked out in my pink gear and fuzzy pigs. Nearby, a film crew was watching some of the climbs while on break from shooting a movie. A few of them came over with their recording equipment and interviewed me in the boulder field. They asked my name and where I was from, so I told them.

"Well, Sasha," one of them said, "what are you going to do here today?"

"Today? All I want to do is climb real hard and win one thousand bucks!"

Everyone cracked up. Once they'd stopped laughing, one of the guys said to my mom, "We're gonna have to keep that clip on a loop. Something to play when we're feeling tired or irritable." (The next year, I would return to win the junior competition, but it wouldn't be more exciting than that first time.)

The Triple Crown clinched my decision to keep climbing outdoors, even after the official competition season was over. I loved the competition circuit, but even more than that, I loved the lifestyle. I wanted to spend all my free time—after school, on weekends, and during summer breaks—on a wall. Devoting that kind of time and energy to climbing meant quitting all my other sports and making climbing my number one priority.

It also meant missing out on birthday parties and hangouts

with classmates. I didn't mind, though, because I was more excited to be with my climbing community than with my friends at school. No one at school climbed. No one understood what climbing was, and there was no social media providing pictures and videos. My friends had posters of Justin Timberlake or Britney Spears on their bedroom walls. I had Lynn Hill making the first-*ever* free ascent of "The Nose" on El Capitan, with her famous quip at the summit: "It goes, boys"—meaning she could do whatever the dudes of climbing could do.

Soon, I was climbing two to three hours at least four to five times a week, and competing most weekends. But despite my continued wins, Dad rarely made it to my competitions and seldom asked about practice, though he did tell Mom that he thought bouldering was dangerous—*No rope!* She countered that it wasn't any more dangerous than ice hockey and football. I imagine that Dad never directly told me his concerns about my climbing because he knew I could be more stubborn and single-minded than he was. I was in fourth grade the last time he said to me, "I'm the dad and I make the rules," to which I responded, "Well, I'm Sasha and I make my own rules."

I know that Dad got a genuine kick out of hearing I'd won a competition, but he was way more interested in watching his favorite sports on TV or taking in one of Charlie's ice hockey games than spending an afternoon sitting through a climbing competition. He loved ice hockey more than any other sport and understood everything about it. He showed up for all Charlie's games at home and away, standing behind the opposing team's net, scrutinizing Charlie's every move.

Afterward, he would pick apart Charlie's game. *Why'd you pass? You had a clean way out. And why didn't that idiot pass to you? He should have passed to you. You could have made the play.*

I wanted Dad to stop bugging Charlie about his game, but I also wanted to yell: *Why is hockey so much more important than climbing?* Dad imagined Charlie pursuing an ice hockey career, but he'd never heard of anyone making a living climbing.

It was true that most climbers—even the most expert and accomplished, even some of the legendary ones—didn't make a living climbing. And with the exception of a small, elite group of women climbers, like my idol, Lynn Hill, and women like Beth Rodden and Katie Brown, "names" in climbing were muscular, twenty-something *guys*. But despite all that, it never occurred to me that I *couldn't* make a career out of climbing.

Mom must have felt the same way, because she never hesitated to take me to a competition, no matter the distance. She genuinely seemed to love climbing as much as I did—loved watching it and talking about it with me—and she understood the time and commitment needed to succeed.

We'd both been looking forward to the Chelsea Piers Climbing Cup in New York City. Chelsea Piers had one of the best walls in the city, if not the state, so at the crack of dawn on a Saturday, we drove the four hours into Manhattan. The junior events took up the morning, but Mom and I stuck around for hours into the evening to watch the highlight of the Cup and the real reason I wanted to go to this particular competition: pro climbers from all over the nation competing in the women's and men's Open. I'd hoped to soak up any moves I could by watching from a distance. Instead, I wound up meeting the person who would spend the next couple years teaching me how to reach the next level in climbing.

Vadim Vinokur was a successful international competitor from Ukraine. Right off the bat, he stood out from the competition—his climbing was stealthy and exacting. He attacked every climb with a steady pace, confident of his plan.

I knew at twelve that that was the way I wanted to climb—understanding every maneuver before I made it, not wasting any energy on extraneous moves. I went up to him after his win to congratulate him.

As we were leaving, Mom noticed a poster on the wall advertising private lessons with Vadim. She called as soon as we got home and told him that I wanted to advance my climbing career—Claudiu had moved to Atlanta to head a program there—and that I needed someone to help me do that.

"The little blond girl?" he asked.

A week later, early on a Saturday morning, Mom and I began our new routine. Every other weekend we'd travel to New York City and stay in a hotel overnight so that I could train all day with Vadim. Sunday night we'd head back home. During the week, I continued to train with my team.

Unlike Claudiu, Vadim expected me to talk through every move so that I understood exactly why I did each one. He'd say, "Look at the climb and decide your full plan, and then tell me. Where is the crux—the most difficult section? Where are you going to clip on the wall? Are there any rests? Talk to me about your pace through each section." I felt a little like a secret agent in a spy movie, discussing the details of an important mission over and over to drill it into my brain.

He taught me to climb fast but efficiently through the hard sections on a wall, and slower through the easier sections. "Slow is smooth, precise. If you go faster through the hard parts, you won't have to stay too long on the difficult holds. You need a plan A *and* a B and C going into a climb, so that if plan A doesn't work, you can quickly switch it out." He said that I had to compete in Europe if I wanted to be an international competitor. "Sasha is much better than the American competition," he told my mom. "She is ready to compete against the European climbers."

A few months later, as we prepared for an upcoming competition, he told me that the week before he competed, he would diet and lose three to five pounds. Losing weight made him climb better, he said. Back at school, I told a friend that I might need to go on a diet. I wasn't sure what a diet was, but in my mind it made me sound like a legit climber.

In hindsight, I'm fairly certain that Vadim—or any other coach at that time—had no idea of the possible repercussions of telling an adolescent girl that it was a good thing to lose weight. That was just his approach, born out of experience and practicality. It was common for many elite athletes to "lean out"—lose a few pounds—before a performance. Unfortunately, all I understood from his advice was that lighter meant better, so I thought, *Why not be light all the time?* Little did I know that that mindset would plague me for years.

I was quickly picking up momentum—winning competitions, becoming the girl to beat in my age category—when I was invited to an international stage: the Serre Chevalier Junior Invitational, to be held the following summer in the South of France. By then Claudiu had become one of the U.S. National Team coaches, and he and Vadim thought that it would be a great opportunity for me to learn the international field. It was a "must" for climbers in the top ranks from all over the world. It would also be my first overseas competition, my first time competing against people outside of North America, and my first event outside of USA Climbing.

Mom was determined to make it happen even though my dad didn't think it was worth it. Unlike government-sponsored teams in other countries, if USA Climbing team members wanted to compete internationally, they had to pay their own travel and hotel costs. Along with entry and registration fees, the money added up.

"You would support this if it were hockey," Mom told Dad when he argued against it. "Charlie went to the Czech Republic for a hockey tournament. This is just as big a deal for Sasha."

"Charlie was with a team," he said, as if it were safer to go with a team than with your mom. "Besides, it sounds completely disorganized. How do you even know where you're going?"

"We'll figure it out," Mom said, dryly. After all, she had traveled the world for work before marrying Dad.

Despite my enthusiasm, it took days if not weeks to wear him down, but Mom's stubbornness easily matched my dad's . . . and mine. In the end, as was typical, Mom won out.

We received an event schedule and a packet of information in the mail, and were otherwise left to our own devices in reaching Serre Chevalier. Mom and I dragged four bags weighing as much as the two of us—mostly my climbing gear—from planes to trains, up staircases to more trains, stopping to unfold maps and timetables. Toward evening we finally made it to a small hotel—walking distance to the artificial outdoor climbing wall in the town square—but it was too late and we were too exhausted to take in much else.

With a whole day before the start of competition, my mom and I went out for a nearby hike. The area was dense with wooded mountains, trails, and ski slopes—popular year-round for skiing, hiking, and biking—so we decided on a gentle trail beside a stream. We breathed in the lavender that washed over the mountain from nearby fields and mixed with the cool, mineral smell of fresh mountain water. Midway up, we stopped to fill our water bottles. I was suspicious of drinking the water, but Mom assured me that it would be like drinking Evian.

Afterward, we wandered through the village, down pristine streets lined with flowers, quaint restaurants, creperies, fresh apricot stands, and boulangeries on nearly every corner—all of which created the most irresistible smells imaginable. Next to the Invitational itself, I would remember the amazing meals Mom and I had, with the exception of the rabbit she tricked me into trying by telling me that "lapin," the dinner special, was chicken. But when I said it had a strange taste, she admitted it was rabbit and that she didn't think I'd have tried it if I knew. *Exactly right!*

The Serre Chevalier Invitational drew spectators and climbers from across Europe. My qualifier routes were graded 5.12 or so, not unlike the grades I'd competed on, but the climbs felt different. Unlike the indoor gym walls at home, Serre Chevalier took place on an artificial outdoor wall, so the spectators—a big, boisterous, international crowd—spilled throughout the town instead of being confined to an indoor venue.

The wall itself was more "featured" than the flat walls in U.S. competitions—meaning that some of the holds were attached to big prism- and rectangular-shaped chunks of wood or fiberglass that created a three-dimensional climbing surface. In U.S. competitions the routes were confined to existing walls, but the Serre Chevalier wall was specifically built for this particular competition, with an overhang so steep that I was nearly upside down on my climb. Back home, competition was straightforward—hands leading, followed by legs. At Serre Chevalier, as at most competitions in Europe, there were steeper wall angles and more intricate sequences that required me to swing my feet up above my head and hang from the tips of my toes while suspended upside down.

The difference was like going from sprinting to hurdling. Still, instead of being nervous, I was psyched to represent the U.S. and discover this whole new world of competition-style climbing.

I reached the top on all my qualifier routes, the only girl

to do so without falling. As I stood readying myself for the final round, "Born in the U.S.A." started cranking over the loudspeakers, and I could hear the crowd roar. I was floored, because I was sure that being a foreigner competing against European favorites would work against me. Instead, I felt embraced by the crowd and stoked not to let them down. It was as if I were buoyed to the top and into first place. I found myself surrounded after the climb by a group of young French fans all talking at once and waving their programs for me to autograph. That had never happened before. I was flattered and a little overwhelmed by their enthusiasm for me—and more so for *climbing*.

Little by little, climbing was gaining popularity in the States, but the top levels of competition remained in Europe, with its deep history of the sport of rock climbing, born out of more than two hundred years of mountaineering. The general consensus was that the bar for climbing was higher there, and that Europeans trained harder than Americans and climbed more difficult routes. European teams also had greater incentive to compete on the World Cup stage, given that many of them were supported on a federal level. Teams like those from France and Austria traveled with entire entourages—coaches, physical therapists, and a person whose sole job was to attend the technical meeting the night before the competition, where officials reviewed the rules, such as when a climber had to arrive at isolation, when the qualification rounds started, and the running order.

Not surprisingly, U.S. representation was pretty minimal at international competitions, and when U.S. climbers did show up, they didn't do well because they weren't consistent in competing at international events. With few exceptions, Team USA was basically Mom and me. Mom would joke how she was my therapist, cheerleader, and designated note taker all in one, but it was disheartening how little support climbers from the U.S. received in comparison to their European counterparts.

BY THIRTEEN I was riding pretty high in my little climbing bubble, feeling very adult. I'd been written up in several magazines, and I was winning a thousand dollars here and a thousand there, with my sponsors matching my prize money. I had my own bank account and I'd made it to my first Junior World Championships—in Imst, Austria.

Imst was the exception to the general lack of U.S. participation in Europe. The Junior World Championships was the one international event a year that the USA Climbing organization supported with coaches and staff. As the next level up from Nationals—where the top four climbers qualified to compete in the World Championships—it was the biggest youth climbing event of the year. Imst was what our team had been training for, our most important competition to date. We were determined to show the world that the U.S. could hold its own on an international stage.

Going into the semifinals I ranked in the top eight, so it was looking good that I would move on to finals. In reading the route, I decided there were two possible directions to follow, so I chose the one to the right and planned my sequence. Halfway through the climb, I realized the route actually wrapped around to the left, but I was too spent at that point to backtrack. By the time I realized I'd misread the sequence, I couldn't down-climb my way out of it. I wouldn't even make finals.

I was angry with myself. I'd failed because I miscalculated, which was worse than running out of steam. I'd disappointed my coach and, more important, my mom, who had pooled all her resources to get us to Imst. She believed in me. I wanted to be the best. I wanted to win, not only for my team and me, but because Mom deserved a medal for all her hard work. She was nearly as competitive as I was, even though she always appeared very chill. Mom never hid her joy in my successes, but she also never tried to hide her disappointment when I didn't win. When I'd fail, I'd think that Mom felt all her sacrifices of time and energy hadn't been worth it, but that was never the case. I know now that she was disappointed for me because she knew I could do better, and because she knew, more than anyone, how determined I was to succeed.

I called my dad. He gave me his usual reaction when I didn't win: "Oh, well." That was that. *Oh, well.* Not positive, not negative, not reassuring—more like, "Shit happens," which I interpreted as "Too bad you blew it. I would have loved you to have 'won' or done better, because I made a big financial commitment to get you there."

When I called him after winning an event, he was always excited, but whenever I lost, our conversation was short and awkward, as though he'd lost interest. What he *was* interested in was whether I did well in school. He wanted me to have fun doing something I loved as long as it didn't distract me from my education, which would ultimately lead to an impressive, lucrative career and a successful life. As far as he was concerned, climbing wasn't one of the cornerstones of that success.

Dad still viewed the climbing community as a bunch of deadbeats. To him, they all looked scrappy and unkempt, which translated into "unmotivated." He had it in his head that "those people"—meaning my climber friends—would somehow lead me down some rabbit hole of dereliction. The more I climbed, the more he and I butted heads.

Over dinner one night, when Mom and I were talking about

the plans of one of the kids on my team, Dad asked, "Is he going to college?" I said that I didn't think so. "Oh, he's just going to be a do-nothing," he said, clearly annoyed. "Seems like those people don't even go to college."

When I brought up a friend who was at college, Dad said to my mom, "That one's going to be a bad influence on her."

"What do you mean?" Mom said. "She's at CU in Boulder."

"That's not a real college," he grumbled.

"All the best rock climbers live there, so that's where I want to go," I insisted.

"Over my dead body," he said. *End of discussion.*

I knew I was sending up a red flag, but it was my way of combating Dad's narrow view of my climbing friends. His unwillingness to see the climbing community through my eyes was beyond frustrating. There was no way I'd admit that I had secretly set my sights on a college that was in line with what he wanted for me. No way did I want him to think I was choosing a school just to please him. I was doing it for me—shades of *I make my own rules*—but it was ironic that my climbing would lead me to a choice we could agree with.

Meanwhile, Vadim had stepped up my weekend training, and I couldn't have been more stoked. That meant longer sessions, core workouts, hang boarding (hanging my full body weight by only my fingers), and running in order to increase my endurance on harder climbs. It was exhausting, but the more exhausted I felt after practice, the happier I was, although I was never too tired to walk around Manhattan at the end of the day—that was like plugging into a live source of energy.

One day Mom and I walked all the way uptown and around the campus of Columbia University. I was awestruck by the place—the diversity of the students rushing by, the intensity of the people talking in groups. *I could see myself here,* I thought.

Why not? I'd been traveling all over the world, meeting new people, enjoying the cuisines of different regions, soaking up the energy of walking big-city streets. For those reasons, I fell in love with New York City. I could live in the city, attend school, train at Chelsea Piers, and continue to compete. I let the idea percolate, but I didn't mention it to anyone—not yet. I didn't want to jinx it. I'd keep up my grades and keep climbing, and steer clear of arguing with Dad over my climbing.

Famous last words.

3

"You're not going to mess around in Spain with a bunch of hooligans," Dad told me once I'd pleaded my case. "You're only sixteen."

My teammates Andrea and Gabor had plans to climb in Spain over winter break with our friend Jakob Schubert—a talented climber who would go on to win bronze at the 2020 Olympics—and they wanted me to join them. An opportunity to go abroad for two weeks with experienced climbers—my friends, people like me who were coming into their own as pro climbers—was not something I could miss. Aside from having heard so much about the incredible next-level rock in Spain, I was dying to assert my independence and prove to my parents how serious my intentions were to become a pro. I was at an important juncture in my career. After a summer of outdoor climbing, all I could think of was getting back to it.

"Dad, we'll be climbing," I said. "What do you think I'll be doing?"

"I don't know, but you're not going. There won't be any *adults*," he said.

"Why can't you respect that I'm trying to get better at what

I do?" I argued. "You let Charlie play hockey anywhere around the world, no question. This is what *I* do." It was the closest I could get to saying: "If I were a guy, you'd let me go."

Of course, Dad was worried about my safety—granted, that was his role as a parent—but we were sport climbing, where a climber is attached to a rope that's clipped into permanent anchors that are fixed into the rock for climber protection, and we were taking all possible precautions. Mom assured him that I'd be in good hands. "Sasha travels with Andrea and Gabor all the time. They're focused and responsible and they've always looked after her. They'll just be climbing." Once again, I tried to explain to Dad how free climbing was the safest form of climbing, safer than bouldering—safer, I reasoned, than football or *hockey.*

"Why do you have to leave on Christmas?" he asked. I said that airfare was much cheaper that day, and that I'd have Christmas Eve with the family.

Looking back, I can see Dad's real fear was that he had little control over me. Since I could remember I'd felt that rules were to be broken—and, deep down, I sensed my dad was kind of proud of that. He wanted me to follow my dream, even if he couldn't relate to it. I give my parents a lot of credit for allowing me the liberty and the space to figure out my own path, but I also think they did that because they were a little afraid of how I might have revolted if they'd tried to keep me from my pursuits.

After several weeks, Dad finally decided to pay my airfare as a Christmas present—I wouldn't find out until years later that he hadn't had the money for my ticket, so he'd used his frequent-flier points. That only made me wonder how different our relationship might have been if he'd told me the truth.

On Christmas Day, Andrea, Gabor, Jakob, and a friend of theirs, Magnus Midtbø, a pro climber from Norway, picked me up at the airport in Spain. I was so stoked just to be riding in the car with everyone. There I was—just having traveled alone, a serious climber, in Europe, with my friends. Even our room at the hostel—a spare, simple space lined with bunk beds and zero privacy—was new and exciting. My only embarrassment would be how much I'd overpacked (an issue still, after so many years), considering how beautiful and mild the weather was.

The five of us split our time between Santa Linya and Margalef—rock-climbing paradises with hundreds of bolted single-pitch routes to choose from. Both areas were renowned for their limestone walls, the kind of rock I'd never before climbed but that would become my favorite rock to tackle. The beauty of the limestone in Spain lay in its incredible features—protrusions, pockets, cracks, bouldery routes, overhangs, and tufas. I had never even heard of, let alone climbed, tufas—porous spires formed thousands of years ago from calcium-rich underwater hot springs. They looked like things one might see on a prehistoric landscape. At Margalef we climbed over one hundred feet out of a cave, up steep, pocketed, gold-and-black walls.

We could have climbed twenty-four hours straight every day of the week and never repeated a route. It was all new and exciting, and it was easy to take for granted how strong and skilled we were. Strangely enough, when a friend asked me what climbing felt like, I didn't know how to describe the feeling in terms that were understandable . . . until years later. *It's like hiking with skis for hours, sweaty and out of breath, in order to reach the top of a mountain after newly fallen snow. But the burn in your muscles is all worth it for that magical feeling of a perfect run on fresh, untouched powder, with the sun overhead, the wind vibrating against your jacket and the fresh air filling your lungs.* That is what I wished I'd told my friend.

Andrea, Gabor, Jakob, and I were considered emerging talent in the world of rock climbing, but Magnus was already an established pro—he was the one to watch. His focus was laser-sharp and his climbing was so graceful and fluid that he made every move look easy, almost like magic. At twenty, he was the oldest and most accomplished among us. He'd won the World Youth Championship and, at thirteen, had "onsighted" his first 5.13b—successfully climbed a route without falling on a first try and without having seen the route before. He didn't talk much, but he clearly had an inner confidence, as if he didn't need to shine the spotlight on himself or his expertise. Even though he'd been killing it in international competitions, he seemed way more motivated by his love of climbing than by winning. He was about six inches taller than me, thin, muscular, and blond, with hazel eyes, a dry sense of humor, and a laugh reserved only for the things he thought were genuinely funny. He also smelled really nice. I kept finding ways to get just a little closer to him in the hopes of cracking through his cool exterior.

I felt completely comfortable around Magnus, probably in part because I'd spent so long feeling awkward around the boys my age at school—my first kiss didn't even happen until a friend's "hot tub" party in eighth grade. When some of my friends started dating in junior high, I was off the hook because I didn't have *time* to date. Because I was traveling and competing internationally, my classmates assumed that I had some kind of jet-setter social life that included dating and partying in exotic places, but nothing could have been further from the truth.

By high school I'd realized how much of a bubble my classmates were in—consumed with popularity and who was dating whom and what basement house party to crash. I felt like an outsider in that world, but in the world of rock climbing, I felt on the same wavelength with other climbers, including

Magnus. I wanted to be near him, to win him over, but I couldn't tell what he was thinking. *Did he think of me as just the kid along for the ride? Did he think I was cute? Did he want to get to know me as well?*

One night at the hostel, halfway through the trip, Magnus and I were lying on the floor at "lights out"—I don't even remember why. *Had someone co-opted my bed before I could get to it?* Our heads touched, and I could sense that my hand was close enough to his arm for me to extend my fingers and faintly brush his skin. I thought: *Is he asleep? Is it my imagination or did he just move a little closer?* We both leaned in for that first kiss. I wanted to pinch myself. *Did that just happen? Is he going to wake up tomorrow and pretend it didn't?* Our relationship had shifted, though our only outward change was to sit next to each other at dinner and to secretly kiss each other good night.

By the end of the trip, we were making plans to be together again. Since I'd be competing in the U.S. Adult Open in Salt Lake City, Utah, he'd compete there as well in order to see me— because he's Norwegian, he wouldn't otherwise have participated in an American national championship. Afterward, he would come back to Alexandria with me.

Magnus drove me to the airport in Spain and I fought the urge to cry nearly the entire ride—except for when I was distracted by a flat tire, miles from the airport. We were in the middle of nowhere and there wasn't a crowbar in the car. Magnus didn't even blink, didn't get upset or angry for a moment. Very matter-of-factly he used his bare hands to loosen and then tighten the screws. That was the story I chose to describe Magnus to Dad, because I thought it would impress him more than anything else—and I was right.

Mom came with me to the Nationals. The weekend gave her a chance not only to get to know Magnus but to see what a talented climber he was. She and I watched as he took first place, and the two of them hung out together and cheered me on when I did the same. Mom liked Magnus immediately. (To this day, she still laughs when she remembers how he referred to the tracksuits worn by American men as barbecue suits, because when he watched American TV shows growing up, men at barbecues always wore polyester tracksuits).

Back home, Mom prepped my dad for Magnus's visit. "I have a good feeling about him," she said. "He's soft-spoken, polite . . . a total gentleman." Dad asked what he did for *work*. "He's a professional climber." Mom and I waited for the blowback, but there wasn't any. I was nervous because Magnus would be staying at our house—a kind of trial by fire for him—but I needn't have worried. Dad and Magnus wound up bonding over their love of ice hockey and a good, medium-rare steak, which was my dad's favorite meal to cook over the barbecue (without the tracksuit).

That summer Magnus and I traveled together to all the World Cups throughout Europe. In between competitions we climbed outdoors in Rodellar, Spain, a miles-long gorge of massive, overhanging orange limestone walls alongside a winding river. It was an eye-opening experience, not only for the spectacular climbing—hundreds of long, steep, bolted routes—but also because we kept running into the same thirty-something couple from Russia, a husband-and-wife team also training outdoors and competing in the World Cup circuit.

In the U.S., climbing a hard 5.13 or an easy 5.14 was considered an incredible feat, especially for a woman. At that point, far fewer American than European women had climbed 5.14, and only Josune Bereziartu, a Basque climber, had climbed a 5.14d (a 9a, according to the French grading system). In 2005, Beth Rodden climbed "The Optimist" at Smith Rock, Oregon, becoming the first American woman to climb a 5.14b. She went on to climb a 5.14c in 2008, the hardest ever climbed by an American woman. But that Russian couple at Rodellar was challenging themselves on *seven or eight* routes a day of hard 5.13s and 5.14s, just as a matter of course. Their climbing was way above the level of expectation in the U.S. I felt inspired by them. I wanted to be as strong as that woman. I'd never even attempted a 5.14. *Five-fourteen* was some mystical number reserved for super-hard-core climbers—the best of the best—and I couldn't possibly be there yet. But watching that Russian woman made me realize that I was being stymied by a number. I had to change my thinking from *I can't do that climb* to *Why don't I try that climb?*

Magnus helped me tackle that kind of "high-end" climbing for the first time—climbs with a difficulty of hard 5.13s and 5.14s. I started to refine my climbing *style*—the way I moved my body through each sequence on the wall. Crimpers—small holds that can only accommodate fingertips—became my favorite type of hold, probably because of the size of my hands and the strength I had built up in my fingers. My finger strength made it easier for me to grasp a crimper than it was for someone bigger, who might not be able to pull up their entire body weight on fingertips alone. My fingers became my superpower.

Every day in Rodellar for a month, we ate breakfast, packed our bags with our equipment—shoes, harness, draws, rope, chalk bag, snacks, belay device, fleece, and jacket—and headed out to climb. I climbed several mid-level and hard 5.13s before trying a 5.14 for the first time. I was nervous, but Magnus reassured me, "This really isn't much harder than anything you've already done." Once he said that, I realized that tackling a 5.14 would be more like breaking through my own mental barrier. I had to tell myself that it wasn't some otherworldly, impossible climb just because of its grade. Once I did that, I found myself steadily progressing through the moves.

I discovered that I not only had the kind of stamina that helped me on longer, more demanding climbs, climbs where big, muscled guys might get "pumped"—get swollen, painful muscles from lactic acid buildup—but that I also had a high threshold for pain. Some rocks were so abrasive that they would rip up my fingers, but that same abrasiveness provided more traction. When my fingertips turned raw and bloody, I would breathe in, shift my weight, and jam my hands into my chalk bag to blot the bleeding.

There was something exhilarating about the feel of a wall shaving my fingertips, something in the pain that felt like an assurance of my connection to the wall. I found myself tapping into a newfound "flow" state—a feeling of all my senses being completely in tune with what I was doing, my thoughts only of the moves in front of me, with every part of my body twisting effortlessly, as though moving through a well-rehearsed yoga routine. Finally, I felt confident in all of my sequences. I knew I could string them together in one single push from the bottom to the top. Breaking through the barrier of my first 5.14 opened the door to a new chapter. *What was next? How hard could I climb?*

My relationship with Magnus had grown stronger after our being together 24/7 for nearly three months. Since he could live and train anywhere in the world, he decided to base himself in Alexandria. He rented an apartment right around the corner from my house. Every morning at 6 o'clock he'd pick me up in the little Porsche convertible he'd bought so we could hit the gym together before he drove me to school. After the exhilaration of the summer, school seemed like interference. I'd zip through my day—keeping up my grades, doing homework at lunch—with one goal in mind: to climb some more and be with Magnus. After school he'd pick me up and we'd return to the gym. At 7 P.M. we'd head back to my house for dinner with my family.

Magnus had an ease around my parents, and they seemed happy to have him there. He'd talk to my dad about his work and compliment my mom on dinner. While I did more homework, he'd work on his business—coordinating his schedule with his sponsors, responding to media and marketing requests, planning his training program. Dad could see how driven and disciplined Magnus was, and how we were working toward the same goals. We weren't partying or experimenting with drugs, or doing most of the things that kids my age were doing—except maybe having sex, which I naively thought my parents had no clue about. Magnus was my climbing partner, my best friend, and my safe haven.

As we traveled around Europe the following summer, Magnus taught me how to take on a *long-term project*—attempt the type of climb that required a commitment, a week or two of breaking down sequences, figuring out moves, and then testing them. Magnus was always trying those kinds of climbs. "You should try a climb that's really going to challenge you," he told me, "a project that you have to try throughout this trip, something that's harder than you've done before."

In Rodellar, Spain, Magnus chose a 5.15b to work on, so I thought it would be cool to try a 5.14b, a climb called "Welcome to Tijuana." Those were our "projects." I'd belay Magnus in the morning, and then we'd go to my climb in the afternoon and he would belay me, or vice versa. In between, we'd do other climbs together that we could onsight—read and execute in one shot—as competition practice, but Welcome to Tijuana was the climb that crept under my skin most of the summer. It was relatively short compared with the other climbs at Rodellar—about twenty-eight hand moves from start to finish—beginning in a limestone cave nestled above a turquoise river that ran along the valley floor. There was a crux sequence at the beginning and one at the end, but because it was a condensed, powerful climb, no part of it was easy.

From the ground, the wall looked blank—devoid of an obvious route—but on closer inspection I found little protrusions in the rock that I studied each day, searching where to place my body. The holds were small—a good fit for my fingers—but steep, spanning wider than my outstretched arms, so the momentum had to come from my hips in order to power my legs and propel me upward. I'd need to execute each sequence precisely, which meant trusting my feet while pulling hard with my arms and keeping my breathing steady—all without letting fatigue take over.

It took everything in me to keep my body from sagging away from the wall and letting gravity win, starting at the steep angle out from the cave. I needed to rely on the friction of my shoes and the tendons in my fingertips, while tightening the muscles at my core. On my first try, I couldn't do all the moves, but I understood what it would take to do them—to squeeze my fingertips harder into the rock, keep my hips tighter to the wall, press my feet more firmly into the slick limestone, and then try harder. For two weeks, I practiced the same routine: warm up on an easier climb, tie in to the rope on Tijuana—lacing it through my harness loops and cinching a perfect figure-eight knot—then pull my skintight rubber climbing shoes over my calloused toes.

On day fourteen I was ready. I knew the moves. I'd not only rehearsed them over and over, teaching my body the dance of staying on the wall, but I'd also visualized them dozens of times on the ground, committing them to memory like the lyrics of a song. Before pulling on to the wall I took three deep breaths. *I've got this. I know this wall. I can do it.* My mind went still and my muscle memory took over. *Right hand, adjust left foot, left hand side pull, right foot adjusts up to 4 o'clock position, drop the knee, reach with the right hand a little higher, adjust position, squeeze my abdominal muscles to keep my core straight, lift left hand to match the right.* I found myself in the flow state I'd discovered the previous summer. At the top of the wall, I clipped the chains to the last bolt. *Oh, my God! It happened!* I became one of a small handful of women to have accomplished a 5.14b.

AT THE END of the summer the college conversations with my dad took a new turn. He now expected me to attend an Ivy League school. It didn't matter that neither he nor my mom had gone to an Ivy; Dad had simply decided that the Ivy League represented the epitome of success. He insisted it would be a waste of time to consider any other type of school. He promised that if I were accepted into an Ivy, he'd pay for it entirely. Well then, I intended to go for my dream school, Columbia University. I reasoned: *Maybe he'll finally be impressed if I go to an Ivy League school, and we'll stop butting heads.*

Instead, the more independence I gained, the more strained our relationship became. We'd slip into yelling matches over the smallest things. When he heard me drive up to the house, he'd watch me through the kitchen window, not trusting me to park the car without dinging it. When I told him I thought he was judging me, he'd wave me off. I'd explode and he would do the same. After a cooldown, he'd remind me about the cookie dough ice cream in the fridge, and I'd offer up that I aced my math test. That was as deep a resolution as we reached. We could never sit down and discuss why we were constantly triggering each other.

It's only now I realize how impatient I was to be an adult, and how impatient that made me with Dad. For his part, Dad couldn't see that I wasn't a little girl anymore; or maybe that's exactly what he saw—that I wasn't his little girl anymore—and he didn't want to let go. Either way, we weren't able to resolve our communications issues. It's only now, after years of therapy, that I realize we never apologized in my house. We just moved on, without uncovering the real, underlying problems—without any analysis. It was the complete opposite of my approach to climbing.

Everything about climbing involved total analysis and understanding. To climb is to focus precisely in the moment, to solve the immediate problem, to avoid mistakes. Climbing made sense, more so than anything else in my life. All I wanted to do was climb, as hard as possible, and the harder I climbed the harder I wanted to climb.

I couldn't eat enough to keep up with the energy I was burning, so I started losing weight, something I didn't notice until online forums started drawing parallels between my "looking skinny" and the fact that I was climbing well—a parallel I'd never heard drawn about male climbers. I was becoming more successful in competition, but I hadn't made the correlation between my weight and my success. I thought I was winning because I'd been singularly focused, and because I'd been working on it most of my life. *Why should I doubt that now?* I wish I'd had the wherewithal to ignore all the online trolling. Instead, I felt defensive: *Shouldn't I be skinny? Isn't that the way I'm supposed to be if I'm going to be successful?*

My role models were an elite group of female climbers, and

the most successful of them were rail-thin. They didn't resemble any of the "normal" adults in my life. There was no question in my mind: *That's the way pro climbers look. Lighter means stronger.* I became obsessed with restricting my food intake and keeping my weight down. I'd always been petite as a child, gangly and lean, and I wanted to stay that way. I didn't hit puberty until my junior year, so I felt a little blindsided by the changes in my body, in my waist and hips and thighs. I didn't want boobs—they'd only get in the way. I couldn't afford any "womanly curves." I wanted to keep my prepubescent body—there was a power in it, in feeling light.

One day, Mom received a call from school. One of the teachers had flagged my weight loss: Was everything okay at home? With me? "Sasha's fine," I heard my mom say, clearly taken aback. "She's an athlete. This is part of her sport." My doctor didn't see anything wrong with my weight either. He pronounced me healthy, *because I was an athlete,* even though I was down to ninety-four pounds. "You look great," Mom assured me. After all, I was climbing well, so didn't it stand to reason that a successful athlete was also a healthy athlete?

My eating wasn't exactly wrong, but it wasn't right—the official term was "disordered." My preoccupation with my diet went hand in hand with an obsession over my training and performance. Food became simply fuel, not something to enjoy at a meal with my boyfriend or my family. If I didn't have a good climbing practice, I felt like a failure, so I'd tell myself that I didn't deserve to have a fun, delicious dinner. I was tired and "hangry" all the time, and my libido all but disappeared. I only wanted to be the best, to the exclusion of having fun, any kind of fun, with anyone. Anything outside of school and my regimented training was disruptive.

I became moody and emotional, as critical of Magnus as I

was of myself. It's only in hindsight I realize my mood swings could easily have been part of my whole hormonal shift, though I wouldn't have listened if someone had told me that at the time. It wasn't surprising that my relationship with Magnus began to suffer. I don't know how he remained as patient for as long as he did. I can only suppose he imagined I'd eventually revert back to the cheerful, fun-loving girl he'd fallen in love with nearly three years earlier.

I managed to snap back to my old self when I received early acceptance to Columbia—despite my guidance counselor's warning that the university would be a "reach" for me. I felt energized and relieved that I'd been accepted to the one school I'd applied to, as if I'd sent an excruciatingly long, hard climb. I'd always had it in my mind to defer school for a year so that I could concentrate on climbing in a way I'd never had time to, so Magnus and I decided to travel the world for a year, competing and climbing.

I was determined to push to the next level in outdoor sport climbing, which was fast becoming the arena where I felt happiest. Outdoors, climbing was an immersive experience—the air, the elements, and the feel of unique surfaces. Limestone was different from granite, which was different from sandstone. At its roots, climbing was an outdoor sport, and to climb outdoors meant to climb a surface that was millions of years old. There was nothing like it.

4

I was twelve when Dad had shown up at our house in a purple forty-foot RV (think: Robin Williams in the movie *RV*)—I'd only later find out it was an impulse purchase he'd made without Mom's knowledge. Dad announced that we were all going camping at the Red River Gorge, in Kentucky (unlike in the movie, we made it safely to the campground after getting stuck in only one tunnel). That trip stood out for many reasons, but mostly for the climbing—the type that would mark a major turning point in my career.

Red River Gorge, Kentucky—"The Red," as it's known—is home to endless caves and cliffs of sandstone walls for everyone from beginners to the most hard-core climbers. But for someone like me, who had always been short, the amazing thing about The Red was how "featured" the rock was—the walls are lined with endless little pockets to put hands and feet in. There was a limitless potential of achievement no matter how short climbers were or how short their reach. I'd been stoked when Magnus wanted to head there on spring break of my senior year in high school. It would be my first visit back since that RV trip.

Magnus had set his sights on a climb called "Southern Smoke," a famously steep, ninety-foot 5.14c with small pockets that required both power and endurance. As I belayed Magnus on the route, I decided to try it as well. No female climber had ever been successful at sending it.

Because climbing is a grade-oriented sport, the numbers themselves can be intimidating. Before even seeing a wall, a climber may think—or be told—that the climb is impossible because of the number. I think this has been especially true for female climbers. When few or no women have succeeded on a particular climb or grade, it can be difficult for a woman to "see" herself as the one to break through. I know this because I felt the same way in the beginning of my career. It's hard to imagine doing something that is so next-level, because *why me?* The better question is: *Why* not *me?* The switch in that kind of thinking is hard to flip, but once it happens it can open up a myriad of possibilities.

To flip that switch is to realize that although men may have a certain biological advantage of greater muscle mass and sheer strength, women can often accomplish the same feats on a wall through strength combined with technique and endurance. Sure, Southern Smoke's 5.14c grade was, at the time, intimidating, but was it really out of my league only because a woman hadn't sent it before me? I didn't have long, powerful arms, but I had technique. I was skillful in positioning my body and feet. What I lacked in arm strength and hand size, I made up for in endurance and super-powered finger strength. Instead of my height being a disadvantage, it helped me be more compact on steeper angles—I had less "body" to pull up the wall.

When I first tried climbing Southern Smoke, I expected there to be a move that felt impossible. *There* should *be,* I told myself, *especially on this level of climbing, the kind I've never even tried.* I continued to think that as I climbed bolt-to-bolt, trying each sequence, so I was completely surprised to reach the top after feeling each section: *That's it? Well, I can do this.* I continued to try Southern Smoke over the next couple days. By my fifth time climbing, I knew the moves.

On my sixth try, they all came together and I knew what to do. I knew where to climb fast and efficiently and where to slow down, where to rest, where to shake out my arms and bring my heart rate back down to a resting state. I could appreciate the gritty sandstone shredding my fingertips as my connection to the wall. When my forearms tired, I pushed hard into my foot to disperse some of my weight, although there were moments when I thought I'd never be able to straighten my fingers or forearms fully again. It was like driving through a blinding snowstorm—there were lots of those during our winters in Mont-Tremblant—gripping the steering wheel for hours as though my life depended on it, then finally stopping, only to feel as if my hands and forearms were frozen in place.

I'm not pumped, I told myself. *Come on, Sasha. Pull. Ignore the fatigue.* Twisting and turning on the steep sandstone, I reached the top and "red-pointed" Southern Smoke, meaning that after practicing it, I completed it without falling, becoming the first woman to do so.

After a rest day I moved on to nearby "Omaha Beach," which I knew could be my first 5.14a onsight—I'd never watched anyone climb it. Because it was so featured, the biggest issue wouldn't be finding something to hold on to. Instead, it would be having enough power in my hands to keep me on such a steep wall. The difficulty was being able to actually close my hands—my muscles would cramp and shut down from all the lactic acid buildup. Before doing any moves, I reminded myself that there wasn't going to be a move I couldn't do. I'd just climbed a 5.14c. This was a 130-foot 5.14a. I only needed not to tire, and in order to do that I had to manage my pump, rest where I could, and climb efficiently. I needed to commit to each sequence, even if it wasn't the "right" way to get through a particular portion of the wall—simply commit, to my feet and hands, and to staying levelheaded.

I finally felt ready, but I was still nervous right before "pulling on to the wall"—the moment when my fingers grip the rock and my feet leave the ground. As I pulled on, I thought the same thing I thought before every competition: *Whether I make it to the top or not, this is my one shot. A slip will cost me the victory. Stay confident and present.* After climbing over a hundred feet at an inverted 45-degree angle, I reached for a hold that immediately felt small and wrong, as if it couldn't accommodate all my weight. To compensate, I turned my hips into position and then hiked my right heel up onto the bulge of the wall and pressed hard into my feet to offset some of the weight on my hand. I twisted my body to make room for my left hand to reach higher. I'd reached the final twenty feet of the climb. *Keep it together. Commit.*

I tightened my grip on the impossibly small holds and settled my body into the best position I could manage. Only ten more feet to go—except that I was so tired and my arms ached so badly that even one more move seemed impossible. All I could think about was getting rid of the pain: *I can let go, just fall back and let the rope catch me, and the pain will instantly subside.* A moment later: *But then I'll have to do the whole thing all over again!*

Over a hundred feet up, I looked down below to the sheer drop and my rope, the width of a dog leash. I thought of how often I'd been asked: "What does it feel like to be up that high?" *Imagine crawling on the ledge atop a skyscraper, connected only to a thin line of rope anchored to the wall—and trusting that line, without a doubt.* Clenching my teeth and lips, I sucked my body against the wall and pulled through my final moves.

Omaha Beach had originally been a grade 5.13d when Katie Brown onsighted it for a first female ascent in 1999, but by the time I tried the route, some of the original holds had broken, creating a distinct crux at the top of the route. The consensus was that its difficulty had been upped to a 5.14a, which meant that I'd onsighted the hardest grade any North American woman ever had.

I had attempted Southern Smoke and Omaha Beach because they were the ones Magnus wanted to try. Before each climb I'd pushed the grades out of my head. They were just climbs, not unlike others I'd done. I only needed to concentrate on the task at hand. When we moved on to the last line of our trip, "Lucifer," a 5.14c climb much like Southern Smoke—on a wall aptly named "Purgatory"—I spent two days working out the moves. On day three, I sent it on my sixth try.

Several online zines did profiles of me, and I made my first cover as an adult in a print magazine called *DPM: Dead Point Magazine*. Their byline was "Climbing Media for the Young and Unruly." I liked that—being singled out for breaking rules. A few weeks later, I was sitting in my senior year calculus class, trying my best to stay awake, when an email from Adidas popped up on my phone. They were launching their line Adidas Outdoor in North America, and they wanted to sponsor me as their first U.S. climber. Was I interested, they wanted to know? *Oh, my God, this is Adidas, the greatest brand in sporting history. Uh, yeah!* I had to stop myself from screaming. It would mean wearing head-to-toe Adidas, and a commitment of eight global appearance days for ads and promotional events. And I would be on salary—the kind of salary that could pay for my climbing expeditions.

After I signed with Adidas, there seemed to be a shift in the way Dad perceived my climbing career. Even if he didn't directly tell me so, I knew he was proud of me, because I'd hear him boast about my climbing successes to neighbors and friends. I might have been equally proud if not for the occasional online blogs and trolls crediting those successes to my weight loss. I shouldn't have given any consideration to the negativity, but I did: *Oh, right, I'm successful only because I'm so small.*

Climbing is about strength, but only partially so, because it's also a gravity sport, meaning that the less weight I had to lug up a mountain, the less power I needed to expend, which would make for more efficient climbing. As long as I maintained my stamina and the strength to pull up my body weight, I could be invincible. The catch-22 was I'd need the fuel (and food) to keep up that stamina and strength. I was back to my preoccupation with weighing and measuring my food, which I rationalized this time by telling myself I was eating "healthy"—fruit, vegetables, and lean protein. I was a *disciplined* eater. I knew what was best for me, and I didn't want friends or family or my school telling me otherwise. With that attitude, something was bound to give.

Magnus was the only one concerned with how thin I'd become, but when he told me I was too skinny I took it as a compliment. He tried to get me to gain weight by telling me that I didn't look healthy, that my training would suffer, and that I'd get injured, but I was too hardheaded to hear his arguments. *Everyone eats this way,* I said. *Besides, my training is going really well, thank you, and what I do is none of your business.* Two weeks later I told him I didn't want to be in a relationship anymore, that I needed to be on my own after graduation.

One of the last things Magnus said to me before returning home was, "You look like a little twelve-year-old boy." He was trying to highlight the truth, but he wasn't doing it very tactfully.

All I could think was: *You're just jealous of my success.* I knew I was *fine* as long as I saw progress in my climbing. I was eighteen and all energy and enthusiasm for what would come next. There wasn't any time or need for introspection, especially since I was climbing so well. I just had to keep moving, keep training, and keep setting goals. Even if it meant a year of traveling on my own.

The day of my high school graduation, Dad drove me to school ahead of Mom, Charlie, and my grandmother, Baba. I was feeling excited and more than a little nostalgic about leaving the school I'd been at nearly my entire life. As I stared out the window, thinking about the end of an era and where I'd be headed in a week, I was happy for the distraction of a Jimmy Buffett song blaring over the stereo—"Cheeseburger in Paradise," one of my dad's favorites.

Dad was in a black suit and the sunglasses I'd given him—swag from a new sponsor of mine—with his mustache neatly trimmed. My entire life, I only knew him with his signature mustache, smooth and jet-black when I was a kid, now steel-gray and Brillo-like. It drooped down over his lips when he was deep in thought, which I usually interpreted as worried or disapproving. If I asked what was bothering him, he would either say something annoyingly ambiguous, or simply, "Nothing." I never believed him, but I had no way of knowing what was going on in his head. All I knew was that the conversation was over.

As we neared my school, he lowered the stereo volume, inhaled deeply through his nose, and then reached under his glasses to wipe his eyes. I felt as if he had something to say, but couldn't bring himself to say it. I took his hand and squeezed. He cleared his throat. "I just want you to know how proud I am of you. In every aspect of your life," he said. "I'm sorry for not always being there. I'm sorry if I've let you down." I held on tightly to his hand, my throat sore from trying to keep from crying as we drove into the school parking lot.

I'd been told I am just like my dad, but I never saw it. My dad was a traditional, Italian, head-of-the-household kind of guy who loved to cook steaks for a crowd of kids, but he could also be like a kid, especially when it came to his toys—the old scooters, bikes, gadgets, and vehicles left as collateral for unpaid docking fees at his marina. He was generous to a fault, even if he wasn't the best communicator, but it was his determination, his ability to dream big and work hard to accomplish those dreams, that most defined him. I couldn't help but wonder if I'd inherited that, if maybe that was how we were alike.

But I didn't say anything. I didn't know what to say. Instead, I checked the mirror to make sure I didn't have raccoon eyes for my last high school pictures.

A week after graduation I flew to Innsbruck, Austria, as planned—except that I was alone. I checked into the sports hostel next to the Innsbruck climbing gym and adjusted my plan to include: Find a friendly face. Somewhere between JFK and Innsbruck Airport, the reality of my aloneness dawned on me. *Would I have friends? Would I remain lonely?* I felt almost paralyzed with worry. *Come on, Sasha,* I told myself, *you know how to make friends. You like exploring places on your own. You don't need a boyfriend to do that.* What I did need was a climbing partner, someone to train with for the World Championships in Arco, Italy, the following month, the competition climbing world's biggest event.

I'd competed in some World Cups and International Invitationals and had a few titles under my belt, so I wasn't exactly new to the international climbing scene. I knew people in Innsbruck, including some of the Austrian climbers, but socializing was awkward because I was on Magnus's home turf, in the midst of his community. We'd been two people who were dating, but because we were both world-class climbers—having been featured climbing together in magazines and online forums—everyone in the community knew about our relationship.

I may have been more independent and well traveled than "normal" teenagers, but emotionally I was still an eighteen-year-old coming out of her first serious relationship. I didn't have any better tools in my climbing arsenal to deal with that than the next adolescent. Several times when I was set to meet mutual friends for dinner, one of them would text to say that Magnus was there, too, so I'd stay home. Most of the time I imagined they were saying what a shitty person I was for breaking up with him. I was worried I'd never fit in, let alone find a climbing partner.

I ran into one welcoming face, a U.S. National Team climber on her way out of the city. She introduced me to a friend living in Innsbruck who was also training for the Arco World Championships and who happened to be looking for a partner. She was on the Austrian National Team and was as motivated and disciplined with her climbing as she was with her diet, which only reinforced what *I* was doing. She weighed her food, so I weighed mine, everything from my oatmeal to my protein. I ate three- or four-hundred-calorie meals—healthy stuff, but not much of it. If I went off my diet and splurged on strudel from the local bakery, I'd feel so guilty I'd have to make up for it by skipping a meal.

Looking back, I believe most climbers on the World Cup circuit had some kind of eating disorder. If climbers wanted to do well, they needed to be super lean. That was the climbing aesthetic—even if no one admitted it out loud. It was the same for women and men, although people didn't comment on men's bodies with the same frequency and ferocity as they did on women's bodies. *Not a surprise.* Climbing competitions were basically endurance-focused, as opposed to requiring more power, strength, and agility, so success was primarily tied to the ability to hang on the wall for a long time, which meant that a climber needed to be light. Light and lean.

Even among some of the best climbers in the world, I was considered thin. The first time I walked into the Innsbruck gym, people stared, but they weren't the admiring stares I'd known years earlier as "the cute little pigtailed girl who could climb." No one spoke to me. No one came close to asking me what was going on with my eating. Instead, I caught winds of whispers behind my back and comments online about my weight. I wanted to shout: *Isn't this what it looks like to be a climber competing on the World Cup circuit?* I remembered a nasty comment I'd read online about my looks after my Red River Gorge climbs: "Ugh, so thin. Does she even get her period? Hahaha." But I wasn't about to change my habits. Instead, I wore baggy clothes to hide my body while I worked toward the upcoming World Cup in Chamonix, France.

There were about eight World Cups spread over Europe and Asia. I hadn't planned to go to all of them, since travel was expensive, but I'd always dreamed of climbing at Chamonix, one of Europe's most legendary World Cups. Chamonix had been a world-renowned ski village at the base of Mont Blanc, the highest summit of the Alps, ever since hosting the first Winter Olympics Games in 1924. The Cup took place on man-made walls in the center of town, amidst thousands of spectators. It was more exciting than most competitions, because the finals coincided with Bastille Day—France's Independence Day—a legendary celebration in and of itself. It was just a matter of finding out how to get there from Innsbruck.

Magnus and I had met several times since I'd arrived in Imst to figure out whether we could be friends, but every time we tried to find our way back to some common ground, we both wound up saying things we regretted. He offered to give me a lift to Chamonix, and then a day later had second thoughts about it. When he again offered, I was the one with second thoughts. We went back and forth until the moment I was in his car en route to the competition. I don't think I'd ever been so silent on such a long car ride.

At Chamonix, Magnus peeled off to be with his friends, the top climbers and "cool kids"—of which I was definitely not a part. They all knew each other and trained together. I was the outsider, the "ex," the only American. Pre-competition I went to the technical meeting by myself and acted as my own coach as I warmed up in isolation. *Yeah, fitting.*

Constant rain delays wreaked havoc with the event schedule, so climbers were eventually spaced in between the downpours. By the time I made it to the finals round, my shoes were soaked, and there was nothing I could do about them or my wavering confidence. I worried about slipping, about my overall performance, and about the prospect of another excruciating car ride. I did in fact slip, but I managed to take fourth place.

When the competition was over, everyone was invited to an after-party, but I was feeling too awkward to attend. *Sure,* I thought. *What'll I do there? Talk to no one and just feel sorry for myself?* Instead, I bought a crepe from a street vendor and brought it back to my hotel room to eat with a book. *Woo-hoo! Good job making finals, Sasha! You won a pancake. Now you can go to bed.* I thought of the time I slipped in my first Junior World Championship on my first visit to Imst. On the drive back to the airport, "Bad Day" had blared over the radio.

Thinking of that song, and how I'd thought my slip was the end of the world, actually made me feel a little better. At least I'd graduated from bawling my eyes out in the backseat of Mom's car. I set my sights on the upcoming World Championships, chalking up Chamonix to a bad dress rehearsal. Before slipping in the finals, I'd felt confident in my performance. I only had to summon that same confidence, focus on what was ahead, and remember the old adage: A bad dress rehearsal leads to a great performance.

5

In Arco, Italy, a week later, the sun finally came out. Claudiu had arrived with my team—twelve of us in all, ranging in age from eighteen to thirty-two—along with my mom. My support system was back, and I was among familiar faces as happy to see me as I was to see them. We'd all made it—from the National Titles to the Continental Championships, which fed into World Cups, and, finally, to the Arco World Championships. Arco was the pinnacle of competitions, a ten-day event held every other year comprising three different facets of climbing: sport climbing, speed climbing, and bouldering.

In sport climbing, success is determined by the height climbers reach on a wall they haven't previously seen. A perfect score means reaching the top in one shot, so the closer to the top, the better the score. Fall, and it's over.

In speed climbing, fastest wins. Competitors race side by side on identical routes on a dead-vertical fifteen-meter wall.

Bouldering, however, involves three rounds—qualifiers, semifinals and finals. Route-setters create series of holds forming sequences of eight or so moves. Climbers have four or five problems to solve and five minutes for each climb, the goal being to reach the top of all the problems in as few tries as possible. The person with the highest accumulated score wins. Climbers compete for gold, silver, and bronze in each event, with the title of Overall World Champion going to the person averaging the best results in all three. My goal was to make it to the finals, and, with any luck, medal in one event.

I was up against the best female climbers in the world, but my strongest competition was Austrian climber Angela Eiter, someone I'd not only looked up to for years, but someone who had always been incredibly nice to me. She was (and still is) a beautiful climber, modest and unassuming. She kept mostly to herself at competitions—a total pro—always sticking to her usual warm-up routine, seemingly unaware of the crowd. At five-foot-one, she was even smaller and lighter than me, and she'd been killing it in every one of her competitions.

Angela was at the top of her game in sport climbing, but not in speed or bouldering. At that point, speed climbing hadn't been as integrated into competition as it would later become. Speed specialists were in their own class and didn't tend to do well in lead and bouldering, and the top competitors for the overall weren't good at speed climbing, so our results really came down to bouldering and lead combined. By the end, no American had reached the finals in any event—except for me. I had the highest average score across all three categories, earning me the gold in the Female Overall World Champion title.

Arco was the pinnacle of competition, so much so that other competitions paled in comparison. It seemed as if the natural progression for pro competition climbers was to move to outdoor climbing. Within the climbing community, it is the "rock achievements"—sport and big wall climbs—that lead to the real global media recognition and the means of making a living. Outdoor climbing was definitely more dramatic and dangerous than competition climbing, but that wasn't the allure for me—I wasn't an adrenaline junkie, and I didn't take unnecessary risks. For me, the lure of outdoor climbing was its freedom and limitlessness. Outdoors it was just a partner, the climb, and me, without the intense combativeness of competition climbing, which relied on route-setters and technical aspects. After Arco, I was psyched to have a whole year of outdoor climbing before starting college. I would focus on "firsts"—first ascents, and first *female* ascents.

I returned to Austria for a few more competitions, one of which was in Imst, where Mom surprised me by flying in to watch me compete. I still loved seeing her at my competitions, and I was looking forward to spending some downtime with her afterward. When she then accompanied me to Innsbruck, it was exactly like the old days—traveling together, exploring parts of a city off the beaten path and discovering fun places to eat. I showed her my favorite cafes, the gym where I'd been training, and where to buy the best apple strudel in town.

As we walked around the city catching up, I could tell something was on her mind. She seemed worried and a little preoccupied. Finally, she turned to me, looking pained. "Dad's not able to pay for Columbia." She wouldn't say what had happened, only that he didn't have the money. That didn't make any sense to me, so I called Dad right away and asked him directly if he wasn't able to pay for school. He was angry that Mom had even suggested he didn't have the money.

"Your mom doesn't know what she's talking about. Of course I can pay for it." I wanted to believe him. I thought Mom must have misunderstood him, or that it was only a temporary setback. "Just go ahead and give the deposit," he said at the end of our conversation. "I'll pay you back. I promise."

Fortunately, I'd made enough money to afford the deposit,

but I couldn't afford the sinking feeling that Dad wasn't telling me the truth. I would come to understand years later that Dad felt he had to protect me from what was really going on in his business, and that it was a matter of his pride. At the time, though, I needed to keep a positive mindset. I couldn't let myself be distracted. I had a huge climb scheduled, the hardest route I'd ever attempted. I needed to focus on that, not on my growing frustration with my dad.

I had pitched the team I worked with at Adidas about my attempting "Pure Imagination," a grade 5.14d climb in Kentucky's Red River Gorge, and they wanted to document it. The first-ever ascent had been made by American Jonathan Siegrist in 2010 and captured in a short film by documentary filmmaker Andy Mann. Siegrist's skills, Mann's awesome cinematography, and the epic nature of the climb had blown me away.

Pure Imagination was an eighty-foot, slightly overhanging climb with three crux sections separated by continuous, on-edge climbing with few rests. It was a beautiful line filled with very small, sharp holds—the kind that would trash one's hands in a "skin-battle." I knew I had to attempt it. If I succeeded, I would be the first American woman—and the third woman in the world—to climb a route that difficult.

Most often climbers document their own climbs by bringing a cameraperson along. If there are images to catch on a groundbreaking climb or a first ascent, sometimes a professional photographer will offer to take pictures. In that case, a climber may go back up to certain pitches, usually the hardest, and redo them for the camera. I always appreciated the work of the pro photographers and cinematographers who came out to my climbs—it felt like a symbiotic relationship. After all, it was their work that ended up with my sponsors and in magazines.

Sponsors were starting to capitalize on outdoor climbing

through social media content, so Adidas set me up with Keith Ladzinski, an amazing photographer—and, in a stroke of pure serendipity, his partner, Andy Mann, who had captured Jonathan Siegrist's ascent. I felt beyond fortunate. If I hadn't had a sponsor, I probably would have attempted the climb anyway, but with one—especially one as big as Adidas—I was in a position to collect professional footage from two of the best documentary filmmakers in the field.

I didn't know Keith or Andy personally, so I reached out to Vian Charbonneau—a climber I knew who was going to be at The Red at the same time—and asked if I could stay with her. When I got off the plane in Lexington, Kentucky, on October 10, 2011, Keith and Andy greeted me. We drove to a little cabin they owned in Slade County, where I met Andy's girlfriend, Sheyna. Our plan was for Andy and Keith to film, while Sheyna belayed me as I tried out the moves for each sequence. It was "next level" in my career—doing a climb with two professional climber-photographers on the wall with me.

Like the climbs I'd done in Rodellar, Pure Imagination was a single-pitch climb, unlike a big wall climb that involves multiple pitches. In order to successfully send that kind of climb I would have to go from bottom to top without falling. The luxury—if anyone could call it that—of single-pitch climbing was that every time I fell, Sheyna could lower me back to the ground. My idea was to spend a week working out my moves and understanding the sequences before attempting the send.

In outdoor climbing, minute details of a move can make or break a climb. There's no "one size fits all" way to climb, which meant that I could use my own style of climbing, largely focused on my body positioning on the wall and leading with my hips, where I had my greatest flexibility. With any climb—

and especially one as difficult as Pure Imagination—my body needed to learn the language of the rock. Pure Imagination was sandstone, one of the most abrasive rocks. Holding it was like sandpapering my fingers, but the upside was that the sandstone provided great friction. The better the friction, the easier it is to make contact with the rock, but first I had to figure out my route.

I broke it down into sections and then strung those sections together, always like figuring out the choreography of a dance on a wall. Temperature and weather were also factors to consider. If the sun was on the wall, friction would deteriorate, making the rock feel grimy and sweaty and more difficult to hold on to. In the cold I could more easily grab on to the rock, but if it was *too* cold, my hands would become numb and feel like wood. Overreaching an inch or pivoting my pinky finger in the wrong direction could mean the difference between successfully gripping particles the size of sandpaper grit and maintaining my balance—or not.

I spent two days in a row climbing, with Sheyna on the ground belaying me and Keith and Andy on their own lines, secured from the top. That way they could let themselves down to find the best places to stabilize in order to film each of my efforts. On the third day of climbing, with Keith and Andy in place, I left the ground. "I'm just going to try and get through this first section," I told them, referring to the first fifteen feet of the eighty-foot climb. Keith was over to my left and Andy was hanging on a rope above me. I needed to stay as close to the wall as possible to maintain friction and ensure my grip on the holds—so close that not even a sheet of paper could slide between body and wall. From over half a lifetime of climbing, my core instinctively knew to engage so that I could concentrate on keeping my breathing steady. If I breathed too heavily, I could fall out of position and off the wall, but if I didn't climb with conviction, I'd lack the power to land on the holds properly.

After I made it through the first section, Andy moved out of the way and I kept going. And going. In what felt like a surreal, slow-motion moment, I reached the top. A moment later I was back to real time and breathing as hard as if I'd finished a marathon run. I couldn't believe I'd made it. I'd become the first woman to send Pure Imagination and the third woman in the world to climb a 5.14d. I hoped that maybe I'd opened a door to more women discovering what was possible for them to achieve.

Andy and Keith had documented the entire ascent in real time—a magical piece of videography on their part. There was no need to redo any moves for the sake of the cameras; amazingly, they'd gotten it all. I was happy, but I felt surprisingly mellow—a case of either overwhelming relief or exhaustion . . . or both. Going into the climb I hadn't been sure of when or *if* I would succeed. That morning, leaving Vian's place, I'd given her the impression I wasn't even close to sending Pure Imagination, so she hadn't come out to watch. When I returned, I walked in and said, "Hey, I did it. I think I'm going to go to bed."

"Wait, what?" she said. "You just accomplished this massive achievement—like, first woman in North America to do this thing—and, *what*? You're acting like it was just any other day at the crag." A few years later, Vian would tell me, "I didn't even know if I could offer you a beer or what to celebrate, because you were underage. I mean, you're pretty Type A, so it's not like I expected you to party hard, but you just went to sleep." I had to think about that. *Sure, just a little Type A, maybe.*

At home, I was suddenly flooded with interview requests from climbing magazines and TV news shows, including *CBS*

News Sunday Morning and Oprah's *Super Soul Sunday* series. Oprah's channel featured a two-minute clip of my climbing Pure Imagination, accompanied by her own voice-over of Theodore Roosevelt's famous "The Man in the Arena" quote—the one Brené Brown, my favorite author, had used as inspiration for her book *Daring Greatly*. It felt surreal. Oprah Winfrey was saying my name! This incredibly powerful woman was mentioning my success on a climb. I was overcome with emotion.

Pure Imagination laid the foundation for my path going forward. I knew I'd need to document my climbing "firsts" so that people could experience them in a visceral way. It was no longer enough to read about the statistics of a climb; people wanted to watch as the drama unfolded, beyond traditional TV news, newspaper, and magazine coverage. For career athletes in niche outdoor sports like mine, social media was becoming a game changer. I figured I was ahead of the game by posting on Facebook and on my blog.

Before we parted ways, Keith and Andy said to me, "You've got to get on Instagram. It's the newest thing." I thought, *I don't really have time for another social media thing.* I couldn't have imagined that one day I'd have half a million followers on that platform watching me hang from precipices around the world—or that one day I'd be using it to document a long, exhausting fight to keep climbing.

WHEN I FIRST started competing, my dream was to make the U.S. National Team and to climb a 5.14. Those were my goals, written on a to-do list on a whiteboard that hung in my bedroom next to my poster of Lynn Hill. I looked up to Lynn, even though we'd had such different beginnings. I was a gym climbing kid from the D.C. area, and Lynn had cut her climbing teeth outdoors in Yosemite Valley. She was of a generation that mostly did climbing-specific training—training solely by doing the sport outdoors—although Lynn had the advantage of having been a gymnast. She had the best body awareness of any climber I'd ever met, and an ability to understand the rhythm of the rock. Her style was graceful and seemingly effortless, yet she'd broken barriers that transcended gender. She had forged her own way. As I transitioned more toward outdoor climbing, I felt as if I was forging mine.

When I climbed outdoors, everything else faded away. In each moment I knew how my feet were positioned on the wall, where my weight shifted, how my fingertips bore down on the edges of rock. There was no room for anxiety or worry—neither belonged. If I went into a climb mentally and physically prepared, having identified and evaluated risks, there was no space for negative thoughts.

I realized that I had to take in more fuel if I wanted to expend the kind of energy I needed for long days outdoors. I was still strict about staying lean and keeping my food healthy and simple, but as I started moving away from the intense and immediate scrutiny of competition climbing, I felt freed in more ways than one. I became less restrictive in my eating habits, allowing myself dressing on my salad, a little cheese, and an occasional dessert without so much guilt—a significant accomplishment for me. I tried to be accepting of my body and the changes it had gone through, especially since I'd become aware of the online climbing community.

The more I was in the limelight, the more people on certain blogs and forums felt the need to critique (and diminish) not only my accomplishments, but my appearance. It had never been clearer to me: If I wanted to be healthy in mind and body,

I'd have to develop calluses around my self-esteem as tough as the ones on my fingertips. I'd also have to stick to my convictions about my plans for school.

When I met up with new and old climber friends throughout Europe, it never mattered where they were from or what their background was. All that mattered was our shared love of climbing. However, my decision to go to college—Columbia in particular, in *New York City*—was a continual source of questioning and disbelief, not only to friends, but to people who didn't even know me. It seemed completely incongruous with a climbing career.

"Sasha, why are you throwing away your career?" I heard over and over from my climbing buddies. "What do you want to be? A *lawyer*?"

"You're, like, at the pinnacle of your career, and you're going to live in New York City?"

"Well, if you choose school, say goodbye to climbing hard."

There was no blueprint for a career in rock climbing that included college, especially at a school known for its rigorous academics. At nineteen, I may not have known where I eventually wanted to end up, but I did know I wanted a life that was multidimensional. What if someday I wanted to start a business, work at one of the companies that sponsored me, go to grad school, or write a book?

I believed the only way to avoid regret was to put myself on the line and commit fully to an objective. I loved climbing and pushing myself past my comfort zone, but I was also ready for a new challenge—one that would stimulate my mind. I needed to throw school back into the mix. That became crystal clear when I was climbing with my friend Matilda Soderlund. Like me, Matilda had shown up at a lot of the World Cup technical meetings as the lone competing member of her team—the Swedish team. Bonding over that, we referred to ourselves as Team "Amereden."

Several weeks before the start of school, Matilda and I were camping in a beautiful remote area in France. Day after day we climbed, made ourselves healthy meals, and passed out from pure, hard-earned exhaustion. When Matilda had to leave two weeks ahead of me, I stayed on by myself—which turned out to be plenty of time for some intense introspection.

As much fun as I'd been having, I didn't want my life to be about bumming around campgrounds, living like a nomad, eating, sleeping, and dreaming climbing twelve months out of the year. Twelve months of having done exactly that made me realize how much I thrived on keeping several balls in the air at once. Besides, what if college could *enhance* my career? I was dismayed that people in the climbing world didn't think I could maintain my status as a world-class climber if I continued my education. My journey was my own, and it wasn't etched in stone.

Of course, I wouldn't have the same time and energy to devote to climbing that I'd had all year. Instead, I would have to work my ass off to prove to my sponsors that I could be a professional athlete *and* a full-time student. I was looking forward to my new life—taking classes, meeting new people, and continuing to compete and make appearances for my sponsors. That last part was most important, because I couldn't forgo any money-making opportunities.

In my family, as in a lot of families, conversations about money had been practically taboo. The idea of talking about my dad's finances seemed as awkward as, say, discussing my sex life. Just, *no*. Even after Mom told me my dad couldn't pay for school, he kept insisting that he could. Mom confided that their finances were tough, but my dad's actions suggested otherwise. He was still picking up the tab after expensive dinners with friends and family, making house renovations, and buying new "toys"—like the yacht named *Big Dog* he bought behind my mom's back.

It wasn't my place to question how Dad spent his money, even when my first semester payment was due. "Just pay the first semester," he said to me. "We'll work that out with the deposit. . . . I'm getting some business deals in order. . . . Of course, I'll pay you back." I didn't feel good about his assurances. Instead, I felt an added layer of responsibility.

I'd come full circle since kicking off a yearlong winning streak at my first Arco World Championships. In addition to red-pointing multiple 5.14cs and 5.14ds during my year off—climbing from the ground to the finish without falling—I was the Pan-American and U.S. Women's National Champion and was ranked first in the world for Female Outdoor Sport Climbing. It was hard to believe that I was the same person who'd arrived in Europe feeling alone and a little sorry for myself—the girl in the baggy gym clothes looking for a climbing partner. I had to pinch myself when I found out I was due to receive the 2012 Arco Rock Legends Salewa Rock Award, one of the two most prestigious awards in rock climbing, for outstanding achievement in the outdoor climbing space.

The Arco Rock Legends Awards were the Oscars of climbing, judged by an international panel composed of representatives from the most important climbing magazines in the world. Just to be nominated was an honor, but to receive the award seemed an affirmation of every minute I'd spent pushing myself harder than I thought possible. As I stood onstage with the nominees—people I'd admired for years—I felt as if a torch was being passed to me. Legends like Reinhold Messner, Adam Ondra, Lynn Hill, and Chris Sharma had all come before me on that stage, and it was now my turn to represent. *No pressure.*

I was on an adrenaline high as I headed straight into the Arco Masters—an invitational for the top-ranked climbers from the World Cup circuit. I felt unstoppable until the semi-finals, when I heard a pop followed by an intense tweak in my left ring finger. I had ruptured my A2 pulley, the ligament that holds tendons close to the bone—a dreaded injury that mostly befalls climbers. Though not uncommon, and not usually serious, the rupture meant that I couldn't open my hand: a nasty bit of luck for someone who was used to pulling her body weight with her fingers.

I was forced not only to forgo my spot in the finals, but also to take a few weeks off from climbing. It was a harsh reality, considering I was already nervous about the balance between college and staying on top of my climbing game. At the same time, it seemed almost serendipitous. Hadn't I wished for some semblance of a "normal" college experience? Hadn't I wanted to fully jump into school with both feet? Well, here was my excuse to do just that. I was as stoked for my first semester as I'd been for any climb.

6

It wasn't a dream. I was at a fairy-tale ball where the guests were some of the greatest female athletes in the world—gymnasts, tennis legends, swimmers, and Olympians.

Juggling life in Manhattan as a professional athlete and a full-time student would have been chaotic enough, but I was also trying to turn my career into a successful business and give back to the climbing community at the same time. Usually that meant pushing past a tough training session, or an overload of schoolwork, or jet lag from traveling to a sponsor event in another country.

But occasionally it meant an invitation to something like the Women's Sports Foundation's Annual Salute. As a recent transplant to New York City, I was only just discovering the city as an epicenter for glitzy, celebrity-driven galas—and the Annual Salute was one of them, an event that drew legendary female athletes, up-and-comers, coaches, and celebrities. I had to pinch myself, or at least stop gawking at the women walking by me who'd been my idols growing up.

I'd recently started working with a sports agent who specialized in female athletes, several of whom were members of the

Women's Sports Foundation—a charity founded by Billie Jean King to advance the lives of girls through sports—and she'd arranged an invite for me. I had no idea what a big deal the Salute was until my agent sent me the roster of invitees. I didn't know much else except that it was black-tie and it was happening on the opposite end of town. If anything, I was excited to have an excuse to dress up—although I wasn't going to blow fifty bucks on a cab when I had a MetroCard, so I took the subway from 116th Street to the Financial District at the base of Manhattan, in full gala dress, makeup, and stiletto heels.

My agent led me through the crowd, introducing me to kick-ass female athletes whose careers I'd followed, like figure skater Sasha Cohen, who had retired and was attending Columbia Business School, and Sarah Hughes, a figure skating champion attending Yale. When we came upon Michelle Kwan—five-time world figure skating champion and the one athlete Mom and I had been obsessed with when I was skating—I was completely starstruck. I tried to be cool, but come on, it was *Michelle Kwan*. I don't remember what I said or if I said anything until she suggested we take a photo together. All I could manage was, "Oh, my God! I cannot wait to send this to my mom!" At the end of the night, she asked if I was going to the after-party. I felt a little like Cinderella as I muttered something about having to finish my homework before dashing out to the subway.

Everything about the event was inspiring—the conversation, the speeches, meeting Billie Jean King. The athletes participating were not only the best in their fields, but they were also women who had moved beyond competition and turned their energy and passion toward business and nonprofit work. I felt validation not only as a professional athlete but for my business acumen and my desire to move my career beyond the niche industry of climbing. As the sole climber in attendance, I felt responsible for representing an entire community. (The foundation is largely composed of advocates in traditional sports: tennis, soccer, softball, hockey, et cetera. Since joining in 2012, I have remained the lone voice of climbing.) I imagined I could help move climbing toward the mainstream and advocate for it as a means of empowerment for other young women.

That night was also the start of building an awesome tribe of female athlete friends outside of climbing, including Sasha, Sarah, and Michelle. There were so many similarities in our lives—not the least of which was an intense dedication to our sports. Those women knew how much time and sweat and sacrifice it took to be the best, and on top of that, what it took to maintain their sport as a career. The only difference between us was that I wasn't anywhere near retiring—I was just beginning my pro career as a climber, despite a rocky start just three months earlier.

COLUMBIA WAS A week into classes when I first arrived, fresh off the Arco Masters. I'd missed orientation and all the "getting to know you" parties. I'd also forgotten to fill out my housing paperwork, so I was assigned a roommate who had also neglected to fill out the forms—apparently the one thing we had in common. We were meeting for the first time, and I was anxious to make a good impression. After a year of almost exclusively being around climbers, I thought: *Okay, cool, I'm making my first college friend.* Nervously, I chatted away, asking my new roommate if she followed any sports (she didn't), what her major was (biomedical engineering), and peppering her with questions to try and keep our polite but awkward conversation afloat.

Lying in bed that night, after a day of trying to find my way around campus, I noticed a taxidermied bobcat on my roommate's desk. I tried to sleep, but I couldn't rid myself of the feeling that its wide glass eyes were staring at me. The last thing I wanted to do was complain, so I placed a baseball cap over its head. When I woke in the middle of the night, the cap was on the floor, so I put it back on. On and off it went—a routine we wordlessly continued for a week until the cap finally stayed put at night, and it became apparent to both of us that we were wildly mismatched.

In my fantasy of college, I'd imagined immediately bonding with my roommate—we'd team up to explore our new surroundings and go to parties together—just as I'd imagined how easy my transition back to being a student would be. Instead, jumping into college in New York City after more than a year of continual climbing was nerve-racking. I felt a flush of panic after realizing the amount of homework I'd already missed and needed to make up. I tried making a list—something I'd do when I had a lot on my plate—but it only made me feel more anxious, because I had no idea where to start.

I was in totally unknown territory. My high school was one building with a graduating class of 110. Now I needed a map to leave my dorm. One of my biggest sponsors was touting me as their only professional athlete who was also in college—an Ivy League college at that—but all I could think at that juncture was: *What am I doing here? Is this really a good idea?* I was excited to be back in class and to be moving my career in a new direction, but I also worried how I'd find a balance between being a pro athlete and being a student—both full-time jobs—and how I'd meet new people outside of my climbing. My life felt like a constant rush of activities—to classes, to training, to interviews. So far, I'd yet to have more than a brief hello and a passing conversation with anyone.

A couple of weeks into the semester I met someone whom I'll call Kelly in a writing workshop. Like a lot of the students I met, she knew me from the news, social media, or the campus paper, which had run a profile of me in their first issue of the new school year. I had already been dubbed "rock climber girl," a title that a few years earlier would have made me feel uncomfortable, but that I was now proud of. Kelly and I had barely spoken; still, I was stoked when she asked me to go to a frat party with her on Saturday night. The only real parties I'd been to in over a year were the after-parties of climbing competitions, where everyone knew everyone else and the conversations invariably turned to rock climbing.

I met Kelly at her dorm and we walked over to the frat house—a brownstone on the other side of campus. The party was crowded and noisy and just like I'd imagined it would be, down to the sticky floor, red Solo cups, and grinding music. Tables loaded with liquor bottles filled corners of the room next to kegs of beer. As I followed Kelly through the scrum of students, I felt as if I'd finally arrived at college for real. Kelly introduced me to a guy who volunteered to bring us drinks. He disappeared into the crowd and then returned with red cups for Kelly and me. Mine tasted like a tequila drink mixed with something sweet and limey—a margarita, maybe.

"He makes a really good drink," was the last thing I remember Kelly saying.

The next thing I knew, I was waking up in a hospital bed. It was early morning, and I was in an empty room, in my clothing from the night before, except for my shoes. I felt a wave of panic. *Why am I here?*

I looked out the window and recognized my dorm across the street. After moving in, I'd been annoyed to find myself across the street from a hospital, because the traffic and noise were constant. Now here I was on the other side. As much as I tried, I couldn't remember a thing after the tequila drink. Embarrassed, I shot out of bed without even bothering to look for my shoes. *I've got to get out of here,* I thought as I made my way across the street in a pair of hospital socks. *At least it's too early for anyone to be up. I can slink back to my dorm without anyone seeing me.*

My roommate was out, which was weird for this early hour, until I saw that my bed was covered in vomit. I took a quick shower, changed, stripped my sheets, did a load of laundry, and kept moving. Despite a dull throbbing in my head, I needed to go to training. I had to be okay. My plan was to continue as if nothing had happened and hope that no one would mention anything about the evening to me. But I did send a text to Kelly: "What happened last night?"

"After the drink you were falling down the stairs and you couldn't stand up, so I brought you back to your room." She had nothing more to tell me.

That afternoon, I saw my roommate. "How are you feeling?" she asked, matter-of-factly. "You were really sick last night. You okay?"

"Why did I go to the hospital?"

"You were throwing up in bed. I was afraid you would choke to death."

I nodded, feeling like a stupid freshman cliché. Thankfully, she must have sensed I didn't want to talk about what had happened, so our conversation ended there. I had homework to complete and wanted to leave the whole embarrassing thing behind me, so I told no one about it.

A week later my mom called to tell me she'd received a bill from the hospital. "Did you take an ambulance?" she said. *I took an ambulance? Oh, my God. My roommate called an ambu-*

lance to take me twenty yards across the campus? "Sasha, what happened?"

"I have no idea. I literally don't know."

"Did you have too much to drink? Did you eat before you drank?" *No, yes.* "That's strange. Really strange. Did you pour the drink yourself?"

"No, someone handed it to me."

"Listen to me, Sasha. I don't want you to ever see those people again."

I didn't ask the hospital any questions, and I went out of my way to avoid Kelly. *What had happened?* I had always imagined I was mature beyond my years. After all, I'd traveled the world by myself; *I had my shit buttoned up.* In my mind, the only way to handle the whole situation was to let it go, like I would a bad performance at a competition.

A couple of weeks later a mutual acquaintance introduced me to Katie Barclay. It was one of those instant connections— like meeting one's doppelganger. At five-foot-two, we literally and figuratively looked at the world from the same vantage point. Katie and her boyfriend introduced me to their group of friends, people who were as stoked to meet me as I was to meet them, and who would become part of my college circle of friends. As far as I was concerned, it was a chance to start fresh.

It was the beginning of doing "normal" things, like socializing with people who weren't eating, sleeping, and breathing climbing—or starving themselves. Some of the people I met were collegiate athletes, so we connected over a shared love of sports and the discipline that went into being an athlete, but athletics didn't consume their lives, not like it did the pros in the climbing world. I eased up a little on my tactical style of eating and started enjoying myself in social situations: going for brunch, not punishing myself for having dessert. I even made an Instagram account where I posted pictures of food and friends like other people my age did.

As far as my academics were concerned, it had been over a year since I'd been in a classroom, so sitting still for hours at a time—something that had always been hard for me—was challenging at first. My brain also needed to make a definitive switch from reading routes to reading textbooks, but the trade-off was well worth it. I was studying subjects I was excited about, nonfiction writing and business management in particular. I studied economics, time management, and building a business. I knew that all of these classes could help in building my own brand. Writing was helpful in learning how to tell my story, since I'd been receiving requests as a keynote speaker, and I'd been my own "business" since I took on my first sponsors at twelve. Now was my chance to learn the real ins and outs and language of business, like the idea of building a team. That meant working with an agent to represent me as I grew my career, in addition to relying on my all-important coaches and sponsors.

My coaches were the people who kept me mentally and physically on point, but my sponsors were the source of my livelihood. I depended on them and they, in turn, depended on me to show up and give a hundred percent, whether it was for a climb, an exhibition, or a commercial appearance. Climbing companies alone didn't pay enough for me to earn a living, so working with more mainstream companies was my ticket to financial independence and stability.

As grateful as I was for all the new things in my life—school, friends, a social life, and some semblance of "normal"—climbing had to remain a priority. I became an expert in time management and setting priorities—two of the first rules of business.

Monday through Thursday I had a full-time class schedule. Thursday evenings I'd board a plane for a competition or photo shoot or appearance on the other side of the world. By Monday morning I'd be back on campus. I went to Paris for an overnight event and Seattle for a competition, and then off to Belgium for a World Cup.

I said yes to everything: *Yes, I'll fly to Germany for an appearance this weekend. Yes, I can be in Italy on Saturday.* I even flew to Japan for a televised competition on a climb *up the side of a casino.* I came in second for that and received eight thousand dollars, which, by climbing competition standards, was good prize money. At the top of the climb, we were all escorted to an amazing sushi spread surrounding a chef slicing up a giant tuna. *Eight thousand bucks and fresh sushi*—I wondered what my ten-year-old self, only wanting to "climb hard and win a thousand bucks," would have thought of that.

Most climbing events were on weekends, but the Pan-American Championship in Venezuela was an exception—and I'd been training for it since returning to the gym from my finger injury. Early in the semester, I learned that an exam for one of my classes would coincide with the championship. Right away, I explained my predicament to the professor and asked if I could take the exam early. She replied, "I don't care if you miss your alarm or you're meeting the President of the United States. I don't make exceptions."

Ironically, if I'd been on a varsity team at Columbia, I would have been allowed more than a few passes for competition. Instead, climbing was simply an extracurricular *thing,* nothing more than a hobby to her. But it was the thing that enabled me to pay for my education in the first place.

Dad and I still hadn't had a straightforward conversation about my tuition, which was an ongoing cause of frustration. As payment came due for my second semester, I dreaded "the money talk." When I brought up tuition on a visit home, he said,

"Go ahead and pay it and I'll pay you back." End of discussion. I was angry, but not because he was unable to keep his promise to pay for college. By not acknowledging that he couldn't pay he was refusing to treat me like an adult. I had become financially independent, so money really wasn't the problem. The problem for me was my dad's unwillingness to acknowledge that independence. All I wanted was for him to say, "I'm so proud of you for making a career out of climbing—so proud of the independent person you've become."

From then on communication with Dad grew more sporadic and strained. Something was up with him, but he refused to offer any insight. Oftentimes, when we did talk, he'd mention paying me back. I wanted to scream, "Stop saying you'll pay me back! I'm not asking you. That isn't the point anymore." Instead, I imagined conversations with my dad that never played out and wrote him letters I never sent. The more independence I gained, the more impatient I became with his inability to have a grown-up discussion with me about what was going on in his life, emotionally and financially. I felt that a little transparency on Dad's end would probably have put an end to our fights, though in hindsight a little more patience on my end might have helped, too.

I was worried about him. He'd grown moody and almost depressed, nothing like the gregarious guy I remembered as a kid. I couldn't understand his increasing negativity and disinterest in his own health. He was suffering from gout and putting on weight; all his meals included meat and rich, high-cholesterol foods. Health nut that I was, I butted heads with him over that as well. We'd run the same "script" over and over. I'd say, "You're killing yourself with your shitty diet. And if you don't care about yourself then that means you don't care about this family."

"I don't need you to tell me how to eat. It's none of your business," he'd say.

We were at a point where I couldn't tell him anything without setting him off, like telling me his health was none of my business. But I felt it *was* my business, because I wanted him around. Growing up, I thought my dad was a great businessman—he provided us with so much. I wanted to be like him in that regard, but as I matured, I could see that his pride got in the way of everything he did. His dream had been to develop a community around his beloved marina, but he was running out of credit and spending money he didn't have. He couldn't hear advice from anyone, and he was too stubborn to admit to making any mistakes, no matter how big or small. Mom was trying to keep a strict budget for the household and Dad was buying boats.

Clearly, Mom was upset with my dad—I could tell by the tension between them—but I think she tried to keep up a good front for the sake of Charlie and me, and also because she was incredibly loyal to Dad.

Mom and Dad had dated for several years. She was thirty-nine and pregnant with Charlie when she gave up her life in Toronto as a successful commercial and documentary producer in order to move to the U.S. to start a family with Dad. She turned all her fierce independence and intelligence to the dual tasks of raising Charlie and (soon after) me and supporting her husband fully in all his ambitious ventures. She trusted his decision-making for as long as she could, until the checks started to bounce.

Looking back on that time, I can see that Mom was more hurt than angered by Dad's reluctance to consult her on his financial decisions. Dad had always dreamed big, but now it was as if a curtain had been drawn back on him, and he didn't want anyone to see, least of all his daughter. The best I could do was to learn from his mistakes and stay the course with my own business.

I SIGNED WITH Red Bull in the spring of freshman year as their first American climber. They didn't have any athletes in college, so they made a big deal out of the fact that I was a student as well as a pro. *Good Morning America* reached out to do a story on me—the angle was how, in addition to being a student, I was also the reigning three-time U.S. national champion. As part of the segment, they would accompany me to Nationals to tape me winning—at least that's what I assumed I'd be doing after winning three years in a row.

I arrived at the competition with a *GMA* correspondent and cameraperson and the Red Bull rep who had signed me, less sure of myself than I'd been in a while. I'd always believed in training so hard that even on my bad days I could afford to make a mistake and still win. But I hadn't done that. Between academics, work, travel, and family stress, I had a lot on my plate, and I hadn't been training nearly as hard as I had in the past. Without realizing it, my priorities had shifted.

My competitors had been training nonstop—they weren't in college. They were primed and ready in body and mind, like they were supposed to be. In stark contrast, I was in the middle of a semester, worrying about midterms. I flew from New York to Denver, Colorado, straight out of my statistics class, from sea level to a higher elevation, which in itself is a huge adjustment. I landed the night before qualifiers, went to my hotel room, and finished my homework. I don't know what I was thinking, but I definitely didn't have my head one hundred percent on the task ahead of me. The minute I started climbing I felt like a sack of potatoes. To the uninformed eye, I looked fit, but I was not prepared—not physically, and worse yet, not psychologically.

I slipped in the finals. I didn't even make the podium. More than feeling disappointed with myself for having messed up so badly, I felt guilty. My new sponsors had been excited to sign me and I had let them down. I was supposed to be able to do it all—be as accomplished a student as I was a professional athlete, able to study, train, compete, and win spectacularly. Instead, I'd failed spectacularly.

I thought I was doing a great job of juggling school, social life, training, competitions, and expeditions, but I'd been wrong. My failure at Nationals was a wake-up call: Maybe I did have too many balls in the air.

But which one could I drop? I couldn't stop training—in fact, it was the thing I most looked forward to—and I couldn't stop traveling because that was a part of my job. I needed to say yes to the opportunities coming my way to grow my career. I wanted to do well in school—a goal I achieved while stress-eating bags of trail mix into the early morning hours and polishing term papers on weekend red-eyes—but I also wanted to enjoy student life. I rushed for a sorority because I loved the women in the group, but I quickly became the ghost sister who wasn't there for any events. The people around me at school were working toward a career after graduation, but I already had a full-time career.

At the very least, I needed to choose between competing on the World Cup circuit or dedicating what little free time I had to focusing on outdoor climbing. I had achieved what I set out to do in the competition world, winning every title I went after. I'd lost my passion for competing on plastic, so why not focus on organizing summer climbs going forward? Why not continue to team up with pro filmmakers like Keith and Andy to create epic content? The more I thought about it, the more it felt like a natural transition.

A week later Keith called, clinching my decision. "Adidas and Red Bull want to fund a film around an expedition of yours this summer," he said. "Where do you want to go? We can pretty much go anywhere."

That was the thing about outdoor ascents—the world was an open landscape of limitless places to climb, especially with the type of climbing I did. I free-climbed, using both traditional gear—gear I placed myself, such as camalots and nuts—and established gear—gear that has been placed before me in the form of bolts, an important distinction to make, since people often confuse free climbing with free soloing, or climbing without a rope. My options, as Keith reminded me, were limitless.

"How about South Africa?" I said.

7

Climbing is a fairly new sport in South Africa compared with places like Spain and Germany, but since the end of apartheid, climbers from all over the world have discovered the country's spectacular crags amidst lush, magical-looking landscapes. I'd been especially keen to explore the climbing there after a chance meeting with the South African climber Arjan de Kock. If ever there was a South African climbing ambassador, Arjan was it. He'd described some awesome climbs, including one in particular that had been bolted but never climbed. He even offered to partner with me if I ever made it to his country.

With Keith, Andy, Red Bull, and Adidas on board, and the license to go anywhere we wanted, it was easy to put the Nationals into proper perspective. I felt fortunate beyond measure. Keith and Andy and I nailed down a plan. First, we would try "Digital Warfare," a route at a "crag"—a climbing area—called Wow Pro, one of South Africa's most well-known sport-climbing areas. Digital Warfare, eighty vertical feet of smooth sandstone, had been bolted by the South African climber Andrew Pedley, but had remained an "open project"—a bolted rock face that no one had successfully sent. Andrew had named the project for the stress and strain it placed on one's "digits"—fingers. *Perfect.* I reached out to Arjan and took him up on his offer.

In early July, Arjan met Keith, Andy, and me at the airport in Cape Town. The plan was to head to Montagu, a small town about a hundred miles away, but as soon as we landed, I received a message from another climber who had been trying Digital Warfare for a couple weeks. She and her team suggested I not try it so that she might send it first. It was an unusual request, because it's not as if a climber can "reserve" a climb. With so many climbs to try, rarely do two pro climbers happen to show up for a first ascent at the same time. When they do, there's no rule book for who has the "right" to a climb, but in an effort to avoid drama, we pivoted to Waterval Boven, a sport-climbing area outside of Johannesburg.

We flew to Johannesburg, rented a car and a house, and then set up for a projected two weeks of climbing. We didn't have a specific climb in mind, so we started out by walking the cliff line across the pumpkin- and saffron-colored mountain plateaus that rose from dense woods. Climbing those vertical, two-billion-year-old sandstone walls would involve rappelling down to the start. It was Keith who first saw it, a beautiful, big, *blank* face—flat and featureless. "Whoa, what's that below us?"

We asked a few locals what the route up the face was called. Turned out it was another open project, also bolted by Andrew Pedley. It's not a hard-and-fast rule, but climbers generally defer to the person who first bolted a climb to make the initial attempt if they so choose, though neither Andrew nor anyone else had sent it. Andrew had dubbed it "The Overlord Project" when he bolted it three years earlier. Since then, it had been designated the toughest single-pitch climbing route in the whole area.

We had to reach Andrew right away, so of course we messaged him via Instagram: "Hey, Andrew, I'm here in Waterval

Boven with a couple friends, and we just saw this striking sandstone face you bolted. Is it okay if I try it?"

"Go for it," he messaged back.

While I hadn't known in advance what route I'd be trying in Waterval Boven, I'd seen photos of the area, so I was familiar with the walls. Based on the type of rock I'd be climbing and the angles involved, I had a good idea of what type of shoe I wanted to use. There were rock-climbing shoes for all different climbs, but the biggest difference between shoes came down to the malleability of the "rands"—the supporting rubber running through the middle of the shoe up to the toe box. On a super-technical climb where my feet had to support my entire body weight on credit card–thin protrusions, I wanted a very stiff shoe for more support. On steeper angles, softer rands worked better, because I needed to feel the wall, using the shoe like a talon to hook on holds and pull my weight from my feet.

To this day I wear my climbing shoes two sizes smaller than my street shoes so that the rands mold to my feet. I pull them on and tie them so tightly as to feel a dull throb, right before there's a welcome numbness as my shoes become a part of my body. Within seconds, the numbness gives way to an intense awareness of every inch of my feet and toes, and that hypersensitivity allows me to place my feet on the tiniest rock crystals to leverage my weight. My feet, in my shoes, become a second pair of hands.

On The Overlord Project I'd especially have to rely on the stickiness of the rands and the friction between my feet and the rock, because the footholds were all "smears"—flat rock with no real gripping area. Every millimeter movement of my body had to be exact. I'd need to press my feet against the wall as hard as possible while gripping onto rock that had nothing to grip—too much air between my body and the rock and I would fall.

I tried not to have any expectations each time I left the ground. If I didn't think about the top, I could concentrate on executing each sequence as smoothly as possible so that when I reached an anchor, it felt more like a gift than a checkmark on a laundry list. The unique thing about going after a climb that has never been done before is learning for oneself whether it's possible. It's like looking at a blank canvas. There's no precedent, no map. *Is it possible? Is it possible* for me? I think of myself as a positive, optimistic person, although I never set out on a climb thinking, *Yeah, this is going to be a blast.* My thinking is always: *Be present, enjoy the journey, have high aspirations and low expectations.* As important as it is to maintain the desire to accomplish something great, success is always a little sweeter when I'm not expecting to succeed.

Every day for two weeks I fine-tuned my sequences of moves, making minute adjustments in order to find the best way to place my body. Once I find the best positions—the best moves—I put them together to make the sequences, which I then practice until they become muscle memory, and then string all the sequences together in order to complete the pitch—much like completing a puzzle.

Every day, no matter if it brought relief, excitement, or stress, I felt an underlying sense of possibility. Some days it was all I could do to find places to grab on to. Other days I was able to string together full sequences. It took me two weeks to finally put all the pieces together, and then six days to red-point the route—free-climb while lead climbing after having practiced the route. With Keith and Andy filming, I made my first-ever *first ascent*—with Arjan belaying and taking the second ascent. As the first person to complete the entire route, Andrew Pedley awarded me the honor of naming it.

I didn't have to think very long about a name. At the time,

Nelson Mandela was gravely ill. Everywhere we traveled around Johannesburg there was a palpable sense of anxiety. It was an easy decision to name the route "Rolihlahla," Nelson Mandela's middle name. In his native language of Xhosa, it meant "pulling the branch of a tree." It was only later I learned of its colloquial meaning: "troublemaker," a fitting new name for Overlord.

We wrapped filming and felt good about the footage we had on Rolihlahla. My sponsors had been relying on me for that ascent. They were also paying a film crew, whose job it was to capture my performance, which came with its own pressure. Even though Keith and Andy were the best, always reassuring me, "Don't worry about us. We're just capturing what you do," they were probably thinking, *Please do this. Please do this.* I'd always wanted to succeed for the sheer joy and satisfaction that came with achieving a goal, but as a professional I needed to succeed for everyone whose jobs depended upon me: my sponsors and the photographers, filmmakers, and production teams. It felt as if it wasn't about only me anymore.

We flew to Cape Town and returned to Montagu, where there happened to be another open project that people were trying—a route on a vast rock overhang that had been established but never had a clean ascent. Because of my success at Rolihlahla, there was no pressure to successfully send the route at Montagu, which made it the perfect challenge after such a long, arduous project. I could climb without the expectation of a send, which sometimes made success a little easier. Montagu could be the icing on the cake . . . and it was. It became my second first ascent. In a more lighthearted spirit, I named it "Miss-Behaving."

In honor of the ascent, the local newspaper, the *Montagu Mail*, featured a photo of me on its front page with the caption: "Amazing Sasha DiGiulian beats the boys to one of Montagu's toughest climbs!" *Beats the boys*. I couldn't help but think of Lynn Hill's famous quip on the poster of her in my childhood bedroom, "It goes, boys!" This must have been what she meant.

I returned to the States for a national invitational in Park City, Utah, called the Psicobloc Masters Deep-Water Solo Climbing Competition. Psicobloc (Crazy Boulder) is a type of solo climbing that involves scaling cliffs or walls over a cushion of deep water. Though it was popular in Europe, it was the first competition of its kind in the U.S., and it drew the entire outdoor industry. Five thousand spectators—the biggest crowd ever in competition climbing—turned up for the event, which involved climbing without a rope on a fifty-foot plastic wall over the city's Olympic Pool.

I was happy to be there, back home competing on the U.S. stage, and reunited with good friends. The atmosphere was fun and festive, different from the European World Cups, where everyone was so intensely serious. Park City was part highstakes pool party and part theater: Lights were dimmed on the audience as a spotlight lit up the wall and an announcer introduced the climbers and did a play-by-play while the crowd cheered.

I made up for my performance at the Spring Nationals by winning the competition. I was also reminded of how thrilling it was to compete—and win. I thought: *Okay, I'm back. I'm doing this.* Maybe I wasn't ready to give up on competing, even after the rush of Rolihlahla and Miss-Behaving. Maybe I was even ready to take on the biggest challenge of my life: a climb that would literally leave me hanging.

8

A couple years earlier at a dinner hosted by Adidas, I'd been seated next to Reinhold Messner, one of the greatest legends in mountaineering. Aside from Messner's hundreds of "firsts"— first solo ascent of Mount Everest, first to cross Antarctica by foot, first to summit all fourteen of the highest mountains in the world—he'd been an activist in the fight against global warming for longer than I'd been alive. This man sitting to my left with sunbaked skin, intense blue eyes, and a wild mane of hair was suggesting my next climb.

At first, I was so intimidated I could barely introduce myself. He shook my hand and introduced himself—*as though I wouldn't know who he was.* During dinner he turned to me and asked about my climbing adventures and shared some of his own, his warmth and sense of humor calming my nerves.

In the middle of a conversation about future climbing projects, he broke into a broad smile and pulled a pen from his pocket. He flipped over the wine menu and started to map out the Tre Cime peaks, three famed peaks within Italy's Dolomite Mountains—Cima Piccola, Cima Grande, and Cima Ovest— often referred to as the Italian Alps. On Cima Ovest he drew a 90-degree "roof"—a completely upside-down climb—about halfway up the thousand foot–plus big wall. He told me that no woman had ever attempted the route, called "Bellavista," and that only a couple elite male climbers had done it. It was known for its massive overhang and dramatic spires, on the most severe summit of the Dolomite Alps. He said that it would be a remarkable feat to take my sport-climbing skills and apply them to a big wall.

I had no experience in big wall climbing, let alone Alpine climbing, where the weather can change on a dime. Alpine climbs are generally defined as above tree line, and often involve long hikes over steep terrain to access routes. Single-pitch climbing was the world I knew—lowering back to the ground after completing a climb. A big wall required hours upon hours of climbing pitches back to back and without returning to the ground. Each pitch is essentially one rope length—fifty to a hundred feet of climbing—separated by an anchor point.

I started making calculations in my head. A climb on Cima Ovest would be divided into ten to twelve pitches—meaning a thousand-plus vertical feet of consecutive climbing. With an average climb time of thirty to sixty minutes for a single pitch, Cima Ovest could take twelve hours of straight climbing, not including the gear management and rope work that would be involved. But for two years, all I could think was: *If Reinhold Messner is telling me to climb the Dolomites, then that's what I have to do.*

I knew that big walls posed the problem of extreme technical challenges combined with the element of *exposure*—an elevated risk of injury, with or without protection. They often required a team to live on the route, hauling equipment and sleeping on a "portaledge"—a hanging, hammock-like setup suspended on a wall. Then again, Bellavista could be a single-day push, despite its massive overhangs and dramatic spires.

I'd been stoked at the idea of taking on Messner's challenge, but I always had reasons why I wasn't ready: convenience, weather, and the question of how far I was willing to go outside my comfort zone. After South Africa, though, I felt a shift in my skills, in my confidence, and in my readiness.

If I succeeded, it could be a turning point. Not only would it be my first big wall climb—which would become the bedrock of my career—but I would become the first female to make the ascent. Without a second thought, I reached out to a Spanish climber named Edu Marin in the spring of 2013 about attempting the climb with me. I had met Edu over the summer when I moved my base from Innsbruck to Barcelona to climb some of Spain's fabled limestone crags. I'd come to know the Spanish National Team, and had sometimes climbed with them.

I'd felt an immediate attraction to Edu—to his charming smile and easygoing demeanor. Around him I felt a little more like the confident, bubbly person I'd been before my experiences in Innsbruck. Although we hadn't had the chance to get to know each other very well, I knew him as a sweet, straightforward guy who was adored by the climbing community. More important, he had experience with big wall climbs. I don't remember exactly how I pitched the idea to him, but in retrospect it must've sounded something like: *Hey, want to go do this mountain together and be alone for three weeks in Italy?*

"*Claro que sí . . . vámanos!*"—*Absolutely, let's go!* he said.

Early that August, Edu and I arrived in Italy. We rented a car and drove to a lodge at the Dolomites, a two-hour hike to Tre Cime. Europe is known for its hut-to-hut hiking, a network of strategically placed huts or tiny lodges on mountain trails—called *rifugios* in Italy. Mostly they're no-frills, like the one we had—bunk beds, flushable toilet, shower, and stove—but after long days of hiking, they can feel as luxurious as a five-star hotel.

The next day we headed out early in the morning and climbed a fifteen-hundred-foot wall in the area. It didn't have any particularly hard pitches, but it was very exposed and high up off the ground, with no protection from the weather. We arrived at the top late in the evening, which made it difficult to find a place to rappel in the dark. By the time we found the descent, rappelled to the start, and hiked back to the hut, it was two-thirty in the morning. We waited out some bad weather (an especially important practice in alpine climbing) and then practiced more single-pitch climbing in the vicinity for a couple days.

Originally, we had planned to climb another big wall on Cima Ovest before trying Bellavista. However, when we hiked to the towering face of Bellavista, we were so excited to see our main objective that we decided to jump in without a warm-up climb. We were also, perhaps, a bit impatient.

We spent the next several days working the route—climbing the first four pitches one day, and the 8c (5.14b) crux pitch the next. After a day's rest we tried the crux again. Each day I learned the skills needed on a big wall, skills that my life would depend on: building an anchor, belaying with twin ropes, belaying while hanging in midair, and "jumaring" (ascending on a rope). Normally I ascend rock with my fingers and my toes, but jumaring is sometimes necessary while climbing big walls as a way to quickly move up on the wall in order to work specific pitches. It allows one to skip certain sections of a wall—essentially by walking vertically up a rope with jumar devices. However, it's not something to do on the push to *send* a climb.

Edu's guidance was good-natured and expert, albeit in

Spanish—which fortunately I'd studied in high school and practiced during my gap year. After trying the next 8a pitch and then rappelling off, we were certain we'd worked the most difficult parts of the climb.

It was cold and damp the morning we set out to tackle the whole of Bellavista. We woke at 6 A.M. and hiked the two hours to the base. We weren't planning on sending it; we were just going to try the crux. It was wet, and we slipped on our first tries, but when I sent it ahead of Edu I yelled back, "Let's keep going!"

"Are you sure?" he asked. "It's already one P.M."

"Yeah! We are sending! Let's do it. The rest is easier climbing," I naively insisted.

By 7 P.M. we were cold and soaked and twelve hundred feet from the ground—about 120 stories high. For two hours we sheltered in a crevice barely big enough for the two of us to crouch, waiting out an unexpected hailstorm that put us way behind schedule. We had been on the mountain since 8 A.M., which had already been a late start to do the climb in a day— typically, alpine climbs start well before sunrise.

Above, the clouds were dark, ominous. Far below, boulders from frequent avalanches littered the ground, as if the mountain were a goliath limestone lizard continually shedding its skin. As high up on the kind of finicky, unpredictable rock as we were, we'd reached a point of no return. We couldn't rappel down the cliff face and we couldn't retrace our steps. My brain started racing. I thought about how BASE jumpers and skydivers from all over the world were drawn to the summit we were attempting. At that point I thought: *If only* we *could jump . . . or dive.*

On alpine climbs like Bellavista, routes could be unclear. I'd heard how climbers often found themselves on previously unexplored terrain—which was exactly what had happened to us. We'd made it to a point where we hadn't yet climbed. Still, the last two hundred feet should have been the easiest because of its less challenging technical grade. However, in alpine climbing there can also be far less protection and *wilder*—meaning less-explored—terrain, especially higher up on a wall. We were striking distance from the top, but instead of the simple marked route, we faced two hundred feet of vertical climbing with no points of *security*—no pitons or bolts, and rock so fragile it couldn't hold any gear, which meant no place to attach our rope.

Initially, we were optimistic about finding some seam in the rock to insert a camalot, or "friend"—gear that can hold a person. But those gadgets required solid rock—the kind of rock that was nowhere in sight. We huddled on a small ledge, unsure of our next move. I expected Edu to come up with a solution. After all, he was the experienced big wall climber; he'd figure it out. But when he broke our silence, it wasn't what I expected to hear. He said we could "simul-climb"—climb tied together on the same rope—meaning that if one of us fell, that person would be certain to pull the other off the wall. Or, we could coil the rope and wear it on our backs.

My mind couldn't compute those choices. "But coiling the rope means we're not tied into anything," I said, panicked.

"Well, yeah, then the rope won't get caught—"

"Because we're not connected!"

No rope meant free soloing, which was a type of climbing I'd never cared to do. I'd never taken the unnecessary risk of near-certain fatality. Free soloing meant that if we fell, it would be our last fall . . . ever. I felt an uncontrollable anger rumbling through my body, like a tennis ball squeezing up my stomach through my windpipe. I clenched my fists. I wanted to beat them against the rock—or Edu. I wanted to scream: "You're the experienced one. Don't you know better? How did this happen? We're going to die!"

Instead, we silently untied our ropes in the dimming light as a swirl of ice-cold mist rose from the abyss below. *Okay. Okay, we can do this. We're going to do this.* I wasn't sure if I was thinking that or saying it aloud, but I did hear Edu say to me, "You can do this, Sasha. I know you can do this."

I followed Edu as he started to climb, my core tight as a knot. Foot, hand, hand, foot. Mirroring Edu's moves, I made my way like a spider, pushing and grabbing, leaving one hold at a time. In a moment between reaches, with my hands and feet mobilized on the wall, the rock gave way underneath my left hand and foot. I watched as it disappeared into the black abyss below. Half my body was left dangling, relying on the other half to hang on with every fiber of strength.

In that moment, all previous thoughts drained away—my negativity, my blaming Edu, my anger, my "what ifs?" I needed to be one hundred percent present in my body and mind. One hundred percent no more bullshit excuses. There was no point in complaining. No point in wasting the energy. There was simply no room in me, at that time, on that mountain, to think, *What if I fall?* I regained the rhythm of my breath. I reattached my left hand to the wall. I found support for my foot. And then I moved on.

At the top I could barely see two feet in front of me in the misty darkness, but I could feel the flat solid rock underneath my hands and knees. I didn't even know I was crying until I heard Edu say, "*Estamos aquí.* No worry." I sat with my hands in my lap and sucked the thick, cold air through my nose. We'd done it! We'd sent Bellavista!

In the very next breath, I realized that we still needed to make it back down.

Crouched in the howling wind, Edu and I talked about the possibility of sleeping at the summit. But surviving the night at the top in our condition sounded like a feat in itself. The temperature had dropped below freezing, we had on damp, layered sweatshirts, and our food supply was down to two Kit Kats. We searched over the next two hours for the way down, but every way we went we faced a dark drop off the edge.

Down-climbing on the fragile rock could prove perilous, because we wouldn't be able to see more than a few feet in front of us through the light of our headlamps. Even so, we continued to search for the descent, mostly because we were too cold to stand still. Suddenly it dawned on me: *I have cell service! I'll call Alex Huber and ask him!*

Incredibly enough, Alex answered his cell. The German climber and I had spoken previously about meeting up in the Dolomites for a climb together, so he immediately started telling me about his schedule and which day would work best for him, as if I were sitting on the couch in my living room ready for a chat. "No. No, Alex," I said. "I'm *currently* at the top of Cima Ovest and we don't know how to get down! Do you remember how?"

"Oh, Sasha!" he said in his thick German accent. "You must sleep at the top tonight. There is no way you can make it down in the night. It is far too dangerous."

Edu and I huddled together and tried to sleep, but neither of us could stop shivering. We decided to keep searching for the descent, but after a couple more hours I was delirious with fatigue. I sat down and passed out the moment I hit the ground.

I woke to a hazy, early morning light and turned to my left—I was perched only a foot from the cliff's edge. To my right, Edu was asleep in a seated position. It was August thirteenth, his birthday. Finally, there was enough light to find the descent. Once we did, we rappelled a short distance and then scampered through crevices and slid along rocks down the backside of the cliff. After several hours we hit the hiking trail. Two hours later we made it back to our cabin, exhausted and exhilarated.

A shower in our tiny bathroom cost five euros and lasted five minutes. Fifteen euros and three hot showers later, I let it sink in that I had made the first female ascent of Bellavista—my very first big wall. Edu and I jokingly vowed to make it a tradition to be somewhere in the world, hanging off a cliff, on his birthday—although I secretly hoped it wasn't just a joke.

ONCE I WAS back in New York City for my sophomore year, my routine was the same—class, climb, home, then a competition or work commitment *somewhere*. Work led to more work, which led to magazine profiles and more invitations to galas and fundraisers. I shape-shifted between dressing up for those glamorous events and climbing to exhaustion in my brutal training schedule. I enjoyed it all, but sometimes it felt as if I was living in two worlds, one valuing strength and grit and sweat, the other highlighting beauty, fashion, and femininity. *Couldn't those two worlds be combined?*

I was as athletic as any male athletes I knew, but I also loved dressing in decidedly feminine clothing—dresses, gowns, hot pink nail polish, and pink anything else—even though it was often hard to find an evening gown in my size that would zip over my muscular back and shoulders. I'd earned those muscles, just as I'd earned my crooked, calloused fingers and bunion toes. For me, femininity and strength were not on opposite sides of the spectrum, though sometimes it was hard to hold on to that belief, especially when certain magazines happened to focus on my looks—petite, blond, marketable—rather than my accomplishments.

I'd gained a few pounds, because I had built up muscle. But

as good as I felt, and as healthy as my eating habits had become, I was still acutely aware of that number. I wondered if I would ever find release from that self-defeating scrutiny. Every morning my bathroom scale still dictated whether I'd feel good going into my training. An added pound could alter my mood, my climbing, and what I allowed myself to eat. I was finally considered "normal" for my height and muscularity, but in the climbing world I felt as if I was practically overweight. After all that I'd accomplished as an athlete, certain climbing websites were still rife with trolls commenting on my body.

Sometimes I'd read or hear rumors about my lifestyle—small digs and disparaging commentary, mostly from internet trolls:

"She definitely doesn't look like a climber."

"Oh, yeah, Sasha's on red carpets and stuff. Why is she abandoning climbing?"

"She's getting sidetracked."

"She's in a *sorority*. Ugh."

Apparently "real" climbers weren't in sororities. They didn't climb in makeup and nail polish. They didn't like dressing up when they weren't climbing. And they didn't look like me. Apparently, being on a red carpet or attending a nonclimbing event was a sure sign that I wasn't a legit climber anymore. Because, of course, I couldn't possibly do both.

I became acutely aware of the ways in which other female athletes were described in the media—"no hint of testosterone in her nature," "so blue-eyed, so ruby-lipped, so twelve-car-pileup gorgeous." Meanwhile, male athletes were "dynamic," "powerful," and "agile." Since becoming involved in the Women's Sports Foundation and joining their advisory committee, I'd heard stories firsthand from world-class athletes reduced to their looks. What would it take to confront that kind of bias? On the smallest scale, I'd always felt that helping kids, especially young girls, discover what they were physically capable of was a means of pushing back and proving that athletes didn't have to look or be a certain way.

I knew what it felt like to be capable enough to "reach the top," and to experience the joy and power of achieving a goal. I believed that kids, especially, needed to be given opportunities to have goals and to realize them. I viewed participation in sports—especially, of course, in climbing—as a way to do that. When Up2US Sports, an organization that provided low-income kids with athletic opportunities, asked me to become their "climbing ambassador," it was a no-brainer.

One of my first travels as "ambassador" was to a climbing gym just outside of Boston. There, I met with a group of ten- and eleven-year-olds, none of whom had ever climbed. They re- minded me of my first climbing team in Alexandria—all energy and enthusiasm. I gave them a quick introduction, and then showed them some basic moves to use while I belayed them. When it was time to climb, I started to ask for a volunteer to go first, but one of the smaller kids had her hand raised before I could finish my sentence.

Right from the start of her climb, she knew what to do—she seemed like a natural—but about halfway through, she froze. It was as if something had abruptly drained all her confidence— perhaps doubt, fear, or the prospect of failure. She wanted to come down, but I knew she could reach the top. "No, come on," I said, "keep going. I know you can do this."

"I don't want to. I can't. I can't do it," she said, as if to herself more than to me.

"Yes, you can. You just have to figure out the next move." I knew that if I let her come down, she'd feel worse for letting her fear get the best of her. "You've got it," I said. "I won't let you get hurt. You're so close. You're more than halfway there."

Seconds later, she continued. She made it to the top, though

I could see she was crying. I wasn't sure if I'd done the right thing, but I just couldn't let her give up. I lowered her to the ground and unhooked her. She ran straight to the bathroom. Two minutes later she returned and hugged me. "Thank you," she said, smiling ear to ear. If that little girl could set a goal, give a hundred percent and push through the fear, she might see that anything was possible. That is what I believed. That's what I wanted the rest of those kids to believe as well.

I thought of Reinhold Messner telling me I could do Bellavista, and the other people who believed I could do something before I believed it—people like Claudiu, Mom, and Magnus. The same was true when legendary climber John Long approached me about making the first ascent of the "Misty Wall Project," a fifteen-pitch 5.13 route in Yosemite right by Yosemite Falls, the tallest, most spectacular waterfall in the park.

Yosemite Valley has been a mecca for amateur and renowned climbers for nearly two centuries—from naturalist John Muir's 1869 ropeless climb on Cathedral Peak, to the first climbs with pitons in the 1930s, to rivalries between climbers of the 1950s through the 1980s, to Lynn Hill's 1993 first free climb of El Capitan, to Kevin Jorgeson and Tommy Caldwell's freeing the Dawn Wall, to Alex Honnold's 2017 free solo.

Some of the most legendary climbers, though, were part of a group called the Stonemasters, one of whose founding members was John Long. Long and his crew were free-spirited adventurers of the 1970s—"self-proclaimed dirtbags and long-haired vagabonds"* barely out of their teens—who basically gave birth to "extreme" sports culture. Long not only made some awesome first ascents, he went on to author dozens of articles and books

---

* https://www.agora.universite-paris-saclay.fr/california-climbing-stone masters -figure-dirtbag/

about rock climbing and eventually to work as a consultant for TV and movies, including for the 1993 action-thriller *Cliffhanger*. In 2009, *Rock and Ice* magazine recognized him as "the most influential adventurer in the world."

In 2017 Long had partnered with Adidas Outdoor and the American Alpine Club (AAC) for his Legacy Restoration Project to conserve and establish high-end free climb routes in Yosemite on old, neglected "aid routes"—routes requiring extensive gear, including "aiders," which allow a climber to stand on rungs or steps to move up a wall. Because climbing was becoming increasingly popular, Long's idea was to clean and upgrade the hardware on older, less popular routes to help disperse climbing traffic. He proposed that I try the Misty Wall Project with pro climbers Jon Cardwell and Marcus Garcia, a route that had originally been climbed in 1963 as a hard aid route. Since then, climbers had attempted free climbs, but no one had ever climbed it "clean"—without falling—in one day.

I was super-stoked for the project, because it would mark my first Yosemite big wall climb. Yosemite had always been a hot spot, but it had recently seen some especially daring firsts: Alex Honnold's free solo, Tommy Caldwell and Kevin Jorgeson's Dawn Wall climb on El Capitan, and the first *naked* ascent of The Nose by two climbers, Leah Pappajohn and Jonathan Fleury—a "first" I was more than happy to let someone else achieve.

The Misty Wall Project was different from any climb I'd done. It involved "crack and trad (traditional) climbing"—a method of placing removable gear such as camalots for safety, instead of having bolts to clip—which meant shoving my fists into the fissures of the rock instead of clamping down with my fingertips on the face, and "offwidths." In offwidth climbing, cracks are too wide to jam in hands and fingers, but not wide enough for a whole body. Instead, I could only ease parts of my body into the crack, while performing a kind of upward slithering movement. It reminded me of doing The Worm—the break-dance move—except I had to do it vertically while ascending a crack in a wall.

At times I felt claustrophobic to the point of distraction. I was cut off from all sounds except the raging Yosemite Falls beside me, like a high-powered drone in my head, and I was in so much pain from the rock shaving my legs and forearms that if it weren't for Marcus's coaching and encouragement, I'd probably have let go.

After several days' working all the pitches, Jon, Marcus, and I bivvied at the base of the wall by the thundering falls. At 5 A.M. we started climbing for the push. Fourteen hours later, we reached the top for the first free ascent of Misty Wall, just as Long believed we would.

9

"Have fun. Be safe. And do your best!" Dad said, as he did whenever he dropped me off at the airport. For whatever reason, we always got along within the confines of his old manual-drive BMW. No matter our prior disagreements, his car was like Switzerland with a Jimmy Buffett soundtrack. Just me and Dad and Jimmy. It felt like coming home.

I was traveling most weekends—thirty-six hours in Seoul for an Adidas Rock Stars event, Germany for a daylong photo shoot, Shanghai for a commercial, Austria for a Red Bull promotion—and taking advantage of those marathon flights to catch up on schoolwork. I usually cut my timing close—hopping from class into a taxi to JFK Airport in Queens for a fifteen-hour plane ride, followed by a taxi to my hotel. After my job I'd reverse the whole routine. *Wash, rinse, repeat.*

One afternoon I had an event in New York City the day before a speaking engagement in Barcelona. I left straight from the event with an hour to spare, but halfway to the airport, I realized I didn't have my passport—I'd visited home the previous weekend and had left it on my desk. Not knowing what else to do, I called Dad at his marina in Baltimore. "Hang on," he said.

"I'll be there. I'm leaving for home now." But "home" meant he was headed an hour in the opposite direction of JFK—to Alexandria. I changed my flight to the last one of the day, the only one left that would arrive in Spain in time for my speaking gig. An hour later, Dad was on the four-hour drive from Alexandria, Virginia, to JFK with my passport.

I told the woman behind the check-in desk that my dad was on his way from Virginia, and then I started pacing. By the time "Last call for boarding" was announced, everyone at the United Airlines desk knew about Dad's race against the clock. Minutes later, Dad came running down the corridor and was met with a United cheering section. He high-fived me and pulled me in for a quick hug. "Love you, Dad. Thanks," I said, my words muffled in his jacket.

SPRING SEMESTER OF sophomore year, I'd sometimes fit in a weekend visit home. It was an easy two-and-a-half-hour ride on Amtrak—a welcome escape from my nonstop schedule. I could sleep in my own bed, enjoy Mom's cooking, and catch up on training at Sportrock, where Mom would belay me. I didn't see nearly as much of Dad—he was still spending a lot of time at work—but when he did join us, there was a new ease in our relationship. Maybe he'd finally started to see me as an adult, or maybe it was because I'd let go of the resentment I had about him not paying for school or not being as involved in my climbing as I would have liked. Whatever the reason, he felt comfortable enough to open up about how his business wasn't going the way he'd planned, and to share how proud he was of Charlie and me.

Occasionally we'd have some one-on-one time, usually around a trip to the nearby grocery store. One Saturday he boasted about a new "toy" he'd acquired, an old Vespa scooter that a tenant had left at his marina in lieu of rent. "Let's take it for a spin to get groceries, Sash." Mom warned us that the scooter wouldn't make it, but my dad insisted. "Come on, it'll be fun."

I squeezed behind him on the back, and we rode through our neighborhood to the nearby Safeway. After shopping, we crammed our bags into the hatch and hopped back on. Dad hit the ignition, but it was no-go. He hit it a dozen more times before we looked at each other and wordlessly agreed that we'd need to walk. We pulled the scooter home between us, balancing the groceries. My dad looked so dejected, but I had to laugh. "Oh, Dad, Mom's gonna be so like, 'I told you so.'"

"Yeah," he said, and then smiled. "But it was fun, right?"

It felt like only yesterday that Dad had finally bought himself an iPhone and asked me to show him how it worked. He could only understand (or only had patience for) the basics. He never got the knack of writing emails, let alone messaging. After seeing one of my competitions on some cable sports channel, he'd send me an email, but they read like telegraph messages in the subject line: "Watched You Today Great Win Keep Going," "Have Fun Stay Safe Looks Beautiful," "Miss You Your Cat Is on the TV," followed by *This Message Has No Content.*

In June Mom flew up to Montreal for my brother's graduation from McGill University, while my dad drove to New York City so we could take a road trip together to meet them. He arrived in time to watch me tape a segment for The Weather Channel with NBC's Al Roker, about how climbing was contingent upon weather. On the drive up, Dad told me how self-assured I seemed in the taping and how excited he was about Charlie's graduation. Mostly he appeared happy and at ease, although I could sense in the silences that he was stressed out about something. I figured it was work.

After graduation, Charlie and Mom flew back home and I returned with my dad. I had a climbing trip scheduled in Wyoming, so he dropped me off at the airport just like he used to when I was in high school. An hour later I learned that my flight was canceled, so I booked one out for the next day and called Dad. He came right back for me and we headed home.

That night, he, Mom, Charlie, and I all went to Chadwicks, a local sports pub at the end of our street, for half-priced-burger night. We cheered on the Rangers playing the L.A. Kings for the Stanley Cup. We talked hockey, my summer plans, and Charlie's joining my dad's business for the summer. I ate the maraschino cherry from Dad's manhattan—served straight up, no ice— something I hadn't done since I was little. Everything felt right. The next day he dropped me off at the airport. "Have fun, Sash. Be safe. And do your best," he said before driving off.

My plan was to spend the first two months of the summer climbing in Lander, in central Wyoming, where I would have my pick of incredible sport climbing on limestone cliffs. I was staying in town with my friends Mandy and Brian and climbing every day. I started to feel as if I was back in a flow state. I felt confident and happy. After a couple weeks of great climbing, I took a rest day on a Sunday. I walked a ways from the house, down a quiet river path, and thought about how grateful I was for everything in my life. I dialed my dad for our usual weekly catch-up, but instead saw an incoming call from Mom and answered it.

"Sasha, Dad just had a stroke. I'm in the ambulance," she said, her voice thin and tinny. My brain couldn't compute the information. I thought that maybe I'd misheard her. *No, that's not possible. I was just calling to talk to him,* I thought. "I don't know what's happening," Mom continued. "I'll keep you updated, but it's bad. You should look into flights and come home as soon as you can. Tonight or tomorrow. You need to be here. We might be losing Dad."

I could feel my heart racing. I didn't have time to think of anything except getting home. I ran back to Mandy and Brian's house. "Mandy, my dad just had a stroke, I need to go to the airport. I don't know when I'll be back. I don't have time to get all my stuff, I'm just going to leave my suitcase." Mandy offered to drive, but I had a rental car I had to return. Gulping air and wiping away tears, I drove to the tiny local airport. It had one kiosk and one plane going out. I bought a ticket and waited an hour before hearing an announcement that the flight had been canceled. No other flight would be leaving that day due to inclement weather.

I ran to the kiosk, my face swollen from crying, my voice cracking, "Ma'am, it's not even raining!" I said to the attendant. "Are you kidding me? What is happening? How can I not leave?"

"Well, you could go to Casper, which is about a two-hour drive. That's a bigger airport, so there may be flights out tonight from there."

I jumped into my car and took off, checking in with Mom and Charlie on the drive. "He's going into surgery," Charlie said. "They're draining the blood from his brain. We really don't know anything yet." At the Casper airport I managed to catch a flight that would arrive in D.C. by 6 A.M. Mom and Charlie met me at the airport. As the three of us embraced, I felt the beat of Mom's heart through her sweater. It scared me how hard and fast it was pounding.

We arrived at Fairfax Hospital and went straight to the Neuroscience Intensive Care Unit. I felt as if I were walking through quicksand as I followed Mom's and Charlie's hurried steps down the hall to its double doors. I sucked in a deep breath, knowing my world would be changed forever once I pushed through those doors. We stopped for a moment outside Dad's room and then entered as though in slow motion. I gasped. *That couldn't be him.* He was unconscious and nearly unrecognizable. Tubes connected to beeping, humming machines swirled around his swollen body. I'd never seen him look so vulnerable. *What if he can't talk? What if he can't walk? What if I don't have a chance to tell him how much I love him?* I remembered to breathe and to hope, instead of thinking the worst. I took his hand. *At least I'll be by his side when he wakes up.*

While we waited, Mom admitted that she'd been keeping me from knowing the full extent of Dad's financial troubles. She told me how Sunday morning she, Dad, and Charlie had been at the dining room table talking about Charlie helping with the business over the summer. The bank had cut off Dad's line of credit and there was no money left for the development. "Well, then what are you going to do?" Charlie had asked. Dad hadn't even a chance to answer—the very next moment he fell from his chair. When Mom yelled that she was calling for an ambulance, the last words my dad said before falling unconscious were, "Don't. Don't call an ambulance!"

We took turns talking to Dad and holding his hands, hoping for a sign from him. Wednesday night Mom asked the attending neurologist if Dad's speech would be badly impaired. The doctor took a breath and said, "I don't think that's the question you should be asking. *If* he wakes up—because there is no certainty that he will—it's unlikely that he would be able to understand you or you him."

Mom looked disbelieving at first. She took several minutes, as if she were computing all the possible outcomes, and then turned to us. "That's not the life Dad would want," she said. "We'll pray for a miracle and see what happens over the next couple days."

Life moved in slow motion the next few days. I dragged myself to the store to buy toothpaste and couldn't understand how everyone around me was going about their day so *normally*. At the cashier line, when someone cut in front of me, I thought: *How can you be so rude? Don't you know my dad is dying?!* But I was living in my own bubble, in my own story, and everyone around me was living in theirs. I thought about how weird and confusing it is that none of us can ever really know what's going on in another person's life, especially a stranger's. I looked around and wondered if anyone else had a dying parent.

It had been a while since I'd spent this much time with Charlie—surprising, really, considering how close we were growing up. Charlie had chosen to go to boarding school for high school—Phillips Academy, in Andover, Massachusetts. After he left I more or less became an only child at home. I visited him for hockey games throughout the school year, and he came home for holidays and summer vacations, but by high school, I was spending most of that time on climbing trips. I felt sad about it sometimes. His first year away was the toughest, because I went from seeing him daily, at home and at school, to hardly at all. When Dad had his stroke, Charlie had just moved back to D.C. to work with him for the summer.

"I've been gone so much," I said to him, a few days into Dad's hospital stay. "I wish I'd spent more time with you and Dad and Mom. I miss the days where we spent the whole summer together in Tremblant."

He smiled and hugged me, as if I didn't have anything to apologize for. "Dad understood that. Besides, you're here," he said.

I searched for something to say that might make him feel better, if only for a moment. "You know, Dad was so ridiculously proud of you when you graduated from McGill. The whole ride up he wouldn't stop talking about it."

We took turns serving up memories of Dad, the good and the somewhat absurd, like the time he took us all out on his boat the evening after 9/11. Not a good time to stall in the middle of the harbor in Washington, D.C., with zero reception, and shoot emergency rescue flares into the nighttime sky. The Coast Guard surrounded our boat while the D.C. S.W.A.T. team arrived in a helicopter and descended upon us with guns drawn. Charlie laughed for the first time in days. He said, "You yelled, 'What's happening? Why do these people have guns?'"

"Yeah, then they realized it was just some dumb family out on a boat ride. Crazy." Suddenly Charlie and I were both lost in thought—maybe thinking about how Dad did what he wanted to do, whenever he wanted to do it, or maybe thinking about that miracle we were hoping would happen. I'd always kept a journal, so during those days of uncertainty I turned to writing to help me sort through my emotions. I bought a new notebook and began it with "Dear Dad." I filled it with memories of my childhood, along with everything I was feeling and everything I still wanted to tell my dad.

On Thursday, Charlie, Dad's brothers, Mom, her sister Deborah, and I met with the chief neurologist. He spoke with us for an hour, answering our questions and explaining Dad's condition. "There's been too much bleeding on both sides of his brain," he said. "If he regained consciousness, he would have little or no control over his physical and cognitive functions. He can't be taken off sedation because his blood pressure will spike, and as long as he is sedated, he'll have to be on a ventilator."

So now we knew. The machine was his source of life—a life that, moving forward, would mean lying unresponsive in a bed. It was up to us to make a choice.

On Friday night, Father Enzio, the priest from the Italian church my dad attended growing up, came to Dad's room and read him his last rites. Mom, Charlie, and I held on to each other and cried. Saturday, more family members arrived. My aunt contacted the crematorium and took Mom to buy an urn. On Sunday we took Dad off his ventilator. I thought: *How is it possible that it's only been seven days since I was sitting by that river in Wyoming?*

A nurse gave Dad morphine. We stood by his bedside as he labored to breathe on his own, taking in less and less oxygen as the hours passed. I wanted it to end, but at the same time I was terrified that it would. We played his favorite songs— "Cheeseburger in Paradise" and other great hits of Jimmy Buffett, which seemed as absurd as it was fitting. "He would love this," Charlie whispered to me. "That we're playing his favorite music, you know?"

A collection of moments played in my head: Dad yelling "Be safe, do your best" as I'd run off to catch a flight, Dad greeting me at the airport upon my return with a bear hug and a latte, Dad pulling me on a Radio Flyer sled, Dad barbecuing more food than his friends and family could eat in a week, Dad peering through the kitchen window watching me park the car, Dad driving to my high school graduation. A nurse came into the room to wheel away the computer monitors, at which point Dad opened his eyes. *Was he waking up?* My godmother, Reggie, reached out to his face and gently lowered his lids. He was gone. I felt frozen in that moment for I don't know how long. It was as if I were imprinting the movie of my life with him forever in my head.

Dad's death flipped all of us upside down. As much as I couldn't wrap my head around the fact that he was gone from our lives, the hardest part was seeing Mom and Charlie so utterly brokenhearted and knowing there was nothing I could do or say to help. At twenty-two I had no experience dealing with real grief. In the past, when I felt hurt or sadness or disappointment, my way of coping was to move on emotionally and psychologically and to keep moving, but my grief felt like all those emotions together times ten. I wasn't sure what to do—or how to grieve—so I decided to follow through with my commitments for the summer. I hoped that would be a way of somehow working through my feelings.

I was scheduled to be a keynote speaker at the International Climbers' Festival back in Lander, but the speech I'd prepared a month earlier no longer felt right. I spent the night rewriting it as more of a tribute to Dad. In front of an auditorium full of climbing enthusiasts, I spoke of how my father taught me to dream big, and how he insisted that I could accomplish whatever I set my mind to. If he thought about failure, he didn't express it. He stated his aspirations as certainties, without any doubt they would come to fruition. He may not have accomplished all his dreams, but he put them out there, always believing that anything was possible. That was his legacy, that and his unconditional love for us no matter what.

I managed to finish my speech without becoming emotional, but afterward I was hit with a wave of exhaustion, as though I'd just run a marathon. Was that what it felt like to begin to process my dad's death?

On the plane back home, I thought, *I have to call Dad and tell him about the festival!* Then I remembered. Those kinds of lapses would continue for years, but there would also be those times when I distinctly felt his presence.

I wasn't sure how to process Dad's death. How was I supposed to be grieving? How long did it take? I had no road map for how to move through the sadness and the anger I had about him being gone. I wondered if I needed more time to be with my family before leaving to go back to my life, but I'd committed to a climb that summer. I'd never been one to bail on a commitment, and I didn't want to start now. What was I supposed to do?

Mom assured me, "Dad would have wanted you to stick with your plans. Dad would have wanted you to keep climbing."

A FEW WEEKS later, I arrived in Sardinia, an Italian island in the Mediterranean Sea, and felt a small wave of relief—I was excited and ready to climb. Edu, Keith, his co-cameraperson Colette, and I were there to attempt "Viaje de Los Locos" (Madmen's Journey), a seven-pitch limestone route that had been bolted and sent by Dani Andrada in 2002, but never repeated.

I'd climbed in Italy before, but being there after Dad's death gave it new meaning, because he'd always been so proud of his Italian heritage. We were in Cala Gonone, a seaside town founded by fishermen a hundred years earlier, walking distance to a nearby pier. Dad would have loved the place, and especially loved that I was there, cooking a huge carbo-load meal of pasta with a Bolognese sauce for my team the night before our climb—a dish that happened to be one of his favorites. I felt connected to him in a way that made my heart just a little lighter.

Viaje de Los Locos was a thousand-foot climb that started with a 5.13d and that, at the time, was deemed one of the hardest multi-pitch climbs in the world. The second pitch was a 5.13a, the third a 5.14a, followed by a stack of hard pitches: 5.13c, 5.13a, 5.12c, and a 5.12b. Edu and I traded off on leading, divvying up the pitches based on our strengths. He led the first one because it was more his style of climbing—powerful, with big, long moves. I led the 5.13a and 5.14a, which were more technical; vertical climbs with small crimpers—more my strengths. In the beginning I struggled on some long reaches, and I fell close to the finish of a couple pitches. Those falls were especially long and frightening.

Falling on a climb feels like being suspended in time. My breath catches in my chest as I move from weightlessness in my harness to crashing against the wall, ideally with feet first and knees bent to soften the collision. Oftentimes, as I fall, I don't even have a moment to think, *Here we go!* It's like being abruptly dropped from the top of the highest roller coaster. Caught off guard, the best I can do is to be as present as possible. Preferably, I'm also at the end of a rope with enough stretch so that there is some buoyancy in the "catch"—the moment my fall is stopped.

Unfortunately, not every fall is perfect. A climber can fall from different angles and end up with head and feet in any number of positions, which is why I at least try to be aware of how my body is moving in space in order to try and position myself for the safest possible impact. A fall may take only a second or two, but it can feel so much longer.

It was taking hours on end to complete the pitches, with little time to rest. I thought, *Too hard . . . this is too hard for me,* but we kept working on our moves for the next several days. As we hiked to the climb at the end of the week, we weren't yet certain this was the day we would make the send, but the air felt cooler than it had during the previous days and the rock felt sticky and fresh. There were also more clouds in the sky, which meant added protection from the glare of the midday sun.

After reaching the base of the wall, we laid out our gear, organizing everything we'd need on our harnesses and in our day pack. I pictured the moves ahead and reminded myself to enjoy the uniqueness of the climb and trust that I was fully prepared. As we progressed up the wall, successfully knocking out pitch after pitch, I thought: *Everything is going according to plan. Stay positive and visualize success.*

Right then, the sun briefly broke through the clouds. Gentle wisps of wind wrapped around me like beams of energy willing me on and whispering, "This is it. This is the day." I took a moment to take in where I was, to be grateful for being there, and in that moment, I was sure I could sense my dad's presence. It was an intangible thing—like knowing that a send is imminent—but I felt he was there, watching over me. Edu and I continued our ascent, which became another first female ascent for me, and a first feeling that Dad had been with me the whole time.

10

"An obsession for the mentally deranged."

That's how *The Alpine Journal*, the oldest mountaineering magazine in the world, once referred to the Eiger, a thirteen-thousand-foot mountain in the Bernese Alps of Switzerland. Although I consider myself risk-averse, I couldn't get the idea of the mountain out of my mind. Every year since high school I'd made a goal of challenging myself on a climb that was beyond my comfort zone, and the Eiger seemed just that kind of challenge.

In the spring of 2015, a friend told me about "La Paciencia," a route on the Eiger's North Face—notoriously nicknamed "Murder Wall" because more than sixty climbers have died attempting it since 1935. The North Face even had a Hollywood action movie named after it—Clint Eastwood's *The Eiger Sanction*, which was filmed on location and cost the life of one of the movie's stuntmen.

At the time, the hardest free climb up the Eiger's North Face was La Paciencia—just under three thousand feet of alpine climbing broken up into twenty-three pitches. What made it so dangerous was the mercurial alpine weather. Climbing the route would require me to bivvy—create a sleeping ledge on a wall by shoveling rocks out of the way—and navigate very cold, wet conditions while managing all my gear, neither of which I'd done before.

This route on the North Face had also never seen a female ascent, so I pitched the climb to Adidas. They offered enthusiastic support and assembled a film crew while I reached out to fellow Adidas climber Carlo Traversi, who had some experience with big walls. Carlo said he'd be stoked for the adventure. He had his own résumé of first ascents, having grown up climbing the walls, cliffs, and boulders of the Sierra Nevada. We knew each other from our years in the competition circuit and from an Adidas climbing trip to Japan, but climbing the Eiger would be our first big wall together.

Early in August 2015, Carlo, Adidas cameraman Frank Kretschmann, photographer Mary Mecklenburg, and I flew to Zurich and then drove to the village of Grindelwald, Switzerland, at the base of the Eiger. We knew we'd have to reckon with minute-by-minute changes in the weather, but we weren't prepared for all the rain, hail, and snow we faced from the moment we arrived. The local climbers told us that unusually warm weather was causing ice inside the North Face to melt, making for slippery climbing. But Carlo and I remained optimistic that the weather would improve and give us a solid window to climb.

Falling rock and ice are the most difficult variables to mitigate in climbing. As much as one can reduce risk by watching weather patterns, navigating away from rock that appears unstable, and always keeping an eye on the route above, larger walls come with added risk. Typically, they see less traffic than sport-climbing crags. Over time that can mean that routes that were once "tested" by a previous climber may have been unknowingly altered—often severely—due to exposure to the elements and changes in climate.

La Paciencia was one of those routes. From the get-go I struggled with feeling that maybe I wasn't experienced enough to have taken it on, but I also knew that stepping outside my comfort zone was the only way to grow. I prided myself on rising to the task at hand. *I can do this,* I told myself.

As we worked the Paciencia route, we found ourselves climbing in tandem with a couple of men developing a parallel route to our left—soon to be named "Odyssey." One of the climbers, whom I'll call James, was a European alpinist. The first thing he said to me when we came upon him was, "I don't know if little girls belong on the Eiger."

I was dumbfounded. I pretended not to hear him, but it didn't stop there. He continued to say things like, "You know, there's a well-known sport-climbing area nearby. Maybe you would enjoy that," basically telling me to go do single-pitch climbs. Another time he said, "I just don't know if this is very safe for you." Carlo ignored him, but I couldn't.

I was always polite, because there was a certain respect that I afforded fellow climbers, even if they didn't reciprocate. "Well, I chose to be here, and I'll be fine. Thanks for your concern." What I wanted to say was, "Hey, I'm here doing my thing and you do yours. Leave me alone."

There was no way of avoiding James, because we were forced to share a bivvy. Carlo and I tried to sleep that night, but James snored like a locomotive. We'd hung our fixed lines nearby, one for hauling up gear and another one for the photographer to jumar on—to climb with aids for his hands and feet, such as a nylon ladder-like foot strap.

One of the most indelicate things about spending a long time on a big wall, especially overnight, is that climbers must relieve themselves at some point—yes, I mean *poop*. The responsible and recommended way to do this is by using a bag, which then gets stored in a "poop tube," an approximately ten-by-four-inch section of PVC pipe, with a plug on one end and a cap on the other. That way, climbers can carry out their waste along with everything else they're hauling.

Apparently, James didn't bother to bring his poop tube, or he didn't take into consideration that there would be anyone climbing nearby, or maybe he just didn't care about anyone but himself. He moved away from our bivvy, and without taking note of where our gear line was fixed, he let it rip down the face of the Eiger. The next morning when we pulled up our rope, it ran straight through his waste. I can honestly say that there aren't a whole lot of things I find disgusting enough to make me nauseous, but finding James's little surprise on our gear line was enough to make me want to puke. The best Carlo and I could do was hope we didn't come down with giardia.

We moved past our bivvy and left James and his companion behind, but then we were stymied by the increasingly bad weather. Snow and hail combined with rain formed cascading waterfalls all around us. From thousands of feet above, I could hear chunks of ice breaking off the wall like missile fire, though it was difficult to see where they were falling because of a giant cloud hugging the mountain, obscuring our view in every direction. At times I'd look down from on lead, unable to see Carlo. I'd yell to make sure he was okay, or to tell him to feed me more rope or take in some slack, but between the white noise of the waterfalls, the whipping wind, and the distant echoes of cracking ice, my voice was lost in the void. Even though I knew he was there,

I felt more alone than I'd ever been. As soon as our communication resumed, we agreed it was time to retreat and wait for better conditions.

Back at our lodging near the foot of the Eiger, Carlo, our crew, and I tried to stay positive, but the next day Carlo wasn't feeling well. I went to work on the crux pitch of the climb with Frank, but even though he was a very experienced belayer, I felt unsure of myself. I didn't know if it was because Carlo wasn't there with me or that I was more fatigued than I'd realized, or both; but not too long into the climb, I became paralyzed with fear. I started replaying in my head the recent news of a climber's death on the mountain—something I never allowed myself to do, because I'd always been very thorough about my preparations in managing risk.

Most deaths in climbing occur from rappelling accidents on descents, or because of avalanches or falling rock or ice. I knew avalanches weren't an issue on the Eiger, since they were more common on high alpine climbing and we were mitigating the risk of falling rock or ice as much as possible by climbing on terrain that was relatively protected by roofs of rock above us.

Still, I couldn't stop thinking of worst-case scenarios. I tried deep breathing, but the danger felt more real than imagined. As I stood on a ledge, trying to push away the negative thoughts, I heard James's voice in my head. "I told you. Little girls don't belong on the Eiger." My temples started to throb.

My fatigue and disappointment swirled together with the anger that was welling up inside me. I pressed the heel of my hand into one eye socket, then the other, while scolding myself, *No, Sasha! Do not cry. You don't cry. Don't do it.* I didn't feel as if I belonged on that wall. Adding insult to injury was some man telling me I couldn't do it, that I should go home. *No, he can't win. Who is he, anyway? I do belong.*

Frank and I returned to our lodging, where we reconvened with Carlo and Mary. We had less than one week left before I had to be on a plane bound for New York and the beginning of my senior year. I would already miss the first few days of classes, but I couldn't afford to miss much more. We were faced with the decision to continue with Paciencia or abandon our plans completely. We needed some guidance.

We got in touch with Roger Schäeli, a Swiss alpinist with over fifty complete ascents of the Eiger's North Face, who was climbing on a nearby line. He suggested we try another route known as "Magic Mushroom"—a drier, bolted route that had also never seen a female ascent. Magic Mushroom received more sun than La Paciencia, so the rock dried quicker after the bursts of wet weather. We could salvage our trip if we acted right away.

I felt enormous pressure to succeed in tackling the Eiger's North Face. Sure, I was responsible for the demands I placed on myself, but this time the media had expectations of us as well. Carlo and I had been chronicling our trip for Adidas by doing live dispatches, which had been released to several news outlets. NBC had called me to Skype on a live broadcast from the bivvy. ABC News, *Time* magazine, and some online zines were covering the climb as well. Attempting the North Face of the Eiger was feeling less like an adventure with a climbing partner and more like a media circus. As a relative newcomer to the big wall climbing space, I felt embarrassed by the excessive attention. I felt bad that people cared about what I was doing on the Eiger, especially since other climbers were accomplishing feats all over the world. But the attention was already beyond my control.

After committing to Magic Mushroom, Carlo, Mary, Frank, and I needed to set up a base camp near the new route. For six hours we hiked two round trips with seventy-pound packs of equipment on our backs up the West Ridge of the Eiger so that we could approach the top of our new climb. Unfortunately, we didn't have time to rig for cameras as we ascended, so we needed to set static line—the lines for the videographer to climb and hang from to shoot downward—in order to capture our climb on film. We decided to approach from the top and descend our static lines to the base of the climb and set up a new base camp. If we didn't rappel down with our equipment, we wouldn't be able to hang those lines for Frank to film us on. However, according to traditional alpinist standards, that was not the best "style" of climbing—the preferred method was to approach a climb from the base whenever possible.

Despite the favorable weather, Magic Mushroom turned out to be challenging in its own way. On Paciencia we had our Airbnb to return to when we tired from working the climb, so we weren't climbing multiple days in a row. With Magic Mushroom, the clock was ticking on my return flight. It was our last chance for a send, so we committed to staying on the wall until we succeeded, returning each night to our bivvy on top. We were all exhausted, pushing ourselves all day, every day, to make progress on sending each pitch. We would wake up in the mornings barely able to open our hands because they were so stiff and overworked. Our forearms felt like lead. First thing we'd do was slather our bodies in Voltaren, an anti-inflammatory cream, hoping to ease the aches and pain.

News of our climb traveled quickly, despite our intermittent cell service. When service did resume, I had a text from Mom saying that she'd received an email from her sister: "Do you know Sasha's on the murder wall!" To Mom's credit, she has never tried to stop me from pursuing a climb. Instead, she would research the area I was headed for and look up the details of my intended climb in order to acquaint herself with any risks. Instead of saying to me "I wish you wouldn't . . ." she'd ask me questions to make sure I understood the particulars of my climb. But this time, Mom said she had panicked and called Charlie—by then he had taken a management job, coincidentally enough, with Adidas Outdoor, where he kept a close, unofficial eye on all my expeditions. He, along with everyone else in his office, had been in the loop for our live Eiger updates, and had been closely monitoring our progress.

If anyone had confidence in my climbing abilities, it was Charlie. Throughout the years, no matter where I said I was headed, no matter the difficulty of a climb I was undertaking, his reaction was always some variation of "That's awesome!" or "Yeah, that'll be super sick." He was the eternal optimist in my family, so when Mom called him, he said, "First of all, the Adidas team in Switzerland has been sending her all the weather forecasts, and she's listening. She's as safe as she can be on that mountain, and she won't take an unwarranted risk. But she is an extreme athlete and she's doing what she loves, and you can't stop her now." Even so, Mom told me she'd held her breath until I texted back.

At the end of three grueling days of climbing, we made it to the top. I'd become the first female to send Magic Mushroom. I felt overjoyed, especially because the trip had hit trouble at every turn. Magic Mushroom may not have been our original goal, but in climbing, as in life, adaptability is key. Things don't always go according to plan, and sometimes that means finding an alternate path to the top.

Despite being elated, I felt an immense amount of pressure to get home. I'd already missed the first week of my senior semester, so I made the decision to take the easy way down. That "easy way" involved calling a helicopter to retrieve us.

As a newcomer to alpine climbing, I'd been unaware of certain unspoken traditions. According to traditional alpinist standards, a climber had to hike all their gear up, and then hike it all down—but I'd found myself in a bind. When several climbers later lambasted me on social media, I learned the hard way that I'd bypassed an established, unwritten ethic of alpine climbing by calling in a helicopter. Though my decision to make that call didn't take away from my experience of the climb, I did come to regret it. However, the flip side of that regret—the positive takeaway—was my understanding that I'd always have more to learn, no matter how "expert" I became.

I have deep respect for the values of climbing purists—most of whom are of older generations. They're protective of the deep-rooted traditions of climbing and the way climbing used to be— meaning niche and hard-core . . . and somewhat elitist. Most purists aren't happy with climbing as a "popular" sport or as one that includes commercial sponsors—but I wouldn't have been able to put myself through school and devote myself to climbing without my sponsors. I had to strike a balance between appeasing my sponsors by introducing media coverage of my climbs and respecting the purists, who sometimes griped online about "big companies" entering the climbing world.

I flew home the day after ascending Magic Mushroom. By the time my plane landed I was inundated with messages of congratulations, invitations to morning show appearances, and some criticism on social media that had nothing to do with the helicopter. As I'd always tried to do to stave off reacting to criticism, I focused on the things I was grateful for. I was fortunate enough to have the kind of high-powered sponsors that were willing to support almost any challenge I undertook, and after seventeen years of climbing I was in the upper echelon of my field. I'd also cultivated the biggest social media presence of any female climber. With those distinctions came a fair amount of attention—most of it appreciated, some of it not so much.

I knew that achievements by female athletes were often more closely scrutinized than the achievements of male athletes, so I should have been prepared to be put on the defensive. I'd been the first female to free-climb the route known as Magic Mushroom, on the North Face of the Eiger, but as was sometimes the case in reporting ascents, the media misinterpreted my "first," claiming I had made the first female ascent of the Eiger. There are many different routes up a big wall, which means that there may be many "firsts" on that same wall.

I hadn't made the mistake in distinguishing the particular route I took, but I caught a lot of flak from the climbing community (mostly from male climbers) for that media blunder (which I continue to correct), as if I had deliberately offered false information. It wasn't the first time I took some mean-spirited critiques, but I'd learn to cope with it over time.

I FILLED EVERY minute of every day of my final year at Columbia. In addition to training four hours a day, five days a week, I scheduled frequent climbing trips and speaking engagements—including a TED Talk at Yale about my Dolomites expedition. I was active with nonprofit organizations—advocating for climbing, fundraising and volunteering to teach inner-city kids how to climb. I appeared at sponsored events around the world, and was featured in ad campaigns and commercials for Adidas and Ford. One of those had me as "a city girl" jumping into my Ford Escape and racing out of town for an adventure in the wilderness—which couldn't have been a more accurate illustration of the last four years.

As much as I enjoyed the kind of "fast lane" life I'd created for myself, I couldn't envision living in Manhattan when school was done. As I sat daydreaming on the subway, or in class, or in my apartment, my thoughts turned over and over to the same thing: climbing. It was a continual craving. Sometimes I felt as if my drive to climb had to do with the exhilaration of conquering what seemed unconquerable, but sometimes I simply missed the rhythm and flow of being on a climb—the feeling of pushing past a physical barrier with my focus solely on reaching the top.

Climbing was when I felt most in control of my body and mind. My world on a wall was silent, except for my breathing and the sound of my feet and hands gripping rock. My only worries were about holding on to the next little crimper or whether I could twist my body into a position necessary for the next move. Clipping a chain was like grabbing onto a little bit of confidence. On a wall the subtlest of moves made the difference between success and failure. At the top of a climb, I would feel overwhelmingly joyful in a way that had nothing to do with what anyone else thought of me, or with how I looked in the mirror or how I presented myself to the world. That feeling beat all the galas, events, and awards, hands down. I just needed to figure out where I might land after graduation.

My whole family flew in for my graduation ceremony—Mom, Charlie, Baba, my aunts, uncles, and cousin Sadie. Afterward, I played tour guide around my adopted city, from Harlem to Lower Manhattan. In SoHo, we turned down Spring Street toward Adidas's giant flagship store. From three blocks away it wasn't hard to spot the two-story-high billboard above the store featuring a picture of me and the words: "Sasha DiGiulian . . . rock star, globe trotter, full-time student."

Baba lit up at the sight of "giant" me—she stood quietly, smiling broadly, looking from me to the billboard. I put my arm around her and squeezed, remembering my visits to her Toronto home early in my competition days. The first time I asked my grandmother to drop me off at a nearby gym for some practice, I didn't expect her to wait for me, but she settled into a folding chair, telling me, "Climb as long as you need. I'll be right here." It was a smelly, chalky old gym, so I kept checking in with her. "We can go now," I'd say, but she kept insisting she was having a wonderful time. She sat for several hours watching me climb.

It became our routine whenever I'd visit. She'd bring along homemade cookies or cinnamon buns, fruit, and nuts to keep me fueled, along with promotional photos of me that she'd insist the gym display on the walls. In between my visits to Toronto, we wrote each other letters, and when my climbing started to take me around the world, I sent her postcards from wherever I landed. Standing on that SoHo sidewalk, I felt a rush of love for Baba, for my mom, and for my whole family. They'd always been behind me.

Of course, the one person missing was Dad. I was deeply touched that his brother and best friend, my uncle Lenny, who looked and sounded exactly like Dad, came for the celebration as his unofficial stand-in, though throughout the weekend none of us could help but feel Dad's absence. There were so many times when someone would mention how happy Dad would have been to see me graduate, how proud. That night we all went to The Palm, an old-school steakhouse in Midtown and one of Dad's favorite restaurants. In honor of him, I ordered his usual cocktail, a manhattan—straight up, no ice, just as he liked it. The maraschino cherry was still my favorite part.

Later that night, when everyone had gone back to their hotel rooms, Charlie and I went out to continue the celebration with mutual friends. Red Bull had reserved a table for the group of us at a downtown club, complete with unlimited champagne and Grey Goose vodka. It had been so long since Charlie and I had been out partying together. While we had vastly different lives— Charlie's was essentially nine to five—we shared an appreciation for good food, sports, and skiing. He insisted we plan a trip to JAPOW together. I laughed because I thought he was making something up after one too many drinks, but he explained that JAPOW referred to "Japan Powder," the iconic low-humidity snow in Hokkaido, Japan, said to offer the best ski conditions in the world. "Okay, JAPOW!" I said.

The day after graduation I woke up and finally realized that I was done living in the pressure cooker of the past four years. I wouldn't have to bike the six miles from Chelsea Piers to campus in the rain because that was the only way to squeeze in my cardio workout between strength training and class. I wouldn't need to stay up all night on a red-eye to Europe so that I could submit a term paper the minute I landed. I could wake up leisurely and spend as much time as I wanted training, without stressing about homework and exams. It was totally unfamiliar territory.

So, what next? I thought. *Should I relax? And what does that even look like?* Just five days earlier I'd hopped on a plane for a GoPro event in Australia and returned with hours to spare before graduation. I was so conditioned to thinking that I had to be on the move that I felt if I wasn't doing something "productive" 24/7 I was wasting time. Sometimes I wondered whether I deserved my success. I'd come across female climbers who were stronger or more talented than me, so why me? I worked hard, but was I really working hard enough and climbing as well as I could? More to the point: *What could I do now to challenge myself?* That, at least, I could answer: Find a new climbing goal.

II

Somewhere along the line, I had unofficially become the face of female climbing.

When media outlets wanted a take on what was happening in the rock-climbing community, they would often ask my opinion. By the summer of 2016 I already had years of experience giving interviews and talking to the media, and since I was already at the Olympic Games in Rio de Janeiro as a spectator, NBC and the Olympic Channel asked me to serve as their climbing correspondent.

I'd just completed a climb in Brazil with my longtime friend Felipe Camargo, a fellow Red Bull athlete. We'd made the first ascent on a route named "Planeta dos Macacos" (Planet of the Monkeys) on Pedra Riscada, one of South America's biggest rock monoliths and a 2,200-foot granite cliff bolted by a Chilean team that had failed to climb it. Red Bull filmed us as we attempted—and accomplished—the first ascent. Afterward, Felipe and I headed to Rio to watch the games and hang out with other athlete friends.

In the days leading up to the games, I was expected to explain the finer points of climbing to the mainstream viewing audience on the heels of the International Olympic Committee (IOC) announcement that sport climbing would be accepted as an Olympic event at the 2020 Tokyo Games—along with baseball/softball, karate, skateboarding, and surfing. I'd spent a couple years as an athlete representative on the International Federation of Sport Climbing (IFSC) trying to move climbing onto the Olympics' global stage. Now, finally, it was going to happen. It was a tremendous step for my sport, though, ironically, I was no longer sure that being an Olympian was in my future. I had moved on in other directions.

I'd already experienced more opportunities in my seventeen years of climbing than most people experience in a lifetime. Climbing had fostered in me the importance of determination, hard work, and goal setting. It had given me the chance to learn what I was capable of. I knew it could do the same for other kids, which is why I wanted to see the sport gain as much exposure as possible. Granted, climbing had gained popularity since I'd started in 1999, but I still so often had to explain to people what it meant to be a professional climber. "You do what? Where do you do it? How does a climber compete?" Rock climbing as an event at the Tokyo 2020 Olympics might explain all that.

I'd never been to the Olympics. It wasn't until I was there that I understood what exactly people mean by "Olympic fever." The excitement that ran throughout the Village was palpable and contagious—a kind of collective positive vibe that I'd never felt anywhere else. The countries represented had their own houses they'd reserved outside of the Olympic housing, where athletes could come together and hang out. Not to be outdone, various sponsors had set up their own rental houses with food and drinks, music, and lounges for the athletes and VIPs to mingle. I spent most of my time hanging at the Red Bull house.

They had great food, a DJ, and, because the house was on the water, Jet Skis for the taking.

Wherever I went I met athletes who had been training their entire lives for the Olympics, which they viewed as the pinnacle of competition. I couldn't help but wonder how amazing it would be to participate in the games. After all, I'd had the Olympics in the back of my mind ever since my ice-skating days.

A part of me wanted to reenter the competition circuit and set a goal of making the U.S. Olympic Team, but that would mean my next four years of training would look much different from how it would for expeditions. Doing well on the competition circuit would mean dedicating myself to competing throughout the year and practicing the style and components of each competition—not traveling around the world to climb outside. I wasn't sure if I wanted to miss out on those experiences to return to training in a gym.

To me, climbing outdoors represented freedom of expression, a cathartic journey, a chance to immerse myself in nature and focus solely on the task at hand, undistracted by the chaos of everyday life. The only thing I could do and the only thing I could control was my movement on the rock. The only problem to solve was how to progress up the wall. Outside I felt part of the elements around me. I understood the grooves and protrusions of the rock surface and the feel of the wind high above the ground.

Rock affords a lot of creativity, because climbers of different builds may ascend a wall in completely different ways. Different climbers, different strengths. In stark contrast, rarely are there multiple ways to do an indoor climb, where a route-setter has the power to decide which plastic holds are used and where they are placed, thereby dictating the flow of a climber's moves.

As enthusiastic as I was about climbing's inclusion, I didn't agree with the Olympic format, which would require climbers to compete in speed climbing, sport (or lead) climbing, *and* bouldering. While this was the basic format of the Overall World Championship I competed in, national and international competitions had never given equal weight to each version, which is how the Olympics was doing it. They'd never required a participant to compete in all three categories, but since climbing was a "trial" sport, the format catered to the IOC's most "user-friendly" version, not to the most authentic. There was only room for one gold, one silver, and one bronze medal, not three different disciplines with three sets of medals.

When I competed in the Overall World Championship, speed hadn't carried the same weight as sport and bouldering. Few climbers even trained in speed climbing. In speed, climbers start as if they're at the running gate of a race—both hands on the start hold, one foot up, one foot on the ground. When the buzzer sounds, climbers tear up the wall as fast as they can, with each climber competing on the same set of holds and sequences.

Competitors in the Overall World Championship used to rely on their results in bouldering and lead, the type of climbing that paralleled the type of movement one more often finds on rock—small holds, intricate sequences, and technical terrain. Since my competition days, the styles of bouldering and lead climbing had shifted more toward a combination of parkour-meets-gymnastics-type movements—leaping onto the wall and landing with a double clutch on two plastic holds and then swinging upward, carrying momentum like a gymnast performing a parallel bars routine.

I felt the IOC had missed the mark on how best to represent climbing, despite the fact that every year the IFSC had made a case for the IOC to include climbing. More so, it seemed as if they had a lack of understanding of how climbing worked. At the same time, I knew that speed climbing was the most digestible way to "sell" climbing to an Olympic audience—a way for climbing to get its foot in the door. "Fastest to the top wins" was far easier to explain than the nuances of problem-solving and sequences. Besides, the IOC left no room for negotiation. Their stance was very clear: This is how it's going to be if you want climbing included.

Despite their format, the idea of being an Olympian remained somewhat seductive. I wasn't yet ready to rule out an Olympic run, even though I was enjoying my role as correspondent and not competitor—there was so much less stress and pressure involved. I could actually relax and enjoy the events and cheer on friends, although there were moments when I missed the feeling of excitement and anticipation I used to have before competing. Part of me felt sort of relegated to the sidelines, even though I was coming off a big first ascent. I'd have to wait and see how I felt about returning to the competition arena once I had some distance.

WHILE I WAS in Rio, Edu called and asked if I wanted to come to Barcelona. We'd been texting back and forth, talking about our summer plans since my graduation. Up until then our relationship had been as friends and climbing partners—purely platonic—although there had always been an unspoken chemistry between us. It was something we'd skirted around for as long as we'd known each other. He'd flirted with me and I'd crushed on him over the years, but the timing never seemed right to move out of the "friend zone." Now, for the first time in four years, I had no immediate commitments, no school, nowhere I had to be. But instead of either of us saying, "Oh, let's see if our relationship can be a romantic one," Edu simply invited me to visit him and climb in Spain for the summer.

He picked me up at the airport and we dropped my bags off at his apartment. Right away he whisked me off on his motorcycle to a fancy dinner high on a mountain overlooking all of Barcelona. That was the moment I knew we were on a real date. From then on, we were constantly together. For six weeks we climbed throughout Spain, purely for fun. In between, we cruised around Barcelona on his motorcycle so he could introduce me to his friends and his favorite places to eat. I couldn't help but feel as if I were in an old European movie, navigating the highways and cobblestone streets of a city on the back of a motorcycle behind this sexy, super-attractive guy.

Edu organized our days and nights, which I was happy to let him do. It was nice not to have to make all the decisions for a change, not to be the one doing all the planning. In my heart, being together with Edu in Spain made sense, and so did the plans we made to climb all over the world. Most of the time the romance felt like part of a natural progression, though it did briefly occur to me that maybe we'd moved too quickly into this new phase of our relationship. But I decided to push any doubt aside.

Spending so much time outdoors in Barcelona cemented my decision not to remain based in New York City. As much as I loved the life I had in the city and the friends I'd made at school, Manhattan was definitely not conducive to an outdoor-oriented lifestyle. I knew from having spent a lot of time in Colorado that Boulder was pretty much the epicenter of American climbing and the climbing community. The climbing in Boulder spanned Rocky Mountain National Park and the Flatirons—giant, slanted sandstone rock formations with rock grades ranging from beginner 5.0s to hard 5.14s. Basically, if there were a "poster child" for climbing, it would be the Flatirons—a world apart from my Manhattan home.

In New York City I was always "leaving the party" to climb. In Boulder, the party happened outdoors. Socializing in Manhattan meant brunch and booze or a cocktail date, but when I was in Boulder, socializing involved a climb with friends and grabbing a green juice at the local vegan shop. If I really wanted to return to the climbing community and have incredible gyms and wilderness climbing at my doorstep, I had to move to Boulder.

I didn't waste any time contacting a friend who worked in real estate in the area. She told me about a rental and I took it, sight unseen. I hired a service to pack up my New York City apartment and move me across the country. It was official. Come October, I would be a resident of Boulder, Colorado.

Edu came back to the States with me and helped me settle into my new place. I was excited to have him there with me— opening boxes, arranging furniture—but I was also glad to be back in Boulder, in my own home.

A week later we went to Rocktoberfest, a big annual climbing festival at the Red River Gorge, where I was looking forward to introducing him to some of my friends. By that point I spoke Spanish reasonably well, though I was frustrated that Edu hadn't made much of an effort to learn English. I had to translate conversations when we were with other people, which meant that I could rarely leave Edu's side—and he rarely left mine, being dependent on me to translate for him. I understood his frustration, because I knew what it was like to be new to a language; I remembered how insecure I'd been when I first tried to carry on conversations in Spanish. But that had only spurred me on to learn the language as best I could. When I was in a group of Edu's friends in Spain, I made a concerted effort to listen and understand the conversation.

But Edu didn't make the same effort in return. In fact, the popular, chivalrous guy I'd fallen for in Spain—the one who loved to laugh and had more friends than anyone I knew—became a quiet, brooding presence when we were with my friends. I wanted him to at least find a way to show he cared.

Edu returned to Barcelona after the festival, and I went back to Boulder. Neither of us was ready to pick up and move halfway across the world. Besides, I was looking forward to being by myself for a while, in my own place. I think of myself as an extroverted introvert, meaning that I enjoy my time in big groups of people, but I need to refuel and find my center alone, so having my own place was a no-brainer. Edu and I agreed that he would live and train in Barcelona and I'd do the same in Boulder. The rest of the time we could travel the world together, exploring new climbs. It would be good for us to have a little time apart, although a small, nagging thought was forming in the back of my head: *Was our passion and admiration for each other enough to sustain this new phase of our relationship?* I wasn't yet sure.

I quickly acclimated to living in a small city and was happy to reconnect with old friends and get to know the Boulder community. I decided to throw myself a housewarming party on election night, which was only a week away. A party would serve double duty, as an invitation to my new home and as a celebration of the United States electing its first woman president.

I was excited—for the party, for the election, and for the chance to finally stop hearing the loud, obnoxious ramblings of the other candidate. Boulder is a liberal utopia in Colorado, so everyone at the party had voted decidedly "blue." I'd even bought a blue dress for the occasion. We all milled around the

TV, watching the results pour in. About halfway through the night people started to look worried. When the Pennsylvania results were called, it seemed almost certain we'd lost. That's when everyone started the serious drinking—out of shock... or denial. The next day Boulder was like a ghost town. I imagined that most everyone I knew had woken up with an election-fueled hangover. Ironically, the election of Trump as president couldn't have been more sobering.

It felt as good a time as any to return to Spain—to spend time with Edu and to take my training to the next level with someone who ate, slept, and lived for climbing. That someone, Patxi Usobiaga, also happened to live in Spain, and he had worked with many of the world's best climbers, including Adam Ondra, Daniel Woods, and Chris Sharma. I knew he would kick my ass like no one else—whether to get ready for my outdoor climbing goals or in preparation for the Olympics.

I'd met former World Cup champion and Arco Rock Legends Award winner-turned-trainer Patxi Usobiaga in the competition world, but I had the chance to become better acquainted with him when I was in Barcelona with Edu. He had retired from competition training and excelled at hard outdoor climbs. Working with someone like Patxi, renowned for his grueling training and dietary regimen bordering on the masochistic, would prove I was doing everything I could to be the best climber possible. I hired him to put me through a specialized three-month program to build strength, and I rented my own place in Barcelona.

Training with Patxi involved eight hours a day in the gym— four in the morning and four in the afternoon—with a nonstop variation of weight lifting, pull-ups, push-ups, campusing repetitions (ascending the wall using arms only), hang boarding (hanging from the tips of one's fingers) with weights attached to my body, circuit training, and biking, rowing, or running. At times, when I didn't think I could lift another finger, let alone my body weight, Patxi would say, "It is only when your body is totally broken down that the real training can begin. You have to train at your lowest; you need to be tired, to feel this desire to quit—but fight through this."

I believed in his philosophy. I thought it was the way to be a true athlete. While I was at Columbia, I'd felt as if I didn't work hard enough at my sport, but now that I didn't have the time constraints of school, work, and travel, I could throw myself wholeheartedly into being the best. I thought working with Patxi would be my opportunity to dive hard into training, which I mistakenly thought included suffering in the name of improvement.

Patxi and I would have breakfast together, train, eat lunch, train, and then sometimes have dinner together. He swore by the same restrictive diet he recommended for his athletes, a diet that involved counting calories—in hindsight, not the best practice for someone like me who was trying not to be obsessed with weight. But he was the expert, so I followed his lead like the diligent and determined student I was. He believed that climbers had to be at their lightest—a belief that had always been a trap for me. His recommendation for me: twelve hundred calories a day, barely enough fuel to allow me to keep up with my training, which was mostly about endurance. On days we didn't eat dinner together, I tried to resist my craving for more food, but I often caved to my hunger. Afterward, I would feel guilty about allowing myself a larger portion or—God forbid—dessert.

The idea behind Patxi's training was that in order to be the best, climbers needed to work their body into a deficit. They needed to beat themselves down and deprive their body of adequate sustenance. Suffering was key, and self-care was definitely not encouraged. I was aware that long hours of training didn't necessarily mean quality hours of training, but I assumed that since Patxi was hailed as one of the hardest-working climbers in the community, his philosophy would be good for me.

Unfortunately, climbing became more like work for me than anything else. I was always tired and hungry. I was in a gym for six to eight hours of my day instead of enjoying the outdoors, and when I did climb outside, my body was so tired and achy that I couldn't feel any flow on the rock. I wasn't enjoying anything about climbing.

"*Venga! Va. A muerte!*" (Come on! Go. 'Til death!) Patxi would say—although I sometimes wondered if this wasn't entirely hyperbole.

I appreciated his zeal and climbing expertise. His love of the sport was obvious. Climbing was his life. Contrary to his training regimen, he was a very sweet guy who, through his dedication and focus, fell into the role of guru to a contingency of high-profile climbers. He had earned the title, but by the end of the third month I realized that even though I'd made some big gains in my climbing, Patxi's method of training was not right for everyone. It wasn't for me, especially if my trajectory was in outdoor climbing. (I credit Patxi for helping me decide that I would not be training for the Olympics.) We parted company in March.

Even throughout my training, Edu and I were never apart for more than a few weeks. Since the summer, we had maintained our "long-distance" relationship: weeks apart and then usually a week together. It wasn't an option to casually date and grow the relationship at a slower pace, or to experience regular, ordinary living together without exciting climbs and destinations. When we were together, after weeks apart, we were joined at the hip. We'd climb all day between breakfast, lunch, and dinner, and then hang out together every night—what I imagined a honeymoon to be like.

After my training I flew back to the States for a couple events and a visit with my family, then I returned to Spain to spend most of the next few months climbing with Edu all around the Pyrenees—a mountain range stretching three hundred miles between Spain and France. The area was breathtakingly beautiful, reminding me of how much I loved climbing outdoors.

It also fueled my anger with the new administration's rollback of dozens of environmental laws. If they had their way, they'd build gas pumps on every mountain range in the country. The devastation of climate change was already apparent, and now we had a president who didn't support climate action. People from all over the world enjoyed our national parks, but the legislation protecting those parks was shrinking. Our wild landscapes and pristine valleys and mountain ranges were being subjected to private development and fracking. So many times over the years I'd imagined taking a more political stance regarding environmental protections. After all, I had a *platform*, and enough experience in public speaking to know how to use it.

Growing up, I was often surrounded by adults with strong opinions. Several of our close family friends were politicians— such as Virginia's Senator Mark Warner and Representative Don Beyer—and I was used to speaking with them when they visited our house. Dad was always pulling me into conversations about sports and travel, which made for common ground between us all. Sometimes I would bring up the importance of protecting the outdoors and ask what kind of action was being taken. In college, I often took advantage of opportunities to speak about the impact of climate change on climbing and

Initial days climbing outside, circa 1999, in Val-David, Quebec.

Me and my dad fishing in Knoxville, Tennessee.

How I spent my time while my brother played hockey: climbing in the rafters. The joke was, "Where's Sasha?" "Just look up!"

Our family Christmas card
with Charlie in 2000.

My first Youth National
Championships in Richmond,
Virginia—the finals—before
the slip.

Me on a cover of
Kids of Climbing calendar in 2007.
Photo by Jean-Michel Casanova.

Competing in the USA Climbing Youth National Championships in Portland, Oregon, at age twelve (2005); my first National Championships victory.

A photo from graduation at Columbia University. It was a surreal moment to walk across the stage and receive my diploma.

Scaling the Red Bull Arena in Harrison, New Jersey, to introduce the game ball for a match between the Red Bulls and the Colorado Rapids in 2014. An evolution from climbing the rafters when I was six at my brother's hockey games! Photo by Stan Evans.

Adventuring in the Dolomites in 2013 with Edu. During this trip we climbed "Bellavista."

The crux pitch of "Bellavista," 5.14b (8c), on Cima Ovest di Lavaredo, Dolomites, Italy. My first big wall climb and the most difficult graded alpine wall achieved by a woman. Photo by Jensen Walker Pictures.

This bivouac ledge is where I spent several nights while climbing the North Face of the Eiger. Photo by Frank Kretschmann.

Lobbying on Capitol Hill with Tommy Caldwell and Alex Honnold and meeting with Senator Chuck Schumer to discuss the importance of climate action.

Climbing over the Utah Olympic Park pool in Park City during the inaugural Psicobloc competition: a technical race up a fifty-foot wall with no ropes, where the consequence of falling is landing in the pool. Photo by Beau Kahler.

A photo by John Evans from the crux pitch (5.13-) of the Misty Wall, a first ascent that I established with Jon Cardwell and Marcus Garcia in Yosemite National Park, California. This move required a dyno, when you use your momentum to swing to the next hold, often losing contact with your feet, out the roof of the climb. Immediately after, I swung my feet above my head to continue through the most difficult moves.

Torn by the rock. Photo by Keith Ladzinski.

Hanging out with my mom—aka "mombelay" (a term my mom coined for herself)—in the Red River Gorge, Kentucky.

Crimping down on the microscopic edges of "Pure Imagination," 5.14d (c) in the Red River Gorge, Kentucky. Photo by Keith Ladzinski.

Another shot of climbing in the beautiful Red River Gorge, Kentucky. Photo by Chris Noble.

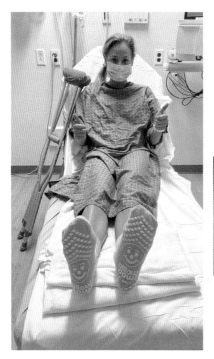

All prepped and ready for hip surgery.

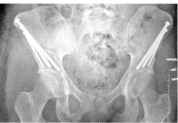

An X-ray image of my hips post-surgery. These four-to-six-inch screws held my broken pelvic bone in place.

Climbing my first M10 (a number equivalent to 5.12+ on the mixed-climbing grade scale), "Flying Circus," a mixed (ice-and-rock) climb in Ouray, Colorado. Photo by Andy Mann.

A family photo with Erik and Moose on a local Boulder, Colorado, trail.

My SEND Bars team during one of our kitchen sessions crafting the recipe of our new bar. I put together this team of women to introduce a nutrition bar packed with superfood ingredients, including a full serving of greens, purposeful adaptogens, and organic whole foods. Photo by Alison Vagnini.

Still reaching new heights: climbing the final pitch of "Rayu," a 5.14b (8c) big wall expedition that I led. This was the hardest big wall ever achieved by a female team, which I accomplished with Matilda Söderlund and Brette Harrington in September 2022. Photo by Jan Novak.

natural resources. I don't think there was any one moment that turned me into an advocate for environmental protections and ecotourism, but after Trump's election it felt like a logical next step.

In the spring of 2017, I was invited to Climb the Hill, an aptly named advocacy event that took place on Capitol Hill, cohosted by the American Alpine Club (AAC) and the Access Fund, a nonprofit dedicated to keeping U.S. climbing areas open and conserving the climbing environment. In climbing all over the world, I'd seen firsthand the damaging effects of climate change on mountains—it was an issue that nearly all climbers could agree on. Climb the Hill was a chance for me to join forces with professional climbers including Tommy Caldwell, Alex Honnold, Lynn Hill, and Libby Sauter, among others, in lobbying for the protection of public lands.

Our team of climbers spent two days meeting with members of Congress, the Department of the Interior, and the U.S. Forest Service to lobby for a number of bills we wanted passed—bills that would not only protect public lands, but would also enact climate change policies and the move toward a greener economy. National monuments were under unprecedented threat in the new administration, and legislation had been introduced that would allow the sell-off of millions of acres of public land and weaken management of whatever was left. As climbers and outdoor enthusiasts, we were especially galvanized by all the environmental protections that were being undone, so, with our various and vast platforms, we committed ourselves to being heard.

We met in person with senators and congresspeople and spoke about our intense connection to the outdoors as professional athletes. We talked about why the places we visited were so important to us, and we shared stories and memories of our outdoor travels throughout the country. We spoke of wanting our children and our children's children to have the same experiences we were fortunate enough to have had.

Lobbying is a slow-moving vehicle, so our aim was to put a face to some of the bills. When I was in a meeting with a senator who told me he was a big fan of rock climbing, it was an opportunity to talk about the country's outdoor spaces and certain pieces of legislation that would benefit those spaces. One of those pieces was to ensure that Bears Ears National Monument in southeast Utah remain protected, since the Trump administration wanted to reduce the area by nearly 85 percent in order to open it to mining and energy extraction.

While I was at Climb the Hill, I spoke with Senator Tim Kaine and Senator Warner, both of Virginia. We discussed how climbing could potentially transform regions through ecotourism by creating green jobs and sustainable systems. Senator Kaine asked me to participate in a climb sponsored by Access Fund in Breaks Interstate Park (known as the Grand Canyon of the South). Breaks is located on the border of Kentucky and my home state of Virginia, in an area with a depressed economy that was formerly reliant on coal mining. The plan was to grow climbing as a way to encourage environmental awareness and conservation. To that end, I bolted some new routes to extend the climbing areas. It was meant to be an ongoing project, one I cared deeply about, because I'd spent a lot of time climbing in Breaks as a kid. It also hooked me on the idea of ecotourism.

Because of my work with Climb the Hill and the AAC, a company called Oru Kayak approached me. They were an eco-minded, high-performance kayak company interested in having me lead a trip to West Timor, in Indonesia's southernmost province. Our crew of twelve consisted of a couple outdoor industry journalists, a film crew, a bolter (route developer), the

Oru Kayak marketing team, and me. We would travel to Mollo, the most fertile region in West Timor, located at the base of a mountain range on the Timor island, where the mining industry had devastated much of the area.

Marble mining had come to West Timor in 1994, and almost immediately people in the outlying villages suffered the consequences. Forests were cut down, creating massive land vibrations and landslides, while mining waste polluted the water, making it undrinkable. By defacing the cliffs and creating tabletop-like formations at the peaks of the mountains, mining companies had ruined the area's natural ability to protect against flooding and the runoff of contaminants created by mining.

In 2000, Aleta Baun, known as Mama Aleta—a mother and homemaker turned activist—led thousands of people from her village of Mollo, along with neighboring regions, to occupy the mining area. After two months, the mining company quit their work and left. Since then, the people of the region, led by Mama Aleta, have organized themselves and united to evict other mining companies in surrounding areas.

The people of Mollo believe in a symbiotic relationship between man and nature. They believe that water, stone, soil, and forest function like the human body. Water is blood-artery; stone, the backbone; soil, the flesh; and forest, the skin, lung, and hair. Life in the region is simple, with minimal electricity and no running water, but Mama Aleta is internationally renowned— the Obama administration recognized her for her conservation efforts. When the Oru Kayak team and I arrived, Mama Aleta and the local activists greeted us warmly. After a discussion of our agenda, they gave us their blessing to explore the mountains and the surrounding area. Our hope was to encourage ecotourism by promoting climbing and sea kayaking, thereby keeping the land in its natural state.

The Oru team and I kayaked in crystal clear waters to our first climb. As we hiked, we were floored by the abundance of awesome stalactite-like limestone formations, towering cliffs, and caves. In stark contrast, the part of the mountain that had been mined was in full view nearby, looking like something out of a sci-fi movie. The entire top half of it appeared to have been sliced off, leaving a desolate expanse of rock, stripped of anything living.

We spent twelve days climbing and bolting, convinced that the region had potential for great world-class rock climbing. If we'd had more time, we could have bolted even more lines. Word of the staggering beauty of the area needed to get out to climbing, kayaking, and nature enthusiasts. Our hope was that ecotourism could provide economic development—jobs and revenue enough to sustain the local community—without destruction of the land and water. None of us could bear the thought of such a paradise lost.

12

To the climbing world, Edu and I were this *climbing power couple*. People left comments online about our relationship and how they couldn't wait to see our "climbing kids." It was a little like living in a fishbowl, and despite the fact that I'd been in the limelight since I was a teenager, I'd always been a fairly private person. As much as I enjoyed the attention I garnered as a climber, I tried to keep my personal life "offline," so to speak, but that was becoming increasingly difficult.

For six months, since the beginning of 2017, Edu and I had been training for "Mora Mora," a seven-hundred-meter big wall route on the East Face of Tsaranoro Atsimo in Madagascar, an island country in the Indian Ocean. Tsaranoro Atsimo is a giant granite monolith, and one of the most difficult big walls in the world. Only one person, Adam Ondra, had successfully "freed it"—climbed it without "aids," and without falling. Translated, "Mora Mora" means "slowly, slowly," or "be patient." But as much as we complied with the "slowly, slowly" part, we were often less than patient, at least with each other.

I met up with Edu in Barcelona. From there we flew to South Africa, and then to Ivato International Airport, in Madagascar's largest city. All of our bags made it, except for a very important one: our portaledge. After tracking it down and ensuring that it would be delivered from Ivato Airport to Tsaranoro Valley, we left the airport and headed to the nearest grocery store, where we loaded up on all the food we'd need for the coming month. There would be no big markets where we were headed. We stocked up on nonperishables that we could easily prepare on the wall, and then boarded a chartered van to drive us the eighteen hours to Tsaranoro Atsimo.

The next morning we arrived at our destination, the Tsaranoro Valley, a remote and mind-blowing expanse of open savanna and tropical and dry forest at the foot of the Tsaranoro massif domes—abrasive granite domes, seven football fields high, with handholds that were small edges the size of peanuts. Climbing would require intense focus, laser-precise foot placement, and slow, slow movements.

Our plan had originally been to do three- to four-day pushes—three nights on the portaledge at a time—but that changed once we discovered that our portaledge had been flown elsewhere. Instead, we spent two weeks unlocking the sequences of the route by setting our static lines up the first seven pitches—about a thousand feet up—to the base of the hardest climb, a 5.14b pitch (8c). Every day we would hike two and a half hours to the base of the wall, ascend our fixed lines (by way of jumars) for over a thousand feet to reach the 8c pitch, climb the pitch to figure out the moves, then rappel back down and hike the same two and a half hours back to our little cabin, utterly exhausted. We couldn't wait for our portaledge to arrive so that we could sleep on the wall and not have to commute back and forth to our cabin after each long day.

We'd almost given up hope of ever seeing our portaledge again, but after two weeks, it magically appeared. It was game on. Finally, we could make a push and remain on the climb for as many days as we needed to make it to the top—I say "finally" because Edu and I were starting to wear on each other's nerves.

Since arriving in Madagascar, we had basically been alone, which was mostly fun and exciting as we figured out our route, but it was also infuriating at times. Being so isolated, we were left to our own thoughts and to the deepening voids in our conversation. It was starting to feel as if we didn't have much else to talk about besides climbing. I loved climbing as much as he did, but I needed to talk about things besides rock sequences— like the politics and the history of the country we were in, or cultural and global events, or books. Before our climb, I'd even suggested we read the same articles so that we'd have something besides climbing to talk about, but that idea didn't work out very well. I wrote in my journal: "I wonder if Edu and I work as a couple outside of climbing. Am I trying too hard to make the relationship work because I think we're supposed to be together? It feels like we don't have much to talk about lately."

Edu's approach to life was to take it day by day—sort of a "Don't worry, be happy" philosophy. That was definitely admirable, but it wasn't the way I approached life. Climbing was my passion, my sport, and my job. It's what kept the lights on, but I also loved to expand my horizons beyond climbing. I was always thinking of how to capitalize on the opportunities I'd been given in order to sustain myself in the future. Edu seemed never to be concerned about the future.

There was no denying Edu and my connection and attraction to each other. We'd shared so many transformative climbing experiences together, along with our passion for climbing and exploring new places. It was almost impossible to imagine not having him in my life. To the outside world, we had a partnership that was unique and enviable, but was that enough to sustain a whole life together? I felt so torn. Here was this terrific guy with the knowledge and patience to teach me rope and big wall techniques, and who relished his role as caretaker. On my recent trip to Indonesia, I'd stepped on a sea urchin, leaving me with a foot-load of prickly thorns. I removed what I'd thought were all of them, but by the time I arrived in Barcelona for the trip we were on, my foot was hugely swollen. Edu immediately arranged for me to see a doctor so I could have the remnants of the thorns properly removed. When he could help, he always did; but there were red flags.

Our director of photography, François Lebeau, joined us during the last week of our trip after we'd successfully climbed the hardest sections of the route. François was there to document our send—fingers crossed. I'd known him since I was twelve, when we met at the Canadian Open Nationals. He'd since become one of the most prolific photographers in the world of rock climbing. Red Bull had hired him to be with us for the final leg of our journey.

Edu and I hiked out the evening before our climb and slept at the base of the wall. First thing in the morning we set off on the route, with François ascending the fixed lines and Edu and I swapping leads as we climbed. I was up first on the 5.14b pitch, and managed to send it from the ground on my first attempt. Edu tried it next, fell, and gave it another try—still no success. At that point, nightfall was approaching, so we set up our portaledge for the night.

Everything is simple on a portaledge, that fragile-looking hammock that hangs from a wall and acts as a temporary "home." Only the essentials are allowed—climbing gear and meals. A climber always wears a harness on a portaledge. I usually start with my harness tightly cinched around my waist, my line like a short leash attached to the anchor. Sometimes the idea of being suspended thousands of feet in the air on what is basically a cot attached to a couple bolts on the wall takes a little getting used to. I'll try and relax, reminding myself that I'm safe in my tiny home. After a while I'll loosen my harness and extend my line to the point where I can dangle my feet over the edge of my portaledge. Cooking my meal or boiling water for coffee is a delicate balancing act that requires the use of a Jetboil—a back-packing stove—carefully positioned so as not to set my home on fire. Eventually, I can appreciate my bird's-eye view from the wall.

First thing in the morning, Edu sent the pitch from the previous day. From there the two of us continued up the final, easier sections of the climb leading to the summit, which would take three days and two overnights. All the while we were climbing, I was supposed to be taking Malarone, an anti-malaria medication, morning and night, but some days I'd forget to bring it. I'd been all over the world and had remained super healthy, so even though Madagascar was considered high-risk for malaria by the CDC, I was confident that I had nothing to worry about. Unfortunately, confidence is not a prevention against tropical disease.

That morning on the wall, I felt the urge to pee, so I moved to the side to hang over an area not too far from our line. Peeing on a wall is just a bit more complicated for women than for men, although it's still easy enough. First, I move off to one side a bit so that I don't pee on the climbing terrain. Since it's not an option to take off my harness, I then pull my pants and underwear down from underneath my harness. Once I've ensured there's no gear or rope—or people—in the line of fire, I push off from the wall with my feet and relieve myself. Pooping is a more involved process, because I need to hold a bag under myself while doing the deed. Afterward, I tie off the bag, place it in yet another bag, and then stuff it into a poop tube so that I can carry it off the wall. A simple process . . . but not this time.

That morning on Mora Mora, after I'd readied myself for a quick pee, I instead felt something rumble through my insides like a locomotive. Without warning, there was diarrhea all down the wall. Because I'd been taken by surprise, I hadn't moved nearly far enough away from Edu and François. I don't think I'd ever felt that mortified in my life.

I moved back to our line just in time to hear Edu say, "What's that smell? François, did you take a dump on the wall?"

Oh, God. If I could have disappeared off the mountain in that moment, I would have. "No, it was me," I managed to croak.

I must have looked a little green or just embarrassingly pathetic, because Edu became very concerned. "Don't worry," he said. "It's human. You're human. Are you okay?"

"Yes, I'm okay. I'm better." I drank some water, ate a banana, and pulled my climbing shoes back on.

We continued our ascent for several more hours, through a range of 5.12 and 5.13 climbing, including a water-runnel feature—a narrow, vertical tunnel of water, almost like a small stream with shallow walls, made from centuries of water runoff. Maneuvering the runnel involved "stemming"—pressing hands and feet against the sides of the wall to use compression to climb, similar to the way I used to climb the arches of our doorways when I was a kid. Farther up, with only tiny granite crystals to hold on to, we had to grip the wall by delicately crimping, our fingers bent like claws, a move demanding a tremendous amount of tension in one's hand and finger tendons.

Fortunately, except for a few rolling waves of nausea, I didn't have any more surprises. Eventually we made it to the top in the second-ever free ascent of Mora Mora and the first free ascent for a woman. We had spent three weeks in the Tsaranoro Valley, with no cell service and no electricity, after months of planning and visualizing and training. I felt so moved and disbelieving. *Holy smokes, we did it!* In the glow of our victory, I almost forgot about how sick I felt.

By the time Edu and I arrived back in Barcelona I had a fever of 104 and was feeling worse than I had on Mora Mora. Edu looked after me for two days, until I was well enough to travel on my own to Toronto, where my mom greeted me at the airport. By then my skin was still a sickly yellow color. Mom immediately whisked me off to the hospital, where I was met with horrified reactions from the staff: "Oh, my God! Where are you coming from?"

When they learned I'd been in rural Indonesia, I was checked in for tropical diseases. That's when I found out that I had malaria. At that point, I had begun to recover—I had managed to control the disease by continuing to take the malaria pills, which are an antidote as well as a preventative medicine. *Good to know.*

A week later Edu joined me back in Boulder. We were still enjoying the whirlwind of attention we'd received about our Madagascar climb. ABC News was preparing a story with the footage of our climb, so they came out to my home to interview us. After the media flurry subsided, Edu and I attempted "real life" together in Boulder, to see what our life might look like outside of climbing. It didn't take very long for me to see how impractical that life would be. Lacking the backdrop of a spectacular expedition, the relationship started to unravel.

I didn't have enough time to be alone or to see friends by myself, because Edu didn't like when I socialized without him— even though it seemed obvious that he wasn't interested in my friends or my life in Boulder. He rarely engaged when we were out in a group, although to be fair, there was a language barrier.

Communicating in English wasn't second nature for Edu, and most of my friends in Boulder weren't fluent in Spanish, but it appeared as if he wasn't even trying. He just looked bored.

I knew Edu had a previous long-term girlfriend who wasn't a climber and who held a nine-to-five job. He was the "star" in the relationship, the professional athlete receiving attention for his impressive climbs, and she was his cheerleader. I knew in the beginning of our relationship that Edu was attracted to my independence, my sense of adventure, and the fact that I liked to make my own rules, but in the light of everyday life, those same things worked against me—they often seemed to rub Edu's ego the wrong way. It was as if the things about me he was attracted to were also the things that drove him crazy.

It was clear that our relationship was disintegrating, but neither of us was willing to say the words to end it. Instead, we did everything but call it quits. We argued, sulked, and ignored each other. But in between, we went through the motions of being a couple.

A month into our "real-life" experiment, we had an Adidas-supported fundraising dinner in San Francisco to attend—a gala for the American Alpine Club. We were still pretending the relationship was working as we got on the plane together, but by the time we arrived, we were barely speaking. The dinner wasn't until the next night—twenty-four hours away. I wondered how we were going to make it until then.

We met up with my brother, Charlie, who was still with Adidas and there for the same event. It was so comforting to see him, like going home. He was one of the few people I felt completely unguarded with, and that night I was sorely in need of a chance to let my guard down and have some fun. I went out to dinner with him and some friends of mine from my Indonesia trip, but Edu chose to go straight to the hotel instead of joining us. When I returned from dinner, everything came to a head. I didn't want to pretend we were the perfect couple, especially at an event with half the climbing community in attendance. It seemed as good a time as any to call it quits. "I can't be with you," I said. "This isn't working. Let's take a break."

I stayed with Charlie. The next day Edu and I agreed that we were past the point of reconciliation. He flew back to Spain, and Charlie and I went to the gala together. That night, as old friends greeted me, it was as if I'd just come out of a long, uncomfortable hibernation. For the first time in weeks, I felt like my former self—until I saw a professional climber I knew, whom I'll call Chad.

He was twelve years my senior, and gatekeeper to what I deemed "the boys' club" of climbing—the dudes who were thought to be the "cool kids." He was someone I'd gotten to know a little over the years as I came of age in the climbing community. I respected him for his route developments, though for whatever reason—because I was a woman, because of jealousy, machismo, whatever—Chad had never returned that respect. I was never a cool kid and I never tried to be "one of the guys." Maybe that was my failing. If anything, a lot of guys looked at my career with disdain, as if my making money as a climber reduced their chances of making a living.

Throughout the years, as I gained more attention in climbing, I would hear of derogatory comments Chad had made about me. Friends sent me screenshots of him wearing a blond wig and holding a Red Bull can, with an obnoxious caption obviously referring to me. When I was eighteen and struggling with my eating disorder, I was told of his online comments about how I resembled the cartoon "Skeletor." After I'd gained back the weight—and then some—he posted an Instagram picture referring to me as Sausage DiGiulian, and embellished it with little daggers—*What the fuck?* It shouldn't have bothered me, but at the time, despite all I'd accomplished, I was grappling with accepting my body as it was—fifteen pounds heavier than in high school. I was upset with myself for allowing my weight gain to bother me, especially since I'd added mostly muscle, but it did. I hadn't become inured to the occasional online digs and snide comments about my size, especially coming from Chad. Over the years I asked him to stop making fun of me and to stop spreading rumors, but it didn't matter. I was just a woman who "couldn't take a joke."

After a cordial enough greeting, Chad asked how I was doing. I said that I was *fine, thanks.* "And how's Edu doing?" he asked.

"He's fine," I said. "He's in Spain." I didn't mention our breakup. It was no one's business, although I had the feeling Chad was looking for some gossip. I politely ended the conversation and moved on. I wanted to enjoy the evening.

I was out as a single woman for the first time in ages. I felt unencumbered as I happily chatted with friends I hadn't seen in a while. I also drank too much at dinner. When the gala was over, I left with the brother of a pro climber I knew.

My hookup meant nothing more to me than a release of all my pent-up emotions. I tried to assure myself that it was no big deal, but I felt terrible for doing it so soon after Edu and I had agreed to take some time apart. I woke up with a massive hangover and realized I'd lost my phone somewhere between dinner and the light of day, which was totally unlike me. In fact, none of what I'd done in the last twenty-four hours was like me. I knew my limits when it came to alcohol—I kept my drinking to a happy buzz—but that night I'd tried to drink away my frustration.

It took a while to try and gain my composure. Coffee, a

shower, and some deep breathing helped. Surprisingly, I soon started to feel strangely liberated, as if I'd finally put an end to my relationship with Edu, even if I hadn't gone about it in the best way. Really, who would even care about my one-night stand?

It seemed that Chad cared. Apparently, he texted Edu to tell him I'd left with "another guy," which was weird because Chad and Edu weren't friends. Edu didn't even like Chad. But that didn't matter—the damage was done. Someone thought my wild night out was *news* and started spreading the word. With a little more digging, Chad found out what had happened and followed up with Edu: "Sasha slept with this guy and she's cheating on you." He didn't know that Edu and I weren't together, although it was none of his business in the first place. Worse yet, Edu apparently had amnesia about our agreement to take a break. Before I knew it, the whole climbing community was in on the story.

I hadn't thought much about the term "slut shaming" until then, but it certainly seemed to describe what happened next. People in the community chose sides, as if Edu and I were playing in a public sports arena and I was the bad guy. The healthy move would have been to not second-guess my decision to end our relationship and to ignore public opinion about my "indiscretion," to embrace my relief and my hard-won independence, and to keep on my own trajectory. Instead, I felt guilt-ridden and embarrassed. I convinced myself I'd made a mistake, that I was wrong to end the relationship. I was determined to win Edu back.

"No, it didn't happen," was the first thing out of my mouth when Edu called the next day and angrily confronted me. I felt trapped, like a deer in headlights. "Okay, yes, it did happen," I finally admitted. I apologized for everything—the breakup, the affair, the gossip. I blamed myself: *How could I even have thought of ending the relationship?* I couldn't lose my best friend, my climbing partner. I forgot everything I'd felt in Madagascar, everything I'd written in my journal about how miserable I was. Instead, all I could think of was how I needed to right my wrongs and reconcile, no matter what it took. My mission was Edu—to gain his forgiveness and win back his trust.

I had a climb planned with my friend Matilda, in Catalonia, Spain, not far from Edu's home. The route, "American Hustle," was a climb I'd wanted to return to after not managing to send it that spring. It was a trip I'd been training for, so I didn't want to cancel, especially since I was meeting up with Matilda. I needed to be with a good friend—to climb and to try to gain back my sense of self. Now, making amends with Edu was also baked into my plan. I flew to Spain with the hope of sending American Hustle . . . and my relationship with Edu.

Matilda and I climbed hard on that trip. I did eight 5.14s, reminding myself that, with effort and determination, I could accomplish whatever I set my mind to do. Naively, I thought the same could apply to my relationship with Edu. When he met me and Matilda for dinner one night, I immediately felt the same electricity I'd always felt when we first saw each other after being apart. I knew that Edu felt the same way, because we spent the next couple days together, but when it was time for me to leave, he told me that he wasn't ready for us to be anything more than friends—perhaps with benefits. Despite our passionate, emotional reunion, Edu wasn't ready to "forgive" me, and I had convinced myself that I was the one who was solely responsible for the crater-like rift in our relationship. We agreed to spend some time apart, at least until the New Year.

I returned home, and Edu and I resumed our emotional roller coaster via texts. His went: "I love you," followed by, "I can't be with you." Mine went: "I love you. I made a mistake. I miss you." I didn't miss our constant, heated battles over the most mundane things, but I did miss him. He was constantly on my mind. Our texts turned into impassioned phone calls. I told him that I wanted us to have another shot. We loved each other and had made so many amazing memories together. Couldn't we just make it work? Couldn't we move on from the incident in San Francisco? Edu would start to give a little, but then he would end our conversations with "But I can't trust you."

How long was I supposed to remain in relationship purgatory? I thought then that Edu was the one responsible for making me feel guilty, but in hindsight I realized that I let him make me feel that way. He wanted me to "behave" and prove that I was a "good girl," instead of respecting the strong, independent, opinionated woman I had fought to become—and that I'd compromised in being with him. Round and round we went, each combative conversation leaving me more and more emotionally drained. Our "power couple" status felt like a facade. Neither of us was happy. I had to accept the fact that no amount of restarts was going to repair the disconnect between us.

13

Climbing is a multifaceted sport. It encompasses rock climbing, bouldering, sport climbing, trad climbing, big wall climbing, alpine climbing, ice climbing, and mixed climbing (a combination of rock and ice). A climber may be a pro in one or two disciplines and a complete novice in another. I knew of climbers who were dedicated to one particular type of climbing—say, rock or ice—but I wanted to be able to do mixed climbing with some degree of expertise.

I'd heard about the climbing objectives in places like Patagonia, a vast paradise of national parks, glaciers, and native wildlife at the southernmost tip of South America. If I ever wanted to climb there or do any extensive alpine climbing elsewhere, I would have to learn how to use ice axes and crampons—spiked traction devices. I never wanted a lack of skill to hold me back from any aspect of climbing, so on winter break in my senior year of Columbia, I learned how to ice-climb.

I'd met Maury Birdwell at the International Climbers' Festival. He's a talented climber and board member of the Honnold Foundation, which advocates for solar power as a proven, environmentally sound solution to global energy poverty. He'd mentioned that he ice-climbed, and I told him that was something I'd always wanted to try. I'd imagined competing in Ouray (Colorado) Ice Park's annual Ice Festival—the biggest ice-climbing event in America, held in Ouray's world-class man-made ice-climbing park—so winter break of senior year I reached out to Maury. He said that he and a friend were going to be at the Ouray Ice Festival and that I should meet up with them the week or so before. It just so happened that his friend Will was a professional ice climber who would become my ice-climbing sensei.

I flew to Boulder from New York City. From there Will flew the three of us in his little Cessna four-seater to Vail for my first lessons on how to ice-climb and "dry-tool"—use ice axes to climb rock not covered in snow or ice. I was stoked to learn the ropes—or, more accurately, the axes—of ice climbing. I knew there would be a learning curve on ice, but I wasn't quite prepared for how steep it would be. The biggest difference between rock and ice climbing was literally the difference between climbing solid rock and *frozen water*. On a wall of ice, axes took the place of fingertips and toes. Instead of using my hands to grab rock, I needed to swing an axe into the ice above my head. My biggest concern at first was that I would accidentally slice my rope in half. In comparison to my new ice-climbing boots, which were equipped with crampons, my rock-climbing shoes looked like ballet slippers. Instead of wedging my feet into crevices and onto rock protrusions, I had to kick the toes of my spiked boots into the ice.

As in sport climbing, I was on a rope for safety's sake, but instead of securing my rope into draws placed into bolts, which are relatively secure and stable on a wall, I had to depend on "ice screws"—long tubular screws twisted into the ice for support, which aren't nearly as dependable as bolts. Frozen water does not have the same strength as rock, so it stands to reason that screws rip out of ice more easily than bolts come loose from rock. At first, the thought of hanging from a screw made me shiver.

In rock climbing I was used to falling all the time. Falls on rock were not only acceptable, they were expected. The point was to get back on the wall and try again in order to improve. But Will had warned me in advance that you never want to fall while ice climbing. In rock climbing, a fall was relatively "clean"—my body would come off the wall all at once—but in ice climbing that isn't the case. Falling with razor-sharp blades attached to my feet made it easier to get caught on the ice in a way that could result in a broken leg or ankle, or worse.

Once I learned the basic safety precautions, I followed Will on the ice, determined to be a star student. We practiced on easy terrain and built up to more challenging routes, including an epic multi-pitch climb on Colorado's Bridal Veil Falls, a 365-foot frozen falls over Telluride Box Canyon—the state's tallest free-falling waterfall and deemed one of the most difficult ice climbs in the country. I grew up skiing in the mountains of Quebec, where it wasn't uncommon to see large ice waterfalls from the chairlift, but I'd never seen anything as big and intimidating as Bridal Veil, and I'd definitely never imagined climbing such a thing.

We hiked for two hours before arriving at the base of the falls. Will took the lead, and I followed after he placed an anchor a third of the way up. Since it was a multi-pitch, we would tackle it in a similar way to climbing a rock multi-pitch—except that I'd never depended upon an anchor in frozen water. It was hard to believe it would be secure enough to support me, let alone Will. When I reached the anchor, I peered at the two screws holding me on a sheath of ice hundreds of feet from the ground. I could see the running water beneath the ice. "Is that normal? Are we okay?" I asked.

"The water isn't as close to the surface as it looks. It only seems that way because the ice is so thick and clear," Will assured me, but I could only think: *All this could just melt off and we'd fall hundreds of feet to our death.*

We still had two hundred feet of vertical climbing ahead of us. Climbing rock high above the ground was one thing, but dangling from ice screws felt terrifyingly unpredictable—and, I'll admit, exhilarating. I'd never been as cold as I was then, except maybe when I skied. As kids, Charlie and my cousin Sadie and I would take to the slopes in such cold weather that we had to occasionally stop and check each other for signs of frostbite—white patches on our face and hands. Looking back, I was grateful that Dad insisted we brave the frigid weather, because I think it made me more resolute.

I remembered an old trick I taught myself to battle those temperatures—counting down from one hundred. If I focused on counting, I could distract my mind from the temperature. Dangling off a wall of sheer ice, my teeth chattering, I started my countdown.

Several days later I was ready to move on to mixed climbing, which required the same axes and crampons on terrain that included varying amounts of rock, turf, snow, and ice. After twelve days I even tried my luck in the Ouray competition.

Over the next couple years, I made several ice-climbing trips with other veteran ice climbers, including professional ice climber Angela VanWiemeersch—a real life "Elsa" from the movie *Frozen*. If it weren't for Will and Angela and other patient pros, I wouldn't have been prepared for my climb with Mark Synnott up Mount Washington—the highest peak in the northeastern U.S. (6,288 feet). Mark is a legendary big wall climber, journalist, and ice-climbing pro based in the White Mountains of New Hampshire. Situated within that mountain range is Mount Washington, notorious for its extreme, subarctic winter weather and high winds—including the highest gusts in the entire Northern Hemisphere at 231 miles per hour. It was a bit of last-minute planning, but in December 2018, Red Bull wrangled me into the climb for the pilot of a new series produced by the company Zero Point Zero.

I arrived at Mark's house late in the evening before our climb, where the Red Bull team had already assembled. Mark introduced me to the crew from the production company—the series' director, a guy named Erik Osterholm, along with Erik's cameramen, Rob and Garrett. After a little small talk, we all went to our rooms to get some sleep. We planned to set out at 5 A.M.

The first thing I did before bed was pack my bag of gear so that I'd be ready to roll as soon as I woke up. When I was done, I laid out my clothing: sports bra, long underwear, long-sleeved top, fleece zip-up, thin down jacket, thicker down jacket, and to top it all off, a hooded Gore-Tex wind and rain jacket and Red Bull beanie.

Laying out my clothing was a routine I'd had since my competition days—though granted, back then my outfit consisted of a pair of tights or shorts and my Team USA jersey. I liked to control all variables that were within my power in order to eliminate as much stress as possible, even down to how I'd wear my long hair (in a braid). I had a similar routine while in school. The night before an exam I'd ready whatever I needed—calculator, pens, sharpened pencils, scratch paper, et cetera. That way I could wake up and focus precisely on the test or task at hand.

Before turning in, I texted Edu. Despite all the drama we'd been through, we had never ceased to share our excitement around climbing and travel. He was a spectacular all-around climber whose passion encompassed every aspect of climbing, including alpine. I wanted to connect with him and share my feelings about the challenge ahead. I told him how cool everyone seemed, and how I was a little nervous about the extreme cold. "You'll do great," he said reassuringly. "It's going to be an epic adventure!"

In the morning, I was the last one up. Everyone else had been awake and packing their bags for a while—I'd later learn that they were a little worried whether I'd be on time, because they'd all been up since 4 getting ready for a 5 A.M. departure. They couldn't have known I'd done all my prep the night before and had even sized my crampons to my new mountaineering boots.

I joined the team in the living room, grabbed a breakfast bar that I'd made for the trip, and chugged enough coffee to catch up with everyone else's caffeine intake. We drove over to the trailhead and began the hike to our route, "Pinnacle Gully." A thick, fresh blanket of snow lay over everything, courtesy of a blizzard just a few days earlier.

Mark and I set out ahead as Erik directed the cameramen around us. We warmed up quickly, so we started shedding our layers. There's a saying in alpinism, "Be bold, start cold," meaning that it's better to be a little cold than to be so warm as to perspire. Damp base layers can chill you to the bone; the sole advice I received from an ice-climber friend was, simply, "Don't sweat." I took off both my down jackets, but kept my Gore-Tex on to keep me dry. After four hours' hiking the kind of terrain better suited to backcountry skiing, we reached the base of the gully, and our climb.

Mark and I pulled out our ice-climbing gear—crampons, ice axes, rope, ice screws, GRIGRI (a belay device), climbing gloves, and some traditional gear for placing into areas of rock—and secured our harnesses. Rob did the same, since he'd be climbing with us to film our ascent while Erik and Garrett went off to capture B-roll and footage of Harvard Cabin, a historic cabin servicing hikers in the summer and ice climbers and skiers in the winter. It was where we would stop for the night. As we split off in our opposite directions, I realized how impressed I'd been with our director, Erik. Since he worked in TV in New York City and Los Angeles, I initially assumed he was a city hipster type, most likely ill-equipped to keep up with us on such a grueling undertaking, but he wasn't even winded by the hike.

Mark and I continued on the climb. Occasionally we had to stop as ninety-mile-per-hour winds took us by surprise, sending loose snow swirling around us in mini-tornadoes, as if we were in a snow globe after a good shake. When it felt as though I might be picked up and tossed around like a toy, I'd lean down on my hands so I could keep four points of contact with the mountain.

I knew in advance that temperatures on the summit could fall to minus 35 degrees, making it the second-coldest place on earth after the South Pole, but I couldn't have known what that would actually feel like. My fingers were frozen like wooden knobs under my thick gloves. When I moved them to climb, I'd regain some circulation, but that resulted in what is referred to as "Screaming Barfies"—when the blood begins to surge back into one's extremities after deadening cold. The sensation felt as if I'd been punched in the gut so hard that I might throw up. I didn't know how many punches I could take, so I tried the Wim Hof breathing techniques I'd learned.

Hof is a motivational speaker and extreme athlete, famous for his breathing exercises, which enable one to weather extreme cold. He was a guest instructor at a Red Bull program I participated in with a dozen other athletes, where he had us all lie on the floor and follow a set of his guided breathing exercises, including moments of oxygen deprivation. At one point in the exercise I had the sensation that I didn't *need* to breathe, and that I could hold my breath for as long as I wanted. Afterward, I did another set, but at the camp I took breaths as I lowered my entire body into an ice bath. It seemed like an insane undertaking at first, but I had to trust . . . and breathe, as I was instructed. A minute in the bath became ten, then twenty, then, finally, thirty minutes. I had what I can only describe as my first out-of-body experience. I felt as if I were floating, observing myself in the bath. It was like conquering my worst fear, which had always been the cold.

As icy winds swirled around me on the mountain, I put Hof's breathing techniques to use. I took deep inhales through my nose, exhaling through my mouth, repeating for thirty breaths. I held the last breath for as long as possible—under different circumstances, that set of breathing would be followed by another and a dip in an ice bath, which, considering our current conditions, didn't sound half bad. Much to my surprise, I beat back the Screaming Barfies.

We climbed Pinnacle Gully and navigated the ridge to the summit, and then hiked back around and down to the descent route. By nightfall we reached the halfway mark of our descent, Harvard Cabin, where Erik and Garrett met us with food and hot beverages. Pinnacle was definitely a humbling experience for me, since I still couldn't "read" ice in the same way I was able to "read" rock. With rock, I could look up at the wall and read the intricacies of its features. In contrast, on ice I didn't yet have the experience to know the best place to swing my axe and with what level of force. However, Mark had been an expert instructor, and the production team was pleased with the footage they got. Soon enough, I crawled into my sleeping bag and passed out.

Making the rest of our way down the mountain the next day was a piece of cake compared to the climb up. By the time we reached Mark's house and I'd indulged in a long, hot shower, I'd almost forgotten how nearly incapacitating the cold and wind had been. My goal had been to challenge myself, to not make one complaint about the frigid temperatures, to remain positive, and to accept the harsh conditions for what they were. And I'd accomplished that. I felt supremely satisfied, so much so that I knew I would say yes to another adventure in ice climbing. I'd already developed my first case of "alpinist amnesia."

The next day, I drove to the airport with Garrett and Erik, who were also flying out to their respective homes. We talked excitedly about the climb and a million other things from politics to books to cryptocurrency. I was fascinated by Erik's behind-the-scenes accounts of *Anthony Bourdain: Parts Unknown*—my favorite TV show—which he had directed for eight years.

I also couldn't help but be struck by Erik's sense of curiosity about people and places, and things other than rock climbing. I imagined that in another time and place, we'd be friends. He'd recently moved to Bozeman, Montana, a ten-hour drive from Boulder, so there'd be no chance of a casual meet. Besides, I still thought that Edu and I would come to some miraculous resolution in our relationship. That was still my goal. Not for a moment did I entertain an alternate ending. Erik and I said our goodbyes at the airport. *Maybe we'll work together again*, I thought.

14

Several months after my ascent of Mount Washington, the highest peak in the northeastern U.S., I was in the checkout line at Whole Foods when the February 2018 issue of *Rock and Ice* magazine caught my eye. For one thing, it was relatively rare to see a climbing magazine at Whole Foods—but then again, it was Boulder. For another, the cover featured Sonnie Trotter high up on the massive limestone face of a striking climb: Mount Yamnuska in the Canadian Rockies. I grabbed the magazine and rifled through the pages. At home, I devoured the article. Of course, it got me thinking.

In the climbing world and beyond, Sonnie Trotter needs no introduction. He's a Canadian climber, known especially for his strength, with hundreds of first ascents all over the world. A photographer and writer, he had written the *Rock and Ice* piece about establishing first ascents of the "5.14 Trifecta"— the Rocky Mountain Trilogy, three of the most difficult 5.14 big walls in the Canadian Rockies, on Castle Mountain, Mount Louis, and Mount Yamnuska. Having done the first ascents, he named his routes: "Warhammer," "The Shining Uncut," and "Blue Jeans Direct." I reached out to him for more information on the climbs. He took no time in responding: He'd be stoked for me to try the climbs and would send any information and pictures that might help.

I imagined two months of the coming summer in Banff attempting the routes—not a bad way to spend time. The town of Banff is nestled within Banff National Park and boasts a Rocky Mountain skyline. The whole area is stunning no matter the season, with its surreally beautiful mountains, lakes, hot springs, and scenic drives. I'd skied there once when I was younger, but I'd never climbed in the area. If I tried the Trilogy routes but wound up ascending none of them, it would at least be an adventure. If I sent even one, I would consider myself lucky. But if I managed all three, I'd be the first woman and second person in history to do so.

Edu and I hadn't seen each other since early December, but we'd talked on the phone every other day trying to resolve the issue of trust. We continued our circuitous messages: *I miss you. I miss you, too. I can't be with you. We should be together. I trust you. I don't trust you.* Nothing we said seemed to move our relationship in a positive direction. He didn't believe he could ever trust me again, and I didn't believe we could move forward in our relationship without trust. Too often when I talked to another guy, Edu thought I was "attention seeking," or worse, "flirting." We followed a lot of the same climbers on Instagram, most of whom were men. Once when he saw that I'd "liked" a photo of a climber who wasn't wearing a shirt, he'd sent me an angry text. Meanwhile, he told me he'd gone on a couple dates with women in Spain, which broke my heart. Things would never be the same, but we both stubbornly refused to recognize the inevitability of our split.

With Valentine's Day approaching, Edu suggested I visit him in order to prove that I was "committed" to our relationship, so

I boarded a plane and flew to Spain. I imagined we'd have time alone to reconnect, but the day I arrived a friend of his showed up to do a two-day video shoot with him, followed by a photographer for a photo shoot. In between, Edu was constantly on the phone planning an expedition to China. Most evenings we met with his friends instead of spending one-on-one time together.

Looking back, I think that he didn't want to suggest we still had a chance, because then he'd lose the upper hand. In the past we'd gone through cycles where I was more casual about our relationship than he was, but now the situation was reversed, and he was in the power position. I wondered, Was my drive to send the relationship simply a consequence of wanting what I didn't or couldn't have? Did I really miss our relationship? Or did I miss the fantasy of what our relationship could have been?

Toward the end of my visit, we finally managed some moments of enjoying each other's company, although we didn't really resolve anything. I did what I thought might inch us closer to a reconciliation—I pitched my plan for the two of us to attempt the Trilogy over the summer. It took Edu no time to get on board. He'd always wanted to climb in Canada and was as intrigued by the Trilogy as I was. At least we'd agreed on something before I left for home: We were going to Banff together.

Having my climbing partner back temporarily eclipsed my uncertainty about our relationship. Climbing often brought us closer together. At the very least we were a successful rock team. Up until then, many of my big climbs had been with Edu, so I assumed I needed him to succeed. I tried to ignore the small, nagging questions in my head: *Had I slipped into a kind of climbing codependence? Hadn't I accomplished so much on my own, even before Edu?* Instead, I focused on the rigorous training schedule ahead.

With four months to go before Banff, the first part of my training had to do with increasing my stamina. With a difficult big wall climb like the Trilogy's three 5.14s, I would need to climb quickly in order to beat down fatigue and endure long days in the mountains without "bonking out"—hitting a wall and becoming completely depleted. I'd learned that sending each pitch wasn't even the hardest part of a big wall climb. Sometimes exposure to crappy weather along with fatigue from hiking three or four hours to the base of a climb was enough to suck every ounce of energy from my body.

I knew, in planning, I'd have to make it through the easier pitches—ranging up to 5.13—and still have power in reserve to fire the crux pitches. The good part was that if (when) I fell, I could lower back down to the start of the pitch and try again. The bad part was how inefficient falling could be. It requires a substantial energy reserve to do the same pitch over and over, no matter how close to the top. Essentially, falling adds pitches to a wall that is energy-sucking enough as is.

Edu and my goal was to climb each route in a single day. Originally, I'd imagined that a friend of mine, filmmaker Tommy Joyce, would head the production crew documenting our adventure, but Edu decided he didn't trust Tommy. He had it in his head that we were "too close" as friends, so if he was in, Tommy was out. Tommy was able to laugh off Edu's jealousy, although he did say, "You know that's not normal, right?" I shrugged. I didn't even know how to respond. Fortunately, Tommy offered to coordinate the self-shot efforts of the trip. It would be up to me to hire a local production crew along the way.

With plans in place to document our adventure, and Edu training in Spain, I took advantage of the awesome climbing in Boulder. In good weather, I was all over the parks. In bad, I hiked the 40-degree-incline treadmill in my house in addition to hang-boarding. I worked on my Treadwall, which allowed me to climb thousands of feet, essentially without stopping. Much like a treadmill that spins an endless belt, a Treadwall is a vertical rotating wall with adjustable steepness, speed, and routes. Without having to worry about any outside factors—weather, wind, ropes, and partners—it could feel at times like total synchronization. An endless, moving, Zen meditation.

First week of May I flew to France to climb in the Verdon Gorge with Edu. With a new joint climbing venture to focus on, I'd hoped we could recapture the fun we used to have climbing. We'd been together only a few hours when Mom called. "Sasha, Baba's fallen ill. She's on her deathbed. I'm sorry, but if you want to say goodbye you have to come back now." I immediately felt my heart twist in my chest. It hurt to take a breath. I had to get home.

Twenty-four hours later I was on a flight back to Toronto and by Baba's side with the rest of my family, but there was nothing I could do except hug my mom and take Baba's hand. I stood on one side of the bed with Charlie, my mom on the other. I kept stealing glances at Mom, her eyes on *her* mother as she struggled to keep her composure. *What is she thinking? Is there anything I can say?* I stood there, images of Baba flashing through my head like clips of home movies—holidays with her, birthdays, the times she'd sit and watch me climb. I felt my phone vibrate. *Probably Edu,* I thought. But it wasn't.

It was a screenshot from a friend of an Instagram post by Chad, which depicted a Latino man obscured by a plus-sized woman. The caption read: "Have fun in the Verdon guys ha-hahaha." Chad, again, and not even from his official Instagram account. Instead, it was posted from a fake account he'd used in the past to make fun of me and other female athletes and climbers. Ironically enough, Chad chose a shot from the feed of a woman who was renowned as a spokesperson for body positivity—*Good going, Chad. It's not enough to poke your macho brand of fun at me. Go ahead and appropriate the photo of a woman you don't even know.*

I was already feeling emotionally and physically wasted, but then the anger and mortification I felt about Chad's post piled right on top. *Am I going to continue to put up with bullshit from someone I've done nothing to?* I didn't have access to the actual post, since it was from a "private" account that I was blocked from—though apparently not private enough, because several female climbers had alerted me to it. I wondered whether it was an account strictly for harassment. I also wondered who was following it.

I stepped outside the hospital room and messaged Chad to take down the post. No response. I called. Again, no luck. I reached out to several trusted friends in the climbing industry, including Lynn Hill and Robyn Erbesfield—another legendary climber whom I deeply respected—and consulted with them about posting a response. They both agreed Chad's post was bullshit and that I had every right to stand up for myself. I called a mutual sponsor of Chad's and mine to lodge a complaint. He said that it wasn't the first complaint he'd received about Chad.

That pushed me over the edge. I wasn't going to put on a happy face for the public. I captioned the response on my Instagram feed "Rise Against Bullying." I shared the screenshot I'd been sent and called Chad out for his actions in a lengthy post, beginning with: "*As a community we need to hold ourselves to higher standards than permitting defamatory, assaulting behavior. I use my social media platforms to share a window into my life—both professionally and personally—yet I also believe that this channel is a platform to have a voice and stand for what I believe in. This includes spreading more love and taking a stance against bullying. I am hurt and brokenhearted to say that I am a victim of a bully and it has crossed the line . . ."*

I'd never understood "I'm just kidding" or "Boys will be boys" as excuses for behavior meant to humiliate or embarrass—and what else was the point of Chad's fake account? I was finally taking a stance, one that felt correct and empowering. Immediately I heard from other athletes, those who had been the butt of his "joking" and those who had watched—frustrated—from the sidelines, worried they'd be dismissed as "not having a sense of humor" or "overly sensitive" for "making a big deal out of nothing."

One woman told me that after my first female ascent of "Era Vella," Chad had started a thread within a group of male pro climbers claiming I'd lied about it. I'd first attempted the Era Vella (5.14d) climb, in Margalef, Spain, in February 2012 with Keith and Andy filming me for Adidas. Despite my best efforts, I wasn't able to send it in the time we had, so that May, I returned with my mom. I was hoping for a double celebration, one for my mom's birthday on May 5, and one for a send of Era Vella. With Mom belaying me, I tackled the crux sequence that had given me so much grief and became the first woman to send the route. Since my mom had belayed me and there was no other "witness" to the climb, Chad figured that the two of us had conspired to lie about the send.

In the days following Chad's post, I was surprised by the outpouring of encouragement I received from people who were also over Chad's particular brand of humor. A large number of those who came forward—including a couple of climbing legends—told me their own stories of having been bullied by someone in their lives.

In reaction to the post, Chad's sponsors summarily dropped him. When that happened, the people who had chosen to stand by their *bro* and the whole elite, macho boys' club came at me. I thought I was ready for the public fallout until I received a text from one of my climbing heroes, a guy whose picture I had tacked on my bedroom door growing up. "You fucking destroyed Chad's career," he told me. His words felt like a punch in the gut.

It took a while for me to be able to own the fact that I'd called out a member of what I deemed a toxic boys' club. My first thought was: *Oh, man, maybe I shouldn't have called out Chad. Maybe I should have stayed small and quiet and rolled with the punches for as long as he felt like doling them out.* But in following my instincts and acknowledging Chad's bullying, I felt as if I'd taken down my own demons. I felt released from the pressure to constantly present myself as cheerful and together. I continued to hear from women and men telling me how courageous I was for standing up for myself, many of whom were eager to share how Chad had disrespected them.

I was grateful when Georgie Abel, a female climber and writer, covered the incident in a May 18, 2018, article on *Medium*. She wrote: "[w]hat becomes important is not that a 38-year-old man created a fake Instagram in order to bully at least two young women, but the fact that he felt supported in doing so. . . . Climbing culture is the thing that gave him that support."

Still, there were some women in the climbing community who chose to take Chad's side—some of whom I'd formerly regarded as friends. A part of me understood. I figured it was more important to them to maintain their status as one of the "cool kids"—and that they might remain "cool," until they happened to be the target of some not-so-cool bullying.

I felt burned by the whole experience—and deeply hurt—but I also saw that letting people in on my struggles as a woman and a professional athlete was part of sharing my journey. We all manage degrees of bullshit and disappointment in our lives.

What I realized in being transparent and vulnerable was that I could empower other women to be the same. I also realized that I had to come to grips with a fear of not receiving affirmation from the climbing community—it was exhausting trying to fit into someone else's idea of what a climber should be or look like. I'd tried hard to make certain relationships work in the community when, clearly, they weren't meant to be.

The first casualty of that realization was my relationship with Edu. When he'd visited me in Boulder, it had become obvious I didn't fit into his idea of what a girlfriend should be—of what *his* girlfriend should be. Aside from not being able to agree on anything, we were still circling the issue of trust. It was exhausting. He'd say, "I don't trust you." And I'd say, "Well, trust is the basis for a relationship, so I guess this isn't going to work." Finally, we both agreed our romance was over, but that we would remain friends, and we'd still do the Trilogy together—in retrospect, a naive expectation at best.

The plan was for him to return to Spain to train on his own, and then meet me in Banff at the beginning of July. Since I was scheduled as a guest speaker for the Bow Valley Festival for climbers in Canmore, Alberta, twenty miles outside of Banff, we would attend the festival together—a great way to launch our adventure and get to know the local climbing community.

A month later, Edu was scheduled to fly into the Calgary airport. But in order to pick him up, I had to make the twenty-hour-drive from Boulder to Calgary myself. It was a marathon drive, but I was used to long stretches of travel. I figured I'd stop halfway to shake out the kinks from sitting so long. Bozeman happened to be the halfway point, where a couple people I knew lived—including Erik Osterholm. *I'll just text him. Why not? See if he'll take a quick hike with me.* He was home, and he was game, so I dropped in. Our rapport was as easy as I'd remembered—it was as if we picked up right where we left off. After a fifty-minute hike, he bought me lunch and packed it in a to-go bag for me. I jumped in my car for the second leg of my drive. "Keep me posted!" he said.

I drove on, feeling happy and refueled. After nearly a day's travel I arrived at the Calgary airport. Edu was angry that I was an hour late, so we wound up driving the final leg of our journey to Banff in tense silence. We should have cut our losses and given up on the friendship right then. Instead, we wound up spending several combative days together, even though there was no way on earth to dig out of the toxic dump that our relationship had become.

Finally, I called it, like a referee calling a fight between two battered boxers. "You need to go back to Spain. Now. We can't do a climb. We can't be friends. We can't do anything!" I felt relief, but only for a moment. My expectations for the Trilogy felt lower than low. For the first time in as long as I could remember, I couldn't summon my usual optimism. Even worse, I couldn't see any road to success.

15

I was in Banff to attempt the Rocky Mountain Trilogy, three of the most difficult 5.14 big walls in the Canadian Rockies, and I was without the most crucial ingredient for a safe and successful climb: a climbing partner I knew and trusted. My plan with Edu had been to spend three weeks on each mountain, Castle, Mount Louis, and Mount Yamnuska, in order to acclimate ourselves to the different types of rock, understand the mountains' unique style of climbing, work out the crux pitches, and film with our GoPros. We had established systems and ways of communicating. We had a certain rhythm and pace and a history of successful climbs together under the most intense circumstances. With Edu gone, all I could think was: *Will all my preparation for the two-month Trilogy adventure amount to nothing?*

Sonnie Trotter and Brandon Pullan, who had helped establish the routes, had enthusiastically provided all the information and photos I needed. I knew they were rooting for me, but at that point I felt unsure that I was capable of doing such big days without Edu. It took time and planning to find a seasoned climbing partner, especially on a big wall objective. Not only would my partner and I be trusting each other with our lives, we'd also need to work out the sequences together, swap leads, and motivate each other.

I'd always demanded the same thing in a partner that I demanded of myself: positivity, a cool head under pressure, and the ability to remain extremely concentrated on the task at hand despite long hours and fatigue. There's little margin for error when it comes to clipping into a safety point and managing ropes and equipment while hundreds (or thousands) of feet off the ground. In addition, I needed a partner who could commit to climbs upward of twenty-four hours at a stretch. It would be a huge ask of anyone.

I arrived in Banff in time for the Bow Valley Festival—a festival for rock-climbing enthusiasts from the U.S. and Canada—where I met up with Mike Doyle, an old friend and the coach for the Canadian climbing team. Mike is also a good friend of Sonnie Trotter, who was there for the festival. After greetings and introductions to some of the Banff climbing community, Mike asked, "Why didn't Edu come tonight? What's up? How are you doing?" It didn't take long for me to spill my whole frustrating—and, I felt, *embarrassing*—situation. "I don't know what to do. I don't have a belayer. Nothing about this climb feels safe."

Mike's response was the first small sign that maybe the climbing gods would be on my side. He said that he would, at the least, be able to belay me on Castle Mountain. Later he joked that he "couldn't turn down a damsel in distress," but I could tell he was excited about the prospect of climbing the Warhammer route. In another stroke of good fortune, Mike also volunteered Sonnie, who would help document the day. I was still nervous, but having a commitment from Mike, someone I knew and implicitly trusted, gave me a renewed sense of hope. Even the local climbers I'd met at the festival had been encouraging me about the routes I wanted to attempt. In fact, some were thinking of trying their skills on one or all of Sonnie's routes. *It was going to happen!*

A COUPLE DAYS later, Sonnie, Mike, and I were on the forty-minute drive to Castle Mountain. We parked and hiked the two and a half miles to the mountain to start laying the groundwork for our climb. Upon reaching Warhammer—despite all the photos and descriptions Mike and I had pored over in advance—we were awestruck by how imposing the wall was in person. The sixth pitch up was the first crux pitch, which consisted of an exposed limestone "nose"—the steepest, narrowest ridge of the wall—high above the tree line. Working the nose would require me to squeeze my core and shoulders and back muscles in perfect unison and create compression between my legs while adjusting my feet. Fifteen pitches altogether, Warhammer would be a long, endurance-oriented climb with not one, but two crux sections. It was time to lace up.

At the start of a new climb, the ritual of replacing my hiking boots with the rubber and leather climbing shoes from my backpack always felt almost profound. This time was no different. I could sense the excitement in my hands and feet, as though they were part of some kind of rhapsody. As I tightly cinched the laces on my climbing shoes, I could hear a faint squeak as laces rubbed through eyelets. I'd chosen shoes with a fairly malleable rand and an "aggressive toe box"—meaning shoes with very downturned toes for powerful, precise positioning in overhanging climbs. I became acutely aware of everything beneath my soles—the feel of every twig and rock particle running through my heel to my calf, to my hip. I felt grounded and ready to climb.

Standing at the base of Castle Mountain, looking up, my excitement abruptly turned to fear. The *idea* of Warhammer was now the *project* in front of me. Until that moment I hadn't realized how emotionally spent I was from dealing with Edu. Even though I trusted Mike and I had climbed tough walls with other people, I felt anxious and raw. I couldn't imagine doing the first pitch, let alone all fifteen. But I was getting ahead of myself. I needed to breathe, slow the rush of fear, and climb—one hand, one leg at a time. *Be in the moment,* I told myself. I moved onto the wall, and Mike followed. Over the next few days, we worked on our moves until we became comfortable with the terrain, and I could feel my old self pushing through.

A week and a half later, with Sonnie along to film the climb, Mike and I set out for the send in the windiest weather I could have imagined. I took the lead at the crux, wrestling through the narrowest ridge of the nose and hugging the wall so tightly I couldn't tell where my body ended and the wall started. When I reached the anchors, I could hear Sonnie and Mike cheering from below. While we still had pitches we hadn't yet tried, there wasn't anything harder than 5.13 left. I felt a surge of confidence. We were going to do this. I willed it. I wanted it.

At the top of Castle Mountain, we still had a final solo of the Eisenhower Tower, a thousand-foot vertical spire, like a little mountain atop a bigger one. Fatigue was kicking in, so we regrouped and decided that we would *free solo* Eisenhower. Several factors went into that decision, the most important being that we'd been told the climb was pretty easy and straightforward, closer to fifth-class "scrambling"—hiking up terrain steep enough to require use of one's hands. Secondly, we needed to take advantage of the waning daylight.

When free-climbing with a partner, it takes time to belay and then catch up with your partner to do the same, increasing the time needed to climb. If we climbed free solo there would be no rope management, so we could climb at the same time, increasing our speed and efficiency. It may not have seemed like the safest choice, but after assessing the situation and weighing the risk of a descent in total darkness, we felt comfortable in our decision.

We made it to the summit with light to spare. Mike broke out the wine gums (Canadian gummies) he had brought for the occasion, in lieu of champagne. Giddily, we devoured them, pausing to look at each other, like: *Dude, we just did that! That was frickin' incredible!* After a brief rest, we began our descent.

Four hours later we were back at the car. It was dawn, and we were running on fumes, delirious after nearly twenty-four hours of endless hiking and climbing. I had made my dream of Warhammer a reality, despite all the unknowns and the emotional upheavals of the months leading up to it. I thought: *I'm the athlete I've always wanted to be. I can endure and persevere no matter the circumstances. I did it—oh, my God!* In that moment, for the first time since arriving in Banff, I felt as if sending the Trilogy was actually within my grasp.

I had allotted two months for the entire project, imagining each climb to take maybe three weeks—three weeks to work out sequences efficiently enough for me to successfully climb bottom to the top in *a day.* With Warhammer in the bag after only two weeks, I was ahead of schedule. I was anxious to take advantage of the next good-weather window and begin tackling The Shining Uncut on Mount Louis. That window came three days later. Thankfully, Mike was still available, so we set out to scout the mountain, renewed and stoked for our middle chapter in the Trilogy saga.

The east side of Mount Louis featured a flat, diamond-shaped portion visible to anyone driving in or out of Banff, known, not surprisingly, as the Diamond. Part of The Shining Uncut's route on the Diamond was a 260-foot, 5.14a crux pitch, a slightly more difficult version of The Shining Uncut's 5.13d route, first climbed by Sonnie and Tommy Caldwell. Basically, the "uncut" route was a greater challenge than The Shining—short for The Shining Uncut—because it involved sending the three routes on the Diamond *in one single effort,* one 260-foot pitch.

To reach the base of the Diamond, Mike and I hiked for four hours, only to arrive at the bottom of a rock gully that turned into steeper terrain of malleable limestone that required scrambling with heavy packs. By the time we reached the base, we had already clocked five hours of continuous hiking and scrambling over twisty narrow trails and inclines. I was exhausted, and the climb hadn't even started.

To go for the send, we would combine the first three of the starting pitches—three extremely technical pitches on small edges with no place to stop. It was more vertical than Warhammer, but the bolts were farther apart—about fifteen feet apart versus the usual five to ten. Although Warhammer had demanded a more gymnastic style of climbing on a steeper angle than the Diamond, the holds had been closer together and easier to grip. Our goal for the day was to work out our climbing sequences, but with only the tiniest rock protrusions for hand- and footholds, the going was slower than I'd hoped for. Mike and I made it up several of the pitches and then came down to the base, having accomplished none of the singular pitches. I couldn't help but feel as if I had gotten lucky with Castle.

Three days later, when the next weather window came, Mike wasn't available. Sonnie had already left Banff, but before doing so he'd introduced me to Dexter, a local climber who was there specifically to work on The Shining Uncut. The good part was that Dexter was motivated to take on the Diamond and that he seemed like a capable partner—he'd been Sonnie's, after all. The bad part was that *I'd* never climbed with him. I felt apprehensive about a new partner and concerned that my long days on Castle Mountain were catching up with me. Worse yet, I worried that my nerves might get the best of me.

Not wanting to lose momentum, I didn't take the time to check in with myself, emotionally or physically. Instead, I headed out with Dexter, feeling totally outside my body— definitely not a place any climber wants to be. Hiking to Mount Louis, my legs felt leaden and my backpack unusually heavy. I had only four hours of sleep under my belt, and the approach wasn't for another five hours. My only hope was that sheer will would kick in and carry me through the intimidating technical climbing ahead—where the pieces of protection were far apart, and the falls as much as thirty feet. On those kinds of long, hard falls, known as "whippers," there's nothing to do except try and position one's body in preparation for the kind of extreme jolt hard enough to rattle that body to its core.

At the base of the route, my first thought was that I couldn't trust my feet or my legs. In the middle of lacing up my shoes, I had the feeling of being completely alone. *This is an impossible climb. What was I thinking?* As we forged ahead, soloing up to the base of the Diamond, I felt too nervous to even take the lead. More important, I was neglecting my overarching goals. Caught up in my desire to triumph over Castle, I was forgetting to have fun, enjoy the adventure, and keep my expectations low. After fifteen straight hours of hiking and scrambling, instead of asking myself whether I was ready to send the climb, I was telling myself to beat this climb before it beat me. I wanted it too badly. Wrong thinking, for sure.

Still determined to keep collecting "beta"—the moves for

each sequence—on the face, I pushed on, despite my increasing fear. When I reached the first of several crux sequences of sheer rock without footholds, sequences that would require intense horizontal pulling, I felt paralyzed. Even though Dexter was belaying me, taking a thirty-foot tumble down the face of the Diamond wasn't an option—I'd built up too much fear to even consider a fall of that length. On top of it all, there had been an unexpected shift in the weather. Castle had been windy but temperate, but the weather on Louis, with its higher, more exposed elevation, was extremely cold, more like alpine conditions. The pleasant summer day we started out with had turned into a chilly fall morning. By the time we reached the Diamond, it was hailing.

Tired and cold, my arms outstretched, I tugged sideways to try and stay on the rock. Suddenly I felt a sharp jab of pain run through my left shoulder. I tried to move my arm, but I could barely lift it. *Don't freak out. Don't freak out,* I told myself. I'm not a crier, but I could feel a lump forming in my throat. *Oh, no, please no tears, not here, not now.* It wasn't that Dexter hadn't been cool or completely supportive—he'd been both those things—but I didn't know him well enough to start processing my feelings while I cried out my frustration. I imagined him telling friends, "Oh, yeah, I went out with Sasha DiGiulian and she cried 'cause it was hard." I grimaced through the pain, trying to keep it together as I rappelled down, hand over hand, carrying all my gear. I would have given anything to disappear off the mountain and be back home.

The next day my shoulder was worse, and the weight of the injury sunk in. Everything I do as a climber depends first and foremost on my physical health—the best intentions in the world can't make up for a physical liability. I felt scared—of my injury, of getting out of shape, of losing momentum, of missing

the next weather window, and of not having a consistent climbing partner. I remembered someone who had reached out to me
on Instagram days after my arrival in Banff, offering support. I
scrolled through my messages. There it was. Serendipity in the
form of one Fabienne Moser: "Hey I know you're in town because I follow you on IG. I'm the physiotherapist for the Canadian Ski Team and I work at Altitude Physiotherapy in Banff. If
you need any physical therapy while you're in town, just let me
know." *YES*, I replied. *Today?!*

I drove out to meet with Fabienne, who insisted I call her
Fabi. She lost no time in diagnosing my shoulder as an AC
joint sprain—the type of injury that can require anywhere from
three weeks to multiple months for recovery, depending on the
grade. Fabi determined my sprain as a Grade 1+, adding that
I should be able to be back climbing in a couple weeks *if* I was
careful not to further separate the joint. If I pushed and didn't
take care of the sprain, I would be looking at *no summer season*
of climbing. She began treating me right away. I took off from
climbing and we quickly progressed into shoulder rehab.

I saw her every day. Initially, treatment involved dry nee-
dling, cupping, and manual therapy. Once she was satisfied
with the results, we began shoulder-strengthening exercises.
Fabi turned out to be not just a physical therapist, but also a
cheerleader, healer, optimist, and, soon enough, my friend.
Throughout the therapy process, she made me feel at home in
her town of Banff. After ten days of therapy and recovery—and
several days of watching weather windows come and go—my
shoulder regained much of its strength and my sense of impending doom faded away.

My biggest concern had been losing the overall fitness necessary to tackle Mount Louis. It had been ten days since I last
climbed, and there was a good weather window closing before

a forecast week of rain. The injury wasn't fully recovered, but I felt more like myself than I had in weeks. Fabi recommended I wait for the next weather window and continue to rehab my shoulder. As anxious and impatient as I was, I knew enough to follow her orders—not an easy thing for me, as patience has never been my strongest suit.

Begrudgingly, I continued to log hours of physical therapy, and I waited. Knowing how antsy I was, Fabi took on the role of tour guide, showing me around town and introducing me to her friends. I went with them to an outdoor concert. We went canoeing. I was having fun! I felt ready, but Fabi didn't want to give the go-ahead until after we hit the climbing gym to test my shoulder, secured with kinesiology tape. Climbing-specific movement didn't irritate it, so she said that if I was careful, I was good to go.

The weather opened up the next day, so I set out at 5 A.M. with Peter Hoang, a new friend I had met a few nights earlier over pizza and beers with Fabi and Mike Doyle. I had a good feeling about Peter, especially because he'd climbed with Mike and he was known as a highly competent and responsible climber, someone who climbed high grades in various disciplines (rock, ice, and mixed), though when we first discussed attempting The Shining, I'm pretty sure Peter had no idea that we would be spending nearly twenty-four continuous hours together. Neither did I. My only thought was to *try* The Shining.

Everything was going smoother than it had my last ill-fated time on Mount Louis. Every move—from the approach to the solo scramble to the first pitches—felt right. I was still nervous on the "runout" 5.12s—long spaces between protection points, creating longer falls—but I could feel a natural connection with the rock that I hadn't come near to before. I trusted my feet, my legs, and my hands.

I made it to the bottom of the crux pitch and yelled to Pete to watch me, because I needed to work out my moves and take some whippers in order to break my fear of falling on the Diamond. He was ready for me to fly off the wall, but as I pulled through the first difficult sections, I stuck to the wall like Velcro, my fingers clinging onto small, blade-like crimps. My body was operating without needing to be told what to do—to me, the ideal state of climbing.

It was happening. Somehow everything was falling into place. I made it through the crux and shouted down to Pete, "Oh, my God! I just got through the crux! Holy shit! I can do this!" I still had a good deal of unknown climbing to go, but after the crux it felt possible.

I returned my attention to my movements. *Be present. Trust.* Pete climbed up the rope to meet me and I powered through the second half, onsighting all of the pitches that followed.

After a few days of rest, I returned to The Shining Uncut. I felt capable of climbing the line, but I was also nervous about the injury I was still nursing. This time, Mike was available to climb with me—a huge relief. Though I was still favoring my injured shoulder and anxious about reigniting the pain, I drew on Fabi's assurance that I was strong enough to continue. On one of the most physically demanding climbs of my career, with Mike belaying and Peter Hoang filming and taking photos, I summited without falling.

The send secured Mount Louis, the second in the Trilogy. Only Mount Yamnuska was left, but first I would have to take a break—having learned the hard way that resting would be of greater benefit than pushing beyond extreme fatigue. Self-care had to be a priority in order for my whole body to recover. I took a week off to do some local sport climbs while my shoulder recovered.

On August 9, I started working on Blue Jeans Direct, the last of the Trilogy routes. Friends of mine from Yosemite drove up for moral support—Justin and Priscilla, both of whom would take photos and film me; Devon, who would belay me; and Ryan, who would help rig the static lines for Justin and Priscilla.

Unlike the alpine conditions on Mount Louis, the weather on Mount Yamnuska was humid and hot. My hands were continually sweaty, preventing me from keeping a tight hold on the rock. As it also happened, British Columbia was experiencing one of its worst wildfire seasons on record, and the smoke from nearly five hundred fires was blowing in from the west, engulfing the wall. The air quality app on my phone showed breathing outside to be equivalent to smoking six to eight cigarettes a day. I couldn't even imagine the devastation people were suffering in the affected areas—or how anyone could deny what was happening to our climate. I had the privilege of having options—I could go indoors and wait, safe and sound (if overly anxious) for the smoke to clear.

Finally, after nearly a week inside, the rain came—not great for climbing, but at least resulting in a respite from the smoke and fire—and with it, a drop in the temperature. I figured it was now or never. I drove over to Fabi's house so that she could tape my shoulder, as she'd done for each of my climbs since my injury. She surprised me with the news that she'd taken the day off from work to watch me send my last climb.

I didn't want to set up any expectations for myself. I told my friends I just wanted to work on the moves—send the first pitches from the ground, up to the crux pitch, to see what it felt like. The crux pitch of Blue Jeans Direct would require an immense amount of power. In comparison to the other two climbs, Blue Jeans Direct was much shorter, but the movements were more condensed and hard-packed. The most difficult pitch of the route, a 5.14, broke down to about twenty-six moves total, with the majority on dime-sized edges atop steep, bulging terrain that involved immense shoulder power in order to cling to the tiniest of rock protrusions.

I glided through the first three 5.12s and the 5.13, before arriving at the base of the 5.14, my fingertips torn and gushing blood. *Did the mountain have different plans for me?* My friends didn't seem to think so. They had climbed up the static ropes Ryan helped set and made it to the portaledge below the crux pitch. On the days I worked the crux, I took breaks on the portaledge with them. They played music and pulled off dance moves on the wall, reminding me to enjoy myself and have fun. I still had a lot of work to do, but during those last few days I knew my dream was within striking distance. I was ready to attempt the crux.

The day of the send, it was just me and Devon, with Priscilla filming from the portaledge. As I climbed, my raw, blistered fingertips bled through the chalk on my hands. I heaved myself upward, shaving off the last of the loose skin and grunting through the burning pain in my fingers—but this time the pain felt like a part of my connection to the wall. Before I knew it, I had managed the crux for the first time! The several pitches left, all graded easier, were within my grasp. When I reached the bottom of the last pitch, I could see Fabi peering down at me from the summit. She had hiked up the back of the mountain with Ryan and Justin to cheer me on.

Sitting on the edge of the summit in a beam of light shining down through parted clouds, I imagined my dad watching over me. I let myself cry, out of sheer joy and gratitude—for the climbing gods, for the weather, and for everyone who had helped make my adventure possible. I had become the first woman and second person ever to have sent the Trilogy. I had free-climbed every pitch and worked out my own beta. My skills and ability as a world-class climber had been validated. I had proved to *myself* that I belonged in the same upper echelon as the best male climbers.

Once again, I was convinced that if I wanted something bad enough, and worked hard enough, maybe, just maybe, I could make any goal a reality. When I received kudos from those climbers who had been silent in response to Chad's bullying, I realized that their "acceptance" no longer mattered. I didn't need them to open any doors for me.

Still, I felt a tiny, gnawing annoyance with myself for having wanted or needed vindication from "the boys' club" in the first place. I wanted to own my success, and I wanted other women to know that they, too, could own their successes. I would find a way to make that happen.

16

Climbing is a sport that is rarely "comfortable." Between my bleeding fingertips, blistered toes, sore muscles, and varying aches, I've always had some degree of baseline pain. As an athlete, pain was something I normalized, especially since I had a high tolerance for it. It was simply an unavoidable consequence of my profession. I had injuries and my body was often fatigued or my muscles were overworked, but that was the trade-off for climbing so hard. Twenty years of climbing had taught me to manage pain. But I'd not yet learned how to listen to my body and distinguish between "normal" pain and the kind of pain that might hint at a more dire problem. Like a horse with blinders, I galloped ahead, blithely unaware that my pain might be a warning.

Nothing could eclipse my joy of having sent the Trilogy—not even the increasingly painful ache in my hips. That was simply a by-product of having achieved my goal. I had arrived in Banff, uncertain about a climbing partner, vulnerable, and overwhelmed by the lofty goal I'd set for myself, and I'd left triumphant. I'd met incredible new friends who helped me to persevere and achieve what I set out to do. I couldn't have done it without them and the Banff community. They made me feel at home and empowered. The whole experience gave me a new-found sense of freedom and independence. Ironically enough, it was that feeling of independence that made me open to the possibility of a new relationship.

I'd been texting Erik during my time in Banff. Every time he texted back, my heart would jump a little. I couldn't wait to update him on my progress and hear about his latest projects. Our communication was easy and lighthearted, and he was continually encouraging of my Trilogy project, but I was still enjoying my freedom as a single person and not having to answer to anyone. I was not looking for a relationship—but, as has often been the case for me, good things have happened when I least expected them.

When I was ready for Blue Jeans Direct, Erik had offered to come to Banff to be there when I climbed. I thought for all of two minutes about his offer, then I texted back that it was too smoky, and that he should wait and visit me in Boulder when I was finished. But that was only partly the reason I asked that he not come. I needed to remain focused on the project ahead of me—and I needed to experience it on my own.

Erik called after I finished Blue Jeans Direct to say that he had a free weekend to fly to Boulder to visit. It felt like almost perfect timing. It was already Wednesday, and he would be arriving Friday night, so I packed up my car and took off the next day for my twenty-hour drive back to Boulder.

When he showed up at my front door with his bags, I wasn't sure what he or I were expecting, but I immediately felt giddy with excitement. *Be cool, Sasha,* I told myself. "Hi. Nice to see you," I said. *Ugh, too formal?* I thought. We exchanged an awkward, tentative hug, and then stood apart as though we were both wondering: *Okay, now what?* I asked him to leave his stuff in the foyer and we went out for dinner. I figured we'd work out our nervousness by dessert—and after a bottle of wine.

Erik and I hung out for the weekend—hiking, biking, and eating in between the kind of long conversations that felt as if we'd known each other forever. There was something so calming about his presence, yet I also couldn't get over how excited I was to be spending time with him. He was lean and athletic, and at six-foot-two, towered over me. It's funny, I thought he was handsome when we first met, but I hadn't allowed myself to even consider that I was attracted to him—until now. It had been a long time since someone had made me smile as much as Erik did.

By Sunday night we were laughing about the fact that neither of us had wanted to assume the other felt the same attraction. Clearly, we were at the very beginning of something promising. After he left, I had to laugh at how naive I had been only four days earlier in thinking that he had offered to fly across the country just to continue a *friendship*. Still, we both wanted to take things slow. I wasn't in any hurry to rush into another exclusive relationship.

As soon as Erik left, I started a running regimen in preparation for the New York City Marathon in November. Before the summer I'd committed to running as a representative for the Women's Sports Foundation, but I'd been too busy with the Trilogy to train over the summer. I figured I would be in good enough shape from all the hiking in Banff. And I was in good shape—as long as I ignored the pain in my hips, which sometimes wasn't easy. The ache soon developed into a deep, hammering pain in my groin area, often followed by a sharp pinch. It felt as if my femur head was on the verge of popping from its socket. I kept kicking out my leg to try and move the femur into place, thinking that would help relieve the pain.

For whatever reason, I had taken my shoulder pain more seriously than the hip pain I'd experienced throughout the Trilogy. In fact, I thought running might help strengthen my hips. I finally went to a local physical therapist, who after a brief consultation told me the pain was all in my head. *Seriously? In my head?* Infuriated, I sought out a second opinion.

Thankfully, the second therapist I consulted, Dr. Laura Schmonsees, gave me some more clarity. She suggested that I get an MRI because she thought that the pain and weakness I was feeling had to do with a torn labrum—the ring of cartilage that follows the outside rim of the hip joint socket. This injury was common in dancers, figure skaters, soccer players, and cyclists—and especially in female athletes.

Considering my reliance on my extreme hip flexibility, her assessment made sense. She said it was a problem we could address with some strengthening exercises. We started working together as regularly as my packed fall schedule would allow. She treated my psoas and surrounding muscles, with the idea that it would help mitigate the pain around the potential labrum tear. Meanwhile, I continued to run, still thinking it would help strengthen my legs and hips. I only had to get past the pain.

I was still running while on a visit to Germany to serve as commentator for the Adidas Rockstars climbing event, so I asked a friend, a professional runner, to draw out a detailed training schedule for me. In hindsight, he must have thought I had more of a running background than I actually had, because he assigned me an expedited training schedule to speed up my prep. I was supposed to start with one eight-mile run, then progress to a twelve-mile run the following week, and then an eighteen-mile run the next week. The plan was to have one long run a week with some shorter five- to eight-mile runs in between.

Although I'd hiked all summer, I'd never run more than

eight miles in my training regimen. I probably should have made that clearer, but I didn't because I didn't think it was a big deal. I went on one of the eighteen-mile runs through Stuttgart—on pavement. When I finished, my shins felt sore. My running partner said that I probably had shin splints— since I'd gone from zero to sixty in my marathon training. He suggested kinesiology tape, so I taped up my shins and continued my routine throughout my fall travels in Europe.

After Rockstars, I met up with Matilda in Spain and we headed to Psicobloc Bilbao, a deepwater soloing competition over a deep river running through the center of downtown Bilbao. It was a pure climbing race to the top: no harness, no help, just climbing shoes and chalk bags. Basically, it was free soloing, with a fall resulting in a fifty-foot drop and a dunk in the river instead of certain death.

From there I headed to Jordan to do a climb for the Jordan Tourism Board, in partnership with Mercedes. That trip turned out to be an unexpected reunion of sorts, because the other pro climber invited was Magnus Midtbø. We hadn't kept in touch after our breakup, but seeing him after so many years turned out to be a blast. We even joked about the fact that while he had taught me a ton about outdoor climbing, I had become the more experienced big wall climber.

When I wasn't climbing, I was still running, despite an increasing pain in my shins. I kept thinking: *I have this goal, so I have to put in the work. The pain is only soreness from pushing my body.* By the time I flew to Germany to sign a new Adidas contract, the pain had radiated up to my hip and I was walking with a limp. My manager at Adidas insisted I have an MRI on my leg and booked me an appointment at the nearby hospital.

There, I received the surprising news that I had a fracture straight through my fibula—the outer of two bones on the lower leg—not shin splints. What wasn't surprising was confirmation of my high tolerance for pain. In the past I'd suffered injuries from climbing accidents—I'd broken a couple vertebrae in my back and had been sidelined by ankle sprains and growth plate cracks in my feet. However disappointing, those injuries had been understandable—the price of a lifetime of climbing—but the fracture in my fibula made me angry with myself, because it had happened during a break from climbing. *Why had I pushed myself?* Not only were my plans for the New York City Marathon over, so were my climbing plans. I walked out of the hospital with an air boot, flew to Miami to speak at the International Women's Forum, and then returned home to Boulder in time for Halloween. At least there would be no decisions to make about my costume. I'd be Peg Leg the Pirate.

Erik showed up a couple days after my return. Since he lived in Bozeman—a flight of only an hour and a half to Boulder—and was between jobs, he was able to visit for several days at a time. With my climbing trips shelved, and no events on my schedule through the end of the year, we were able to take the time to get to know each other—an unforeseen silver lining to my injury. We'd have the chance to see how our different jobs and lifestyles might gel.

Erik traveled the world as a documentary filmmaker, working on projects for weeks at a time. What would it be like to be with someone who had such a different career from mine and to have a life together that wasn't built around climbing? So far it felt like a very good thing. I wanted to fall asleep and wake up next to Erik. He was the person I could talk to about anything. When I thought *What's next?* it had as much to do with my relationship with Erik as with my next climbing goal.

The stress fracture felt like a wake-up call for me to take better care of things closer to home. I started working with a nutritionist and a new trainer who was more in tune with my body's physiology. I started swimming—for the first time since my elementary school swim team days—and adopted a yoga and meditation routine in an attempt to be in the moment, even when the moment wasn't on a wall. All of that helped me develop a cross-training and wellness practice, the likes of which wasn't ordinarily embraced in the climbing community. Historically, the way climbers improved was by climbing more, but I was forced to find alternative workouts off the wall.

Instead of waking up and grabbing my phone or laptop, I began my days with a "media fast," filling in the time by writing in a gratitude journal before diving into the day. I spent a good part of those days looking over the content from the Trilogy climb, which I had financed myself without any big-budget crew or equipment. The extensive footage I'd captured was gritty in a low budget–film kind of way—more like a cool indie documentary— a step beyond *10am on a Tuesday*, the weekly YouTube series I'd been working on in between training for the Trilogy.

I had started *10am on a Tuesday* in April 2018 as a way of documenting my climbs and travel and activism. After years of posting content on Instagram, I was often asked, "How do you cram everything you do into a day?"; "What's your day look like?"; "What do you do besides rock climbing?"; "Do you ever sleep?" (Not only do I sleep, I love sleep.) *10am* was a cool way to answer those questions by regularly showing a day in my life.

The name stemmed from the idea that, as a pro climber, I could be anywhere in the world on any given Tuesday morning. Essentially it was billed as a behind-the-scenes glimpse into my life as a professional rock climber, featuring everything from exploring different parts of the world—both on the ground and from extreme vantage points—to workouts, nutrition tips, local climbs, home training with friends, photo shoots, and conversations with some of my climbing mentors. In one episode, I woke up in Moab, Utah, for a climb, cruised back to Denver for an afternoon training session, and then shimmied into a floor-length gown for a nonprofit fundraiser in New York City.

Unlike my Instagram posts, which had presented a curated version of my life, the series presented the highs and lows of my days, though mostly it was good vibes and positivity. I was pumped about where the series could potentially go and the kind of platform it could be, for everything from fitness to climate activism, sustainable living, and global ecotourism. There were so many athletes, activists, and friends I wanted to interview for my show, people who had inspired or mentored me, people who had encouraged me to take the lead in my life, without whom I might never have reached so many of my goals.

Working on *10am on a Tuesday* and the Trilogy got me thinking about creating a film production company, one that could be a platform for sharing not only my adventures, but also the inspiring stories and adventures of other women. With my own film production company, I'd not only create my own cinematic content, but also own the rights to it.

I had worked with production companies since I was sixteen years old, but I hadn't had much influence over how they used my image or told my story. I wanted to control my own narrative, and have final say over my story. With my own production company, I could work on passion projects, be in on the editing process, and even raise funding to support other women doing epic outdoor adventures. While looking over the footage from the Trilogy, I realized it could be the perfect inaugural project. I even had a name for my company: Female Focused Adventures.

After gathering all the footage I'd shot on my iPhone and GoPros, along with the material I'd hired people to shoot, I reached out to Tommy Joyce, *10am on a Tuesday*'s director and editor, and the two of us started work on the film of the Trilogy. My plan was to eventually license the film to secure funds for an expedition with my new company. In the spirit of empowering other female content creators, I would hire female videographers, editors, directors, and producers. I was stoked. Female Focused Adventures was about to take off.

As it happened, I was scrolling through Instagram when I came upon a photo that looked like something out of *Lord of the Rings*. Friends of mine, pro climbing brothers Iker and Eneko Pou, had posted about a first ascent they'd recently completed on the tiny island of São Tomé and Príncipe, off the west coast of Africa, in the Gulf of Guinea. The photo featured a massive volcanic spire rising out of a dense jungle: Pico Cão Grande. It had all the underpinnings of a grand adventure—a challenging climb, aesthetically different from any I'd ever done, in a mystical place I'd never visited. It hit me immediately: *That's it. That'll be the first official FFA expedition.*

In November I started researching more about the Pous' trip and the features of Pico Cão Grande (Big Dog—coincidentally, the name of the boat my dad had bought without telling Mom). It was the second largest volcanic plug in the world, and Iker and Eneko had just made the first ascent of "Leve Leve" (Slow, Slow), a mostly traditional 5.14a route. The island of São Tomé was tiny, so tiny I could barely find it on the map, and Pico Cão more resembled a giant penis than a big dog—not the most compelling reason to climb it. But I did think about how cool it would be to attempt the first female ascent of that epic tower.

The first person I put that question to was my climber friend Angela VanWiemeersch. Without hesitation, she was in. I knew my stress fracture would be healed by the summer, so we started planning a July expedition. I brought on board the rest of our team: Savannah Cummins, a climber-photographer-filmmaker, who would document the climb; Heather Mosher as second-camera on the wall; Adriane Ohanesian, to film on the ground; Julia Steers to direct; and my friend Kati Hetrick as producer.

For several months we prepped and researched the conditions we'd be facing on the island, an area so remote that it saw fewer tourists in a year than Yellowstone saw in a day. We would be headed into dense rain forest, with stiflingly hot and humid weather—not the best condition for climbing a challenging vertical big wall. At least, we told ourselves, we wouldn't be arriving in the monsoon season. But nature would conspire with climate change to present us with an unwelcome surprise.

Most of our team—Savannah, Angela, Heather, Kieran (our male expedition cook), and I—met up in Lisbon, Portugal. From there we flew on a small plane to the city of São Tomé to meet up with our remaining team members, Julia and Adriane, who were flying in from Nairobi. When our plane first started its descent, it seemed as though we might be landing in the middle of the ocean, until a tiny strip of land became visible—the Central African island country of São Tomé and Príncipe.

Once off the plane, we were instantly hit with blazing heat and 95 percent humidity—when it wasn't dumping rain. I'd climbed in Cuba, where the weather had been suffocatingly warm and humid, but it wasn't even close to São Tomé.

We made our way through the tiny airport to the cargo hold—our plane was too small to carry our sixteen bags of expedition equipment and gear, so it had arrived on a separate cargo plane. We collected our bags and hit our first stop: a hotel on the coastline by the airport, where we spent two days organizing our gear and preparing for our drive to the jungle.

There, we were joined by several porters—two of whom, Paolo and Gabriel, would remain with us to help retrieve clean water for cooking and drinking from a river about thirty-five minutes from our camp. The others would help lug three weeks' worth of food, gear, and cooking supplies. After renting Land Rovers, we all drove to the edge of the jungle to set up our base camp. From there we would hike to the base of the tower. We built our tents and then unpacked all our gear, distributing it among backpacks—forty-five to sixty-five pounds each—to carry on the two-and-a-half-hour hike to the base of the wall.

From the moment we set foot in the jungle, we were hit with pouring rain—a continuous, monsoon-like deluge that threatened to turn the ground underfoot into a muddy waterslide—even though it wasn't monsoon season. But even this weather wasn't my biggest worry. We were in a jungle that was known for a black cobra snake as huge and deadly as the black mamba, Africa's longest venomous snake. We all had on "snake boots," but as far as I was concerned, at knee-high they didn't cover nearly as much skin as I would have liked. We were basically told that if we minded our own business, they probably would, too. Nevertheless, we carried a very expensive anti-venom with us, which, in actuality, would allow the victim of a black cobra bite only about an hour of survival—kind of a cruel joke, considering the nearest hospital was multiple hours away.

I was antsy to get some climbing in after a week of traveling, so Angela, Savannah, and I started out by trying the first pitch of Leve Leve, a 5.12d trad (traditional) line—meaning that we had to carry and place protection devices into the wall rather than clipping into pre-placed bolts. We had to contend not only with slippery wet rock on the line, but with mud and moss on the wall and in cracks. When we tried to place our gear into the rock, not only would it pop out, but whole pieces of the rock would also come loose.

As the days went by, we continued to push our way up Leve Leve, climbing through waterfalls on the face of the cliff, trying to safely navigate with a combination of aid climbing and free climbing. After a little over two weeks, we decided it was too dangerous to continue. We changed plans, switching to a different route, a bolted route called "Nubivagant," meaning Ascent into the Clouds in Portuguese.

Bolted in 2016, Nubivagant would provide better protection from the elements. Also, it was a fifteen-pitch 5.13d that had never seen a female ascent. Fortunately, the first four pitches were somewhat protected from the rain by a small roof, though the rock was laden with thick, slippery moss. I pulled past the fourth pitch and was hit with a torrential downfall. Regardless of our path up the wall, we would face the same conditions. We were all thinking: *The rain has to stop . . . sometime.*

Days passed and the rain showed no signs of letting up, so we started climbing the rest of the route in a rainstorm. It felt as if we were climbing a Jenga block tower. Despite the bolts, the rock was not solid. At one point a terrifying shower of rocks tumbled down, narrowly missing our heads and ropes. Tired, dirty, and frustrated, we were three weeks into our climb and nowhere near where we'd hoped to be. Despite our friendships and our initial common goal—and what I'd thought was our unanimous desire to succeed—tensions had been mounting. I overheard mutterings of: "Do we really want to keep trying this? What's the point? Why are we here? This is stupid."

Nevertheless, I tried to remain the voice of encouragement and optimism and pushed us to continue. I vowed to keep trying to figure out the route, but Savannah and Angela lost their motivation even before we reached the base of Nubivagant. They were tired of feeling scared—fair enough, but I felt confident we could mitigate the risks. They didn't seem open to even considering how we could do that, and of course, I couldn't force them up the wall.

I made one last pitch for us to continue, to no avail. We were nearly four weeks into our expedition and almost out of time. Their minds were made up. I woke up the next morning knowing the decision was final. We were at the mercy of the weather, and it had won. Our plan was to pack up and leave the jungle the following day.

But the next morning, as we began to break down camp, the rain stopped. Just like that. *Seriously, are we part of some cosmic joke?* I felt a surge of hope, but I knew that Angela and Savannah were done hearing my arguments, so I bit my tongue. I would consider our trip a wash.

But the next day, when we were scheduled to hike out, there was still no rain. Angela and Savannah came to me and said that if the weather held up overnight, they were game to finish the climb.

I could barely contain my excitement. All I could manage was, "Oh, my God. Okay. Right. Cool." We spent the evening unpacking and organizing our gear in case the weather actually held. I couldn't sleep that night; instead, I kept praying: *Please don't rain. Please don't rain.*

Again, no rain. We prepared our backpacks and a minimal amount of food, because we wanted to be as quick as possible in our ascent. Free-climbing every pitch—pulling ourselves up with our hands and feet while attached to a rope—ended up not being an option. Despite the break in the rain, the wall was still like a waterfall—it was so bad at times that I wished I'd brought swim goggles. We'd decided to use gear to help our progression up the wall in a safer manner. We wouldn't be following our original plan to free the wall, but it would be a serious victory for all of us if we succeeded in climbing the tower. We would be the first women to do so.

We left the ground at 3 A.M. and climbed through until

nightfall. By sunset we were three hundred feet from the top of Pico Cão Grande. We didn't want to stop, so we climbed into the night—a dangerous move, but there didn't seem to be anywhere to rest. Blocks of rock started to fall around us as we continued up. I looked to my right and spotted a small ledge on the side of the cliff that could just about fit the three of us sitting down. We could sleep there—or more accurately, sit with our eyes closed.

First, we needed some food, but all we had left of what we'd brought were salty, dehydrated breadfruit chips. We hadn't planned on dinner on the wall. In that moment, the chips tasted better than anything I'd ever eaten. Ironically, we were out of water: *Where's the rain when we need it?* Beside us was a little drip coming off the rock, so we balanced a water bottle underneath to collect the droplets. By morning we had half a liter of water. That would have to sustain us until we reached the top.

We were nearly delirious with fatigue and hunger, but by that point our adrenaline was driving us. After six more hours of slow, methodical climbing, we reached the top of the rock face and continued on a grassy, steep hill. We stayed connected on our rope for about a hundred feet, bushwhacking through dense jungle to reach the peak.

Oddly enough, reaching the top felt slightly anticlimactic, because the top wasn't a big reveal. It wasn't as if we were exposed on a rock summit. We could barely appreciate the scale of our climb because of the thick vegetation that seemed to swallow us up. Still, we laughed deliriously, high-fiving each other for having pulled off the climb. We looked and felt drunk from exhaustion and disbelief—the selfies and videos we took clearly back that up.

Meanwhile the clouds had turned ominous, threatening

more rain, so we had to find a place to rappel off the tower and begin our descent—the time when most big wall accidents are likely to happen. With thousands of feet of loose rock and dangerous terrain to navigate on our way down, we knew we were in for a frightening journey, but at least we had daylight. It was roughly noon. Nightfall wouldn't arrive until just after five.

I rappelled seventy meters down a gully that we'd originally thought to be the route of descent. It wasn't, so I proceeded to jumar the rope back to the top, which sucked even more energy from my depleted store. The ground couldn't have felt farther away. I could sense the growing unease and tension among us. But slowly we found our way down, rocks crumbling around us. The thought of my soggy sleeping bag at base camp, caked with a month's worth of dirt, sweat, and bugs, had never seemed more appealing.

As we neared the ground, we heard cheering. Our porters, Paolo and Gabriel, were waiting for us, shaking their heads. "Wow!" said Paolo. "We never—well, we thought you ladies were crazy when you said that you were going to climb this. In our country, we've just never seen women be rock climbers."

The minute we hit the ground, the rain came back with a vengeance. By the time we reached our campsite we were drenched and spent. But we'd done it. We'd persevered and safely reached the top despite the relentless weather. Before disappearing into our respective tents, we all agreed: "We're getting the hell out of the jungle tomorrow!"

We barely had the time to process what we'd accomplished. The first night out of the jungle and back in a nearby eco lodge, all we could manage before passing out were the first showers we'd had in a month. We'd cut it close to our return flights, so we had one day to give some time to the local media and have a little celebration. We treated ourselves to a nice dinner with copious amounts of wine and reflected on our time in the jungle, stripped down to the basics under extreme conditions.

We toasted our fending off of poisonous snakes and tarantulas, our living and working together for so many days in a row, our being some badass women. Still, I couldn't help but feel as if the tension of the trip hadn't completely dissipated. Maybe it was my fatigue or the dull pain I'd come to take for granted in my hips, but so much still felt unspoken and unresolved.

17

Post-expedition blues were inevitable after a big wall climb. I imagined it was the same feeling athletes had after competing in the Olympics. Not only had São Tomé been the Olympic event I was training for, it had been a full-time job prepping to capture the expedition on film as Female Focused Adventures' official launch. Aside from months of training, I'd been responsible for hiring my crew, readying all the necessary gear and equipment, and considering all the logistics of travel and safety.

On expedition, nothing was as important as the mission at hand. In fact, there was nothing except the mission. After an expedition, it always took a little time to ease back into my regular life of enjoying time at home and with friends, and climbing for fun (and appreciating the creature comforts of cooking a real meal and using a real bathroom). What I hadn't counted on, in addition to my usual post-expedition blues, was a certain amount of disappointment.

Back in Boulder, I had time to reflect on my role as expedition leader. My ultimate goal had been to send São Tomé and bring everyone home safely, but the experience had not been without difficult, unforeseen circumstances. I had laid out the particulars of the trip to my team way before our journey, without soft-pedaling what we'd be facing. I had planned on the hot, humid conditions, crumbling rock, and venomous snakes—but not the cockroach-infested tents, limited food resources, stressful climbing conditions, and cases of trench foot.

At different points in the trip my team and I disagreed on whether we should continue our climb to the top. I drove everyone hard, but not harder than I drove myself. In retrospect I realized that not everyone shared my relentless determination to reach our goal. Instead, a couple of my team members were angry with me for having pushed them beyond their comfort zones.

Working with Kati on a trailer for the short film of Pico Cão Grande brought back those frustrating moments. First off, the trailer was turning out to be almost as arduous an exercise as the expedition itself—because of the intense amount of rain, we didn't have as much footage to work with as we would have liked, so we decided to incorporate animation—and watching the footage reminded me of the tension toward the end of the trip. Normally on a climbing trip, I work closely with one or two partners who are as excited about the objective at hand as I am, but São Tomé had felt different. We hadn't all been in sync—in our effort, our intention, or our communication. I wasn't sure what that would mean for my next expedition, except that next time I would make doubly sure we were all on the same page from the outset.

IN MID-OCTOBER I flew to the Banff Mountain Film Festival for the premiere of *The Trilogy*. It was fitting to be going back to Banff, to the community that had so generously supported me. It felt like going home to family. Tommy Joyce had done an amazing job editing the film—Female Focused Adventures' production company's first release—but I was so nervous about its debut in front of such a huge audience. It wasn't blockbuster filmmaking or a polished product like *Free Solo*—the documentary of Alex Honnold's free solo climb of El Capitan—and I had felt so vulnerable in the making of it, but the story line must have hit home with people. It wound up winning the People's Choice Award, which felt almost like reaching the summit all over again—except in heels and without bloody fingers. I was touched in a way that made my heart soar.

I came home on a high, eager to make plans for my next climb—my next epic adventure. I had an idea, one that had been percolating for a couple years, but that I had only recently been reminded of. As it happened with São Tomé, I was scrolling through my Instagram and saw photos that Savannah had recently taken of a climb called "Logical Progression" on El Gigante—the tallest vertical climb in North America, located in Mexico's Basaseachi National Park. She had been hired to capture the climb of two North Face team athletes—both men.

Logical Progression was a legendary climb of mythic proportion. The late Hayden Kennedy, an exceptionally talented climber, had christened the three-thousand-foot limestone tower with a bolted face as "the world's most badass sport climb." The tallest wall I'd climbed, Mora Mora, measured in at twenty-two hundred feet, so El Gigante seemed like an ambitious next step—a project that would require extreme technical skill and endurance. I reached out to Savannah. She and I began planning a March 2020 trip, which we'd pitch to Red Bull.

At that point, Erik had more or less moved in with me, although he'd kept his house in Bozeman. Fortunately for me, he was an amateur climber, so he understood the dangers involved in the projects I'd undertaken. He also knew that I planned to continue the same trajectory, and he was nothing if not supportive. His only ask: "Be careful. I know you will be."

At the end of December, Erik took off for Papua New Guinea for a new show he was producing, and I headed to El Salto, a rock-climbing area in northeastern Mexico renowned for its sport climbing, especially its steep limestone walls. With its excellent winter climbing weather, it was a perfect location to train for Logical Progression. I planned on training pretty much nonstop until the expedition, with the exception of several detours—the first of which was a trip to Sundance to premiere the trailer of the São Tomé expedition.

The third week in January, Erik and I, along with Kati Hetrick, the film's producer, and her fiancée, Amy, all headed out to Salt Lake City and my first experience at the city's most famous film festival. It was surreal in its own way—different from the premiere in Banff—because we were presenting in front of a huge audience that, for the most part, didn't know much about climbing.

Given the incredible content being shown at the festival, I couldn't imagine the Sundance crowd being impressed by our trailer, so I was surprised by how excited people were about it and how interested they seemed in the Q and A with Kati and me. They asked us about everything from controlling fear to remaining positive and, of course, how to go to the bathroom on a wall. It was really the first time I thought: *Wow, Female Focused Adventures might be on the path to creating projects that people will want to see.*

Right after Sundance I headed to Mallorca, Spain, to do a shoot for a luxury lingerie line called Agent Provocateur that was planning a global campaign to highlight strong women. I would be one of the four featured professional female athletes, a marked departure from their usual curvy fashion models with Victoria's Secret–esque bodies.

Despite their intention to show muscular athletes, I'd been initially wary. I'd worked so hard against the sexualization of female athletes and had avoided doing any shoots that included me stripping down for the camera, even on my personal Instagram. I didn't want to risk not being taken seriously, and I felt that way even more strongly coming off Female Focused Adventures' warm welcome at Sundance. I also didn't want to set the precedent for younger female athletes that posing in provocative clothing was something they needed to do to achieve success.

I had spoken with Agent Provocateur's creative director, who explained the campaign's mission and how the athletes would be shot. She told me that the company wanted to show muscular female bodies, underlying the theme of "strong is beautiful." *Okay, they already know I'm a muscular, flat-chested woman and not a model.* I thought about their offer. I'd be proving what I'd always believed, that femininity and physical strength are not independent of one another. It would be an opportunity to own my body for all that it was. Stepping out in lingerie while doing my sport seemed a duality I could get behind. But I'd bring a good friend for support.

I invited Suzu Cornella, my sports psychologist, to come with me. Suzu also happened to be one of my oldest friends. We had competed against each other throughout our youth, but while I'd continued as a professional climber, she'd gone on to get her master's degree in sports psychology. If I didn't become paralyzed with fear, I was hoping we'd have some fun with the whole crazy experience.

Mallorca in January is not the warm, sunny haven that it

is in the spring and summer (it didn't help that I wasn't used to climbing in a bra and thong), but I was game. It was a huge production—easily eighty or so people buzzing around amidst cranes and drones and boom mics. The company had constructed a wall on a soundstage so that they would have more control of the elements than they would on natural rock. Between takes, I wore a bathrobe. When they were ready to start shooting, I'd drop my robe and climb, more physically exposed than I'd ever been in front of strangers. But between the encouragement of the art director and the stylist, and the care the company took with my hair and makeup, I felt beautiful in my own skin. I wasn't exactly comfortable with so many people watching me climb in such minimal clothing, but I was enjoying what the shoot was about. And I was feeling empowered in the process.

By the fourth and last day, Suzu and I were exchanging looks of "This is so hilarious." In the end I felt as if my strength was as apparent as my femininity and my sexuality. And why not? I was owning my body without concern about anyone else's expectations. I was pushing through yet another comfort zone.

From Spain I flew to England for a two-week speaking tour throughout the UK, aptly billed as "Beyond the Comfort Zone." For that trip I wanted my mom as my companion, so she and I traveled together, just like we used to in old times. Right before the tour, I'd begun working with the UK-based Bentley Motors, and they had provided me with their latest-model SUV—an ultra-luxurious two-hundred-thousand-dollar-plus Bentayga—to drive from city to city. I wasn't used to driving on the left side of the road, so I cruised along at a snail's pace, terrified at every sharp turn. Along the way people strained to see who could be driving such an expensive car. *Just my mom and me.*

We listened to books on tape, snacked on copious amounts of trail mix and popcorn, and stopped at climbing gyms in the middle of nowhere so I could keep up my training. We went on hikes through England's Malvern Hills and drank Scotch whisky at a pub in Scotland. After the first two nights of crashing at modern, generic hotels, we told our tour manager that we would take charge of finding our own accommodations. We booked ourselves into little hole-in-the-wall inns with tons of character—paper-thin walls and ancient, rusted skeleton keys.

One night we were in bed at a pub-slash-inn when, just after midnight, I woke from a dream that I was being rained on. I opened my eyes to drops of water falling from the ceiling onto my face.

"Mom, it's raining inside!" I yelled, waking her out of a deep sleep. "The ceiling is leaking!"

She got up and called the front desk. It turned out the person directly above us had passed out while running his bath and flooded his room. Ten minutes later we were in our pajamas dragging our suitcases down the hall.

We hit fourteen cities in fourteen days. Each night I spoke for about thirty minutes and then showed *The Trilogy* film (also about thirty minutes). Afterward I talked about my favorite climbs and what went into accomplishing my goals. My whole life I'd been pushing past my comfort zone. My message to my audiences, which included a surprising number of climbers and nonclimbers, was that they could do the same—they could choose their own paths and dedicate themselves to their passions.

After the first night I told Mom that she didn't need to sit through each presentation, but she insisted on coming every night. I have to admit, it was reassuring to see her during my halftime break while the film showed. She'd bring snacks to the green room and sit and chill with me. When I was done, we'd discuss the evening. She would highlight something that she liked in particular and make suggestions for the next evening, like, "When you talk about São Tomé, why don't you tell that story about how you would bathe," or "I love that photo of you hanging off the side of the cliff on slide sixteen!" I was reminded of what a good time Mom and I used to have when we were on the competition circuit. It also hit me on a deeply visceral level how she had always been my biggest ally, since the beginning.

My mom spent more hours belaying than most people I know, including professional climbers. She belayed me from the time I was seven years old until I graduated from high school, and then she continued to belay me when I visited from college, and even on Era Vella, one of my first female ascents. It's only in the last few years that I began to truly appreciate the fact that I never felt the need to hide anything from her. She knows me better than anyone. She can be brutally honest in her opinions, but to her credit, she'll only offer those opinions when I ask— although I could always tell by the look on her face how she felt about any new boyfriend in my life. I enjoyed her company on that trip more than I can say.

However, despite our good times and a successful tour, my hips were still painful throughout our trip, especially after my daily training. But a part of me decided that the physical therapy had done some good, and that maybe the pain was a by-product of the treatment. There was always some soreness involved in working muscles in a new way, I told myself. That's what I wanted to believe, so I continued with my training. Mom flew home to Montreal after our final stop in Scotland, and Erik met me in Barcelona, Spain.

I had a three-week window to train before shooting a commercial in Spain for Bentley Motors—my last commitment before Logical Progression. Erik came with me to Chulilla, one of the best climbing destinations in the world. Chulilla's massive limestone canyon was a great place to do some rock-specific training. It would have been an exciting and motivating precursor to my upcoming expedition, if my hip pain hadn't been so relentless. Thankfully, it wasn't affecting my climbing too badly, but something was wrong and it wasn't getting better. At worst, I imagined I'd finally have to succumb to surgery to repair my torn labrum, but it wasn't something I planned on dealing with until after Logical Progression. I was scheduled to return from that expedition on March 27, 2020. I figured that before we left I could get a cortisone shot to help manage the pain. Until then I was sure that nothing could go wrong.

I REMAINED IN Spain a week longer than Erik in order to shoot the Bentley Motors commercial. By then my hip was killing me, and no amount of physical therapy or positive visualization was helping. A couple days into the shoot I texted Erik at midnight—4 P.M. Colorado time—and asked him to call an Adidas-recommended orthopedic doctor who happened to practice in Boulder. Dr. Omer Mei-Dan was an extreme sports athlete and stuntman turned orthopedic surgery specialist. He was also a former Red Bull athlete in BASE jumping.

I flew home from Spain on March fourth. The next day I met with Dr. Omer and was sent directly for an MRI and X-rays. Afterward, I sat in a small waiting room, trying to imagine the worst possible scenario: *Okay, since physical therapy isn't working, I'm going to find out I have a torn labrum and will probably need surgery. That sucks, but it'll be arthroscopic surgery, so not invasive. At least I'll know for sure before leaving for Logical Progression.*

It wasn't too long before Dr. Omer came into the room, followed by several somber-faced doctors. *Oh, God, this isn't a good sign,* I thought. I stood as Dr. Omer introduced his team. "Hey, nice to meet you," I said. "So, what's going on with my hips?"

"You may want to sit down," he said. All of a sudden the air seemed to leave the room and my body. *This isn't going to be good.*

He explained that I had hip dysplasia—something I'd only ever associated with German shepherds—and that I was about three to four months away from needing a total hip replacement. *Oh, my God.* I could feel a lump forming in my throat. I wanted to jump up and run away. "But," he said, "there may be enough cartilage remaining in your hips so that we can do something called a PAO—a periacetabular osteotomy, a major surgery for congenital hip dysplasia.

"What's happening is you've shredded through your labrum, and your femur head isn't secure in the socket, so there's movement. You're facing bone-on-bone rubbing, which will eventually crack your pelvic bone. If you don't do the PAO surgery within the next couple months, you'll need a total hip replacement. I don't know if you'd want to consider hip replacement, because it would mean having limited mobility. If you get a hip replacement now, at your age, you're almost certain to need another new hip at some point."

I was trying to take it all in, all his reasons why a hip replacement wouldn't be a good idea for someone like me, and that if I wanted a chance to continue my career as a pro climber, a PAO was my best option. My dysplasia—which caused hypermobility in my hips, an asset and advantage in my twenty-plus years of climbing—was now a liability. It would be my kryptonite if

I didn't have the surgery, and probably the end of my climbing career.

Dr. Omer explained that if I hadn't been a climber my whole life, the dysplasia probably wouldn't have been an issue until my late forties or fifties. But "ifs" didn't matter. I had ignored the pain for too long. Not quite convinced, or maybe not wanting to believe it, I took the results of my MRI and X-rays and met with another surgeon that same day—who made the same assessment. Then I went to one more. All three were of the opinion that I would need hip reconstruction surgery on both sides in order to fix my hips.

I went back to Dr. Omer. He explained that the first surgery would involve arthroscopic surgery on my left side, a procedure involving a fiber-optic camera to view the joint. During that surgery he would clean out the damaged tissue, which meant shaving down my femur head and knitting the labrum back together. The second surgery would involve the PAO on my left hip. After letting my body heal for a few months, he would perform the same arthroscopic surgery on my right side, followed by a fourth surgery for the PAO on my right hip. Meanwhile, three screws on each side, ranging from four to six inches each, would hold the pieces in place as the bone healed. The fifth and final surgery, six months after the second PAO, would be to remove the hardware.

"Okay," I said, after I'd had a chance to put my thoughts together, "I have this two-week-long expedition coming up, and I've been training for it since November. Everything is in place. Red Bull is supporting it. Am I going to be worsening my hips by going?"

"At this rate, you've done the damage. Two more weeks of doing what you've been doing isn't going to make it much worse."

I asked him about a cortisone shot, something to at least keep the pain at bay, and the reason I went to him in the first place.

"I'm not going to do a cortisone shot, because that will further compromise the cartilage. So, if you can handle the pain, then sure, go for it. We'll book the surgery for after you get back, in early April."

Okay, okay, I thought, but there was nothing okay about any of it. My throat felt tight, as if I were having an allergic reaction. I felt a pressure mounting inside my skull. But I made two decisions. I would go to Logical Progression, and I wouldn't tell anyone about my diagnosis—I didn't want it to cast a shadow over the whole project. I would force myself to forget, at least for the next few weeks, that this expedition could potentially be my last. *My last big climb.*

My Female Focused Adventures crew was ready to roll. "Mango"—Mariana Ordóñez Prieto, a climber I'd met on my trip to El Salto in December—was the final addition. Mango was from Chihuahua, Mexico, so it seemed fitting for her to join me and Savannah on our expedition in her home state. In addition to the three of us, we had two riggers—climbers hired to secure static lines—twenty-five-year-old Nolan Smythe, a climber and BASE jumper, and Aaron Livingston, Nolan's climbing partner and best friend. Both were seasoned climbers. They'd flown down to Mexico ahead of us to climb Logical Progression and set up the static lines for the videographer to climb and hang from in order to shoot downward. Nolan was communicating with us via satellite phone from El Gigante, keeping us informed on the project status. Everything was going as planned.

The rest of us were set to leave the next day, so I came home from my appointment with Dr. Omer and soaked in a nice, long Epsom salt bath—my preferred method of decompressing. Afterward I'd dive into the final stages of packing. When my cell rang, I almost didn't answer it, until I saw that it was Savannah. It was odd that she'd be calling so late. I picked it up. "Nolan's dead," she said.

18

Nolan had been on pitch fourteen when the rock he was standing on broke. When he fell, the rock fell with him, slicing through his rope and sending him fifteen hundred feet to the valley floor. It was a crazy, horrible, freak accident, the kind that no one anticipates, especially among the most careful and experienced of climbers like Nolan and Aaron.

Aaron was still on the wall, stranded halfway between the top and bottom, having watched his best friend plunge to his death. To make matters worse, severe weather was headed into the valley below El Gigante. Given Aaron's location on the wall, he couldn't rappel to the ground, but even if he could, he'd be stuck at the base with Nolan's body. Because of the weather, it was too dangerous to land a helicopter. The expedition had not only turned into a body recovery mission, it had also become a rescue mission: Aaron needed help off the wall.

One of the difficulties of Logical Progression was that there was no reasonable way to reach the base by foot. Climbers had to drive to the nearby town, hike two hours to the top of El Gigante, and then rappel three thousand feet to the base of the wall to begin the route back to the top—twenty-eight pitches in total. There was no way to reach Aaron the day of the accident. He had to solo his way up with the use of a climbing aid to his and Nolan's portaledge to spend the night alone, in a state of shock, before help could arrive.

The next day two local Mexican climbers I had worked with, Sergio "Tiny" Almada and Jose David "Bicho" Martinez, arrived in Basaseachi and immediately hiked in to begin a rescue mission. Together they rappelled to the halfway point and fixed new ropes. They reached Aaron and somehow helped him climb to the top, despite his fragile state of mind and body—he was both grief-stricken and exhausted.

The next morning, I took the first flight to Chihuahua along with Savannah, Angela, Jordana, and Aaron's girlfriend. From there we drove the five hours to Basaseachi. By then Aaron was off the wall and the Mexican government had authorized a military helicopter to recover Nolan's body.

First, though, they had to have someone alert the plantation surrounding the bottom of El Gigante—a vast poppy plantation—that a rescue mission was planned. There was some gray area in navigating a helicopter landing in the area, since it was known to be cartel territory. It was important that the plantation owners not view the landing as a siege on their crops. Once the police had alerted the powers that be about our emergency, and they were assured that they could safely land a helicopter, it became a matter of waiting out the storm. No one was flying anywhere near El Gigante in the kind of thunder and lightning gathering around the mountain.

Meanwhile, Nolan's mom, dad, and brother were about to land at Chihuahua International Airport, a short time after Erik was set to arrive—he happened to be in Mexico for a wedding. He called me as soon as he landed. "Nolan's family is about to arrive," I told him. "Would you please meet them at the airport and drive them to Basaseachi? We're here already and hoping the weather will let up."

When they reached Basaseachi, there was still no way a helicopter could take off and land. The wait was torturous, but there was nothing anyone could do to make things move faster. We were all stranded at a remote motel together, waiting out bad weather under the worst possible circumstances. What does one say to parents who've just lost their child? I knew that Nolan was doing what he loved, but I also felt a heavy responsibility for everyone's being there. All I could do was offer Aaron and Nolan's family my condolences and hope for a letup in the storm.

A couple days into our wait, I asked Nolan's family if they wanted to take an easy hike to see the wall that Nolan and Aaron had been on. I thought it might bring some meaning as to why the two of them had taken on this expedition. Nolan's family agreed, saying it would be a great help to see where the accident had taken place.

Mango and I took them to a lookout point miles away from El Gigante. As I walked with Nolan's mom, dad, and brother, I was at a loss for words—I could feel the heaviness in their every step. It was as though we were all walking a tightrope, trying as best we could to keep our balance.

In between stretches of silence we managed some light conversation, mostly about the beauty of the region. At the lookout, we could see the entirety of the towering wall. I showed them the route through binoculars. It was my first time seeing the entire route as well—on a wall that now represented so much heartache. As we observed a waterfall across the valley, Nolan's dad said that he could understand why his son wanted to come here.

After several more days, the rain finally seemed to let up

a bit, but not enough for our pilot to feel comfortable, so Erik found a nearby charter service. We told Red Bull that we needed to forgo the military helicopter and use a private service. They immediately stepped in and took care of all the arrangements and expenses. After nearly a week, a Red Bull–chartered helicopter was able to make it into the valley to retrieve Nolan's body.

I flew back home on March 12, 2020, amidst murmurs of an impending lockdown because of a raging worldwide virus, but all I could think was: *Someone just died. How could it get worse than that?* No matter how many times people told me that Nolan's death wasn't my fault, I couldn't help but feel responsible. My head and heart ached in tandem, clouding my thinking. El Gigante had claimed one life and irreparably altered so many others. A few days later, the Covid-19 quarantine went into effect. My surgery was pushed to early May. The world seemed to have tilted off its axis.

LIKE MOST OF the country, Erik and I went into lockdown. The only thing that felt real was that I was with a person I loved, who offered me support as I talked out all the thoughts and emotions swirling through me. On top of everything that had happened, I was facing a career-ending injury and looking down the barrel of five surgeries. I didn't know any climber who had gone through a PAO. *Was my career done?* And how could I even think that was important given that people were now dying in a *pandemic*?

I knew how fortunate I was—living on a mountain, surrounded by nature as far as the eye could see—yet I couldn't escape the feeling that I was in my final days of freedom. Although most elective surgeries had been canceled or postponed indefinitely due to Covid, my surgery had been moved to early May because it had already been delayed too long. If I didn't take that date in May, there would be no guarantee of when I might be rescheduled. I only had a couple of months left on my hips before the dysplasia would be too severe for a PAO and I would lose them to a total hip replacement.

The PAO is a more complex procedure than a total hip replacement, because it involves cutting through the hip bones and repositioning them with screws in order for the femur to fit correctly into the hip socket. But because I was relatively young, a PAO could provide me with greater mobility than full hip replacement and possibly save me from needing another hip replacement thirty years down the line.

The day before my first surgery, I went climbing with Erik and a couple good friends at Seal Rock, one of my favorite places in the Flatirons. I'd never felt so emotional during a climb, feeling the grit of the rock beneath my fingertips, being in control of my body's every move. I reached the anchors and leaned back on my rope, all of Boulder spread out below me. I was reminded of the immense beauty in life and how much I still wanted to accomplish as a climber. I wanted others to experience what it felt like to be in nature from the amazing vantage point of a climb. I thought: *Even if I never get to do an inspiring climb again, I hope I can continue to encourage more people to climb.*

I gave a teary goodbye to my friends before heading home with Erik for an early dinner. My first surgery was at 7 A.M. After dinner we did a gentle hike on the trail by our house, as we often did to unwind at the end of the day. I could feel the tears welling up and a pressure in my throat from trying not to lose it. I'd never had surgery, so I had no idea what to expect. So many thoughts kept swirling in my head. *Will it be like this next year? Will I climb again? How painful will tomorrow be? What if something goes wrong in surgery?* I had to catch myself: *Positive thoughts only, but . . . When will I walk again?*

The first of the five surgeries was the arthroscopy on my left hip, to be followed a week later by the PAO—the longer, invasive, ten-hour open hip surgery where Dr. Omer would cut each pelvic bone in four pieces to reconstruct it. Then, he'd place in each hip three four- to six-inch-long screws in the bones to hold them in place. Three months after that my body would be recovered enough to withstand a PAO on my right hip.

The less invasive hour-long scope felt like an introduction to the unchartered waters ahead. It was my first time ever going under general anesthesia, which I think gave me more anxiety than the procedure itself, but at least I was allowed to go home the same day. Dr. Omer told me that all had gone well. He prescribed five to ten minutes of no-resistance biking twice a day leading up to the PAO to reduce the chance of blood clots. It was far from the exercise I was used to, but I was at least moving my legs. There was no turning back. I had a week before the PAO.

Despite my scheduled surgeries, I wanted to keep to any commitments I could, especially since so many people around me had had events and jobs and opportunities canceled because of Covid. The global premiere of *The Trilogy* with Outside TV was still happening. Outside TV had licensed the film from Female Focused Adventures to show live on Amazon and its cable streaming channels. As part of the premiere, I was supposed to be on a virtual red carpet along with several friends and pro athletes—but I still hadn't told anyone except family, friends, and my sponsors about the surgeries. I wasn't ready to let anyone else know, especially since I had no idea what my future as an athlete would look like.

The premiere was two days after my first scope, but I couldn't bend more than 90 degrees at the hip. Mom had flown in for support for a few weeks, so she was there to help Erik prop me up on a day bed and make me look halfway presentable.

But that wasn't the biggest obstacle. I was going "live on the carpet," so I couldn't take any of the pain meds I'd been prescribed for fear of feeling—and more important, *looking*—drunk. I skipped the meds and presented the film to an audience of over half a million people, trying to appear relaxed and happy while deep, dull aches clutched my abdominals. Every time I smiled I was afraid I'd make some kind of wounded-animal sound. But despite all the maneuvering, it wound up being a welcome distraction from thinking about what lay ahead in two days—the real-deal surgery.

Monday morning, Erik assisted me through the hospital doors and up the elevator to the check-in, where a nurse met us. Because of Covid, no visitors were allowed past that point. I turned to Erik and said, "I guess I'll see you in a few days or so." He was told to leave, and he went home to wait with Mom.

Although I was familiar with the pre-surgery and anesthesia procedure from having the arthroscopy—and kept reassuring myself, *I woke up, didn't I?*—I couldn't help but feel afraid. Dr. Omer was going to cut through the front and back of my hip, take out my lower abdominal muscles so that he could break my left pelvic bone in four places, move my bones over the femur head to create the correct anatomical structure, and then secure the broken bones with screws in a ten-hour surgery. A thought hit me that almost made me laugh: *All those abdominal crunches I've been religiously doing for so long will be for nothing . . . So much for my six-pack.*

My only memories of overnight stays in hospitals were associated with losing my dad and Baba. Hospitals were sterile, frightening places where people often lived out their final days.

Tragically, Covid was making that the case for so many. It made my heart feel even heavier. There would be no visitors for anyone, least of all me.

Late that night when I came to, alone in my hospital room, I couldn't feel the lower half of my body. I wasn't even sure where I was. I could see that I had a catheter, but I had no sensation of it. I didn't have time to take stock of anything else before the drugs and the IV drip knocked me out for another twelve hours.

The next day Dr. Omer came by to check on me. He said that everything had gone well, and that he had taken extra time to make sure that I would have maximum mobility with my new hips. I asked him what I needed to do to go home. He smiled and gave me a checklist of things I had to be able to accomplish before I could be released, and then he told me not to get ahead of myself. "People typically stay a week in the hospital after this kind of surgery." *A week?! No way. I want to go home tomorrow.* He cautioned that I would have to be extremely careful, as my entire middle was broken, but after he left, I attempted the first item on the checklist: "Get out of bed." *Easy,* I thought, until I realized I had little control over anything below my chest.

At Dr. Omer's request, a physical therapist came by later that day. Normally physical therapy wouldn't start until at least a few days after surgery, but Dr. Omer knew how anxious I was. At least I could try to stand. The therapist wrapped a thick, harness-like safety belt around the middle of my body to help guide me to a seated position. The anesthesia had at least worn off some, so I could feel my legs underneath me, but when I moved the tiniest bit, a searing pain shot through my groin to my stomach. *Oh, shit.*

Sitting up made me light-headed, so I waited several moments and then slowly scooched to the bottom of the bed, where my crutches awaited. *Breathe. Slow. You can do this.* I was sweating profusely. *Why is it so hot in here?* I tried to stand. I felt dizzy and confused, and my vision was blurred. I sat back down and took a couple deep breaths. Again, I attempted to slide an inch or two. And again. Each time it felt as though the air was too heavy to move through. The physical therapist finally told me it was too soon. "This is why we don't usually do this until several days after this type of surgery," she said; I could detect a note of "Dr. Omer told you so" in her voice. "You need to stay in bed," she added, before making a brisk exit.

I knew what I needed. I needed to go home. That was the only way I'd feel better. Besides, there might be people who actually needed my bed. I didn't. I wanted the doctor and nurses to know that. I was healthy. I didn't need drugs or oxygen or around-the-clock care like most of the new surge of patients.

And I surely wasn't going to recover eating hospital food. Prior to surgery, I had consulted with my nutritionist about how I could expedite my recovery through supplements and my choice of foods. I would take collagen for my muscles and joints, 500 mg of vitamin C five times per day, ocean minerals, calcium, and vitamin D3, Athletic Greens, 100g of protein, psyllium husk, antioxidants such as elderberry, and adaptogens—medicinal mushrooms, like Lion's Mane and Chaga, which help decrease inflammation and increase focus, endurance, and natural immunity. The list went on. I'd get none of that if I stayed where I was.

I lay there several more hours before another doctor on the team came in to check on me. I asked him about the light-headedness and confusion, and the sweating. He said it was due to the heavy painkillers—OxyContin, I later learned—and the morphine drip. The morphine was at the top of my checklist—I had to be off it before I could go home—so after the doctor left, I asked the nurse to stop my drip. I knew I'd prefer feeling pain over being confused, and then maybe I could try again to stand. I knew my triceps would have no problem with crutches—I still had those muscles.

A few hours later I was feeling more pain, but I was at least feeling more myself. I begged the nurse to send back the physical therapist. She told me the therapist would be back tomorrow. "Please," I begged, "I am ready. Today." She stared at me as if trying to decide whether she wanted to risk wasting a therapist's time. I stared back until she agreed to see if someone was available. Later in the day, the original therapist appeared in my room, a look of annoyance mixed with disbelief on her face. "I've got this," I said, before she could protest. "Trust me."

Dr. Omer had explained that if I sat more upright I'd be less dizzy when I stood. I brought the back of my bed up just enough to elevate my head, nowhere near a 90-degree angle, but even that was painful. I filled my lungs with air and dug into the breathing techniques I had learned at Performance Under Pressure (PUP), a program for Red Bull–sponsored athletes designed to push them outside their sport-specific conditioning— deep breaths in, hold, exhale, repeat. I sat as far up as I could manage, inched my way to the end of the bed, grabbed the walker, and stood, even if I was a bit wobbly. Pleased with myself, I looked at the therapist for some reaction. She seemed surprised and a bit skeptical before turning to lead me out of the room.

I hopped on my right leg down the hall, alongside her. When she opened the door to the physical therapy room, I thought maybe we were in the wrong place. The room wasn't anything I'd expected a physical therapy room to look like.

Instead of high-tech equipment and massage tables, it was filled with models of basic wood furniture and things one would find in a home—like dollhouse furniture blown up to adult size.

Next on Dr. Omer's checklist was the "stair test." Sure enough, it referred to half a dozen stairs leading nowhere—nothing fancy or automated, just six steps and a railing. The idea was to see if I could navigate moving around in my house. If I could crutch myself up the stairs—without looking like an emergency room risk—I would be closer to going home. The pain had become way more apparent without the morphine and squeezed my hips like a vise, but I'd made up my mind. I had to prove to the therapist I was ready to leave. I made it up the stairs.

With my vital signs stable, I had only one thing left on my checklist to go home: "Pass a stool." Simple, I thought, but not now, not after all the anesthesia and drugs—which I learned would continue to block me up for a while post-surgery. I couldn't leave until I'd done that one last thing. "You didn't pass this morning, so you can try again tomorrow," the therapist said, with one foot out the door. Once again, I begged, "Please, just give me until the end of the day." At 5:30 P.M. she returned and gave me another chance. I succeeded, if barely.

Two hours later, a nurse was wheeling me out of the hospital to Erik's parked car. He and Mom were there, waiting, smiling. As the two of them helped the nurse lift me out of the wheelchair and into the backseat of Erik's car, my mom joked, "All you had to do was give my daughter a goal. Once she has that, she doesn't stop until she accomplishes it."

I'd won my first battle—to go home. Getting into the car was only the beginning of a long line of formerly simple tasks. Next would be making it up the stairs to our front door, then getting into bed, getting out of bed, and going to the bathroom . . . constantly. I couldn't remember ever having to pee so much in my life. Had I developed a UTI from the catheter? It sure felt like it, until I found out that bladder spasms were often a side effect of catheters. Still, despite all the times I needed help from Erik moving to and from the bathroom and around the house, he never blinked.

With Erik as my self-appointed chief caregiver, I had the chance to experience his "producer" mode firsthand. He set alarms on his phone, with varied sounds corresponding to the different sets of pills I had to take. He set alerts as to when to replace the ice packs on my hips. He made a printout of the vitamins I needed and the ingredients for my favorite green smoothie, and he oversaw my meal plan—protein-heavy and no refined sugar.

In the beginning I was too out of it to know my pills from my ice pack, but I knew I was loved. As soon as I had the energy to stay awake, I would let Erik know how grateful I was.

I wouldn't be able to bend my hip or open my legs or put weight on both legs for another six weeks. I couldn't even sit up in bed. Pain was a continual issue, but I was worried about staying on the Oxy, so six days after the surgery I made the decision to cut it out. I would manage the pain with THC, a far safer pain relief alternative than Oxy—with the benefit of antioxidants and minimal side effects.

I was familiar with the effects of cannabis, but that night I woke with severe sweats and shakes, as if I had a bad case of the flu. We called Dr. Omer immediately. A few minutes into the conversation, I thought to mention that I'd quit the Oxy cold turkey. "You're in a bit of withdrawal," he said. "Normally you'd be weaned off it." *Well, that's frightening,* I wanted to say. *It only takes six days to form an addiction?* If I'd been on the fence about substituting THC for the painkillers, that information clinched my decision to use it instead of narcotics.

I knew my legs and hips would be out of commission, but I hadn't realized what intense pain my stomach would be in. My abdominal muscles had been cut out and sewn back, so any little cough felt like a threat to rip my stitches apart. I could only imagine what the force of a sneeze would do.

A couple weeks later I had my first post-op X-ray, right before starting my real physical therapy. Instantly, my mood brightened. My concentration was returning, and slowly I was becoming purposeful in a new kind of way. I knew it wouldn't be helpful to get ahead of myself and imagine the months of immobility that lay ahead of me. Instead, I broke my recovery down into small, manageable goals, just as I would break down a big wall climb into sequences.

I began each day by checking in with myself—writing my thoughts in a journal, even if it was for only five minutes. I set intentions for my day, even if they were as simple as writing emails and doing hand exercises. I couldn't do anything that might engage my stomach muscles or my hips, but I was getting back my motivation. It was time to work on what I could.

Once I was able to sit up, I started a live talk show on my Instagram. Weekly, I brought different people on the show via Zoom—activists and experts in their fields. I spoke with Senator Mark Warner about climate change policy. With Lynn Hill I discussed being a woman in a male-dominated sport. I talked to pro athlete, author, and entrepreneur Rebecca Rusch and world champion cyclist Kate Courtney to learn about what drove them; I've always found it super inspiring to hear how successful people motivate themselves. I conducted cooking classes, preparing recipes via Zoom with a chef and discussing tips and tricks in the kitchen.

I made a list of three long-term goals, one of which was to start the company I'd been dreaming about for years. Given my longtime disappointment in the nutrition bar industry, I'd spent the last decade making my own power bars before every climbing trip. I just couldn't bring myself to eat the crap on the market—"nutrition" bars chock-full of processed sugars and preservatives—so I would blend together dates with different nuts as a base and then add freeze-dried fruits and vegetables. I wanted to create a company around a bar with whole-food ingredients, powered by adaptogens and packed with greens. I already had the name: SEND Bars—bars that I would want to buy to power through my adventures. It was nearly impossible to have access to vegetables on a wall or on the go in daily life, so I wanted to create an easier system of readily available nutrition within some type of sustainable packaging.

My second goal was to finish editing the São Tomé documentary, and my third was to write the book I'd always dreamed of writing. Goals were key to my recovery, as was keeping busy. When I wasn't researching, writing, or editing, I was working with a physical therapist or doing the exercises on my own, four to five times throughout the day. Building up my strength from scratch gave me a new appreciation of my body. It made me realize how I'd taken my health and strength for granted, assuming I'd always have both.

Yet despite all the ways I'd found to keep busy and productive, I was afraid I might not be able to return to the climbing life I once knew. Most of the time I managed to remain optimistic, but Logical Progression remained at the forefront of my brain. Every time I thought about climbing I would imagine falling rock cutting through my rope, and then suddenly I'd feel gripped by fear—which was one emotion I prided myself on facing head-on. I'd even given TED Talks and lectures to help others face their own fears, but I couldn't shake mine. I kept playing back Nolan's accident and wondering why I'd been spared. I was to be the next one on that rope after Nolan and Aaron. *Why wasn't it me?*

Over the years I have lost friends to climbing—two only the year before, in an avalanche in Canada—and I'd heard stories about other talented climbers who had died in climbing accidents. I'd never heard of a rock breaking and slicing through a rope, but then two weeks after Nolan's death I heard of the same thing happening to two climbers in Utah. Was I pushing my luck in wanting to go back to climbing?

Every time one of my sponsors called to talk to me about climbing projects in 2022, I only pretended to be excited, since I didn't have any idea whether those projects would be within reach . . . at any point. I had no frame of reference, because I didn't know anyone who had gone through a PAO. My sponsors weren't familiar with the surgery either, so they assumed I was going to come back one hundred percent. What could I say? "Hey, I don't know if I'll be able to climb again, so those four years left on my contract . . . yeah, who knows?" or, even worse, "Yeah, sorry, I'll probably be too scared to climb again."

For months I'd been protecting my hips in a completely controlled environment, but what would happen if I tried pushing them to do the level of climbing I had done before my surgery? When I climbed, my harness rested exactly on my pelvic bone. Would my hips be strong enough to withstand the intense force of a fall in a harness? There was no room for physical frailties on a climb, and no room for doubt.

When August rolled around, I was still in the process of relearning to walk. I'd graduated to some basic exercises, like riding a stationary bike, swimming, and walking on an AlterG treadmill. The AlterG was an anti-gravity treadmill designed with pants that zipped up to the top of the machine at waist level and filled with air, the amount of air based on the percentage of body weight one could withstand while walking. I started out by walking with only 30 percent of my body weight—like moving my body across the floor of a pool. Each week I'd up the percentage as I remembered and relearned the rhythm and length of my stride.

Before I could walk on my own with my full weight, I started to do some easy, very controlled top-rope climbing with friends. I'd walk with crutches to the wall and then climb using only my hands and my right leg—which didn't make my surgeon very happy.

Looking back, I can see that was probably risky, but I had to keep moving, because I'd always thrived off being in motion. It not only made me stronger, it also helped me to think clearly, problem-solve, and be creative. For me, the mind-body connection was like an open circuit. A break in one signaled a break in the other, which is why the more I forced my body to move, the easier it became to see other goals through to completion. The more clearly I envisioned my goals, the more motivated my body became. I tried not to think about how, at the month's end, I'd be back at square one after surgery on my other hip.

I was allowed just enough time after the surgeries on my left hip to develop strength in that leg to support a newly broken and aligned right side. After the surgeries on my right side, it would be copy, paste, and do over—back to the pain and immobility, back to Erik carrying me to the bathroom in the middle of the night, back to relearning how to walk. *Positive thoughts only,* I told myself, even if I didn't yet believe them.

19

Patience has never been my strong suit. I hadn't taken more than two months off from climbing since I was six years old. For as long as I could remember, my body had always been an athlete's body. Being sidelined made me feel helpless and irrelevant, and hearing about other climbers achieving epic feats kicked my competitiveness into high gear, which only made me feel worse. I wanted desperately to celebrate the successes of my climbing friends, but I was feeling too sorry for myself to muster up anything but frustration that I wasn't climbing and that I still needed to recover.

It was Erik who constantly reminded me that my competitive nature as a professional athlete was what spurred on my recovery in the first place. He was the one person to whom I confided my biggest fears about my future as a climber. He was also my most enthusiastic cheerleader, insisting that I trust the process and believe that I would eventually be able to achieve new climbing goals.

In August 2020, just as I was beginning to feel somewhat like a whole person again, I had the second scope, and then, in early September, the second PAO. Physically, the second set of surgeries was a little easier, since I knew what to expect. I knew what I'd need to do and how I'd manage the pain. Mentally, though, it was more challenging, because I was overwhelmed by the thought of going through another several months of baby steps and recovery.

I knew my body before surgery, but now I had to forge a new relationship with it and understand its latest mechanics— its strengths and limitations. I'd undergone a serious structural change in order to eliminate the pain I'd been experiencing for years. But now I had a whole new pain—the pain of working muscles that had been chopped apart and sewn back together. I had to work out harder than ever to break down all the internal scar tissue that had quickly formed after my surgeries and that had presented a level of stiffness and burning pain like nothing I'd ever dealt with. I added a whole new pre- and post-workout of strength and stretching routines that left me feeling as if my hips had been used as a punching bag.

I had no idea what climbing with brand-new hips—without the kind of flexibility I was used to—would feel like. I would have to relearn how to move my body on the wall and adapt to a new style of climbing with new hips—but would I be able to compensate for that lessened flexibility with the added strength of reconstructed hips? I hoped so.

Even more important than regaining my physical ability to climb would be regaining my confidence. I genuinely missed climbing—the exhilaration of it, the chance to prove to myself that I could accomplish something that seemed impossible at the outset, and the physicality of moving up a mountain. I missed pulling off of small edges with my fingertips, leveraging my body to make my next move, and feeling the squeeze of my core muscles, which were now languishing. It was wild to not feel like an athlete for the first time in my life, but my time off from climbing had given me an opportunity to reflect on just how much I missed it—and how much I loved it. At the end of the day, that love of climbing would beat out the fear.

A month after the second PAO I returned to the AlterG anti-gravity treadmill to learn all over again how to walk with my new hips. By early November I was able to ditch my crutches. I still had only limited use of my hips, but at least I could walk on my own . . . and I could climb. I had to be conservative, since falling was not an option, even in a harness, but I was able to use my arms and legs to a great enough degree to manage a 5.12 on my second day of trying. It was as if a switch had been turned on inside of me—fear had never been my default mode, why let it take over now? Why would I *choose* not to remain focused on the positive? Why would I choose not to believe?

Logical Progression was tragic, but it was beyond anyone's control. It was the kind of accident that could have happened on any big climb. It was not a sign from the universe that I needed to give up doing the thing I loved. In fact, I'd been fortunate. I'd been strong enough to undergo a PAO instead of a total hip replacement. I was still powerful, still motivated. I was ready to work toward finishing the goal I had started—the climb that had haunted me. I had to return. In doing so, I would not only answer the nagging question of whether I could tackle such a climb, I'd have the chance to overcome the fears that had replaced my love of big wall climbing. Impulsively, I called my good friend Laura Capps. "I can climb again. It's in me. I know I can come back. Let's go to Logical Progression."

Laura had been by my side through much of my recovery and had seen me at my worst. She also happened to be a talented climber whom I trusted wholeheartedly. I wouldn't have to worry about her judging me if I had to rest or if I happened to be struggling with hip pain—after hanging in a harness for hours on end—or, in the end, if I wasn't able to send Logical Progression. Her response was what I needed to hear: "Oh, my gosh, Sasha. That'd be amazing. Let's do it!"

Although I'd pretty much made up my mind, I did ask Dr. Omer if I might mess up my surgery by going back to climbing too soon. His response was that I needed to take extra care and listen to my body, especially because I had a lot of built-up scar tissue. Both Erik and Mom were supportive of my decision— though tentatively so. I think they both knew me well enough not to tell me I couldn't do something I'd already set my mind to do.

The next day Laura and I started mapping out what our training program might look like leading up to an April 2021 departure. Although April would be the tail end of the ideal climbing season in Mexico, it was the soonest I could feasibly be ready to attempt such a big, demanding project. After April, the temperatures could make the rock too hot to climb, and I didn't want to wait for another window six months down the line.

I was giving a hundred percent effort in my training, doing physical therapy every day, and working with a nutritionist. I figured that realistically I had a fifty/fifty chance of sending Logical Progression, but once I committed to the project it became my guiding light instead of my biggest fear, despite the emotional roller-coaster ride I experienced daily. Visualizing my climb brought me purpose and direction in my training and forced me to show up for physical therapy three times a day, even when the process felt like watching paint dry, even when progress meant gaining less than a degree of mobility after an exhausting week of effort and sweat. Logical Progression grew beyond being a series of pitches to send. It represented getting back on the horse that threw me. If I was able to do that, with or without a send, I'd know that my psyche, as well as my hips, were on a path to healing.

I was in rehab up until February 17, when I had my final surgery to remove the hardware in my hips. Afterward, I took a week off to recover, and then it was game on. I could begin the real grind of preparation by pushing my body to the extent of its capability—and a little bit further each day. I tired more quickly and felt sore as hell after every physical challenge, but I couldn't imagine pushing less than a hundred ten percent.

Throughout the year, Red Bull had been filming my surgeries and rehab, with the intention of creating a documentary about my recovery. I suggested the series culminate with my return to Mexico, so with Erik's help we came up with a crew to accompany Laura and me on our climb. As the winter months waned, Laura and I set a departure date of April twentieth.

In early April, she and I were set to go on a training trip to the Vegas area—yes, Vegas, which had some of the most concentrated climbing in the country. The beautiful, difficult multi-pitch walls in Red Rocks would be the place to test our skills and put us in prime shape for our expedition. The day before we were to leave, Laura called, overjoyed and in tears. She was pregnant. I was thrilled for her because she was so happy, but then she told me how bad she felt about our plans—she could go to Red Rocks but not to Mexico.

I understood, of course, but as soon as we hung up reality hit: *Wait, who will be my climbing partner?* More to the point: *Do I need to go so soon?* I'd kept plans for my return trip under wraps, so there was no external pressure to go in April. I could forgo the trip if I wanted—take the pressure off myself—but that didn't feel like the right answer. Instead, I became even more hell-bent on making the trip happen. I knew it was what I needed, mentally and physically. It was to be my reward for all the weeks and months I'd spent healing and recovering. I couldn't fathom a delay.

One of the few people I had told about Mexico was my good friend and mentor, Lynn Hill. She had been climbing around Boulder with me since February, helping me train. I called her as soon as I got off the phone with Laura. *Lynn will have a solution.* "Lynn, Laura can't make it. I'm stuck. I don't know what to do!" We talked a little until it hit me. I blurted out, "Hey, any chance you'd want to go?"

Lynn paused long enough for me to think that I'd lost the connection. "Let me get back to you," she said. "It sounds amazing, but I don't know. It's a big climb and short notice. Let me think about it."

We left it at that. I went off to Vegas, as scheduled, to confront my fears about climbing on rock again. Those fears weren't only about falling and rocks breaking—like in my nightmares— they were also about my hips and the potential for pain, and the concern about muscles that had been immobilized and re-wired. *Could my hips even manage a big lead fall—the type of fall that meant over twenty feet of free falling on a rope before being caught by my harness?*

While I was in Vegas, Lynn called. She would go with me to support my climb but asked if we could delay the trip by two weeks. *Two weeks? Sure! Absolutely!* I put aside any concerns I had about moving our climb into hotter weather. It wouldn't matter, because not only would I have a climbing partner, I would also be attempting Logical Progression with my absolute hero, the legendary Lynn Hill. It would be a dream come true.

A week later, Lynn had a family emergency and had to drop out. I was less than ten days away from my new departure date and back at the drawing board. I couldn't imagine who might be able to go with me on such short notice. As I headed out to train in the South Platte of Colorado—an area known for its technical limestone climbing—with my friend Vian Charbonneau, I unloaded the whole disappointing string of events.

"I'll go," she said, as matter-of-factly as I would expect from Vian.

"What?" *Had I heard her right?* "Really?"

"Sure. Why not? Sounds amazing." Vian was a fearless, bad-ass climber—one of those people who didn't labor over decisions and didn't sweat the small stuff. I also knew her to say yes to a climb before knowing exactly what she was in for, only because it sounded exciting. I quickly outlined the plan. She didn't blink. I had a climbing partner! We were going to Mexico!

With a week left before departure, our prep kicked into high gear. Our team consisted of Pablo Durana, a documentary cinematographer who would film on the wall; Kevin Capps (Laura's husband), a rock climber and guide who would help Pablo rig static lines to capture the climb; and Luc Forsyth and Carina Hessner, who would film from a nearby vantage point with a drone and a long lens. Our travel was booked and the logistics arranged. All that was left was some last-minute climbing and the same worrisome thoughts that I always tried to bat away before a big expedition. Only this time those thoughts were a lot less unfounded than they'd been before other big climbs.

What if I don't come back? That was dark thinking, for sure, but it was something I always thought at some point before every expedition. Despite doing whatever was in my power to prepare and mitigate risk, I always hit a patch of sadness. I'd think of how much I loved my family and friends. *What if I never see them again?* Before Logical Progression I was also thinking about the life I'd made, waking up next to the person I loved, with my big, overgrown Bernedoodle, Moosechaga, asleep on top of me. I thought, *Man, I hope I don't go and blow this all, this sweet, sweet life.* But then I made peace with myself, as I always did, by remembering that I really didn't have control over my life, not even when I was doing anything and everything to remain safe.

There are untold dangers in life. I think of how a freak accident could happen in my house or in my car or anywhere at any time. A climber friend once said to me, "Nothing bad is going to happen. Until it does." At first I thought, *How depressing.* Then it hit me how illuminating that was. Going into my Logical Progression expedition, I felt especially reflective about everything that could go wrong, because things had already gone wrong. I didn't want to dwell on those things, but I had to give them some space. Soon after, I was excited to move out of that space and more than ready to climb.

On May 5, exactly one year out from my first hip surgery, Vian, Erik, and I left for Chihuahua, Mexico, where we met up with the rest of our team. From Chihuahua we drove to Basaseachi to spend the night so that we could leave at sunup. We had a two-hour hike ahead of us, but we'd need to make multiple trips, back and forth, to bring everything we needed—one of the reasons Erik had "volunteered" himself. Once in Basaseachi, it was time to organize our gear.

I don't think I'd ever been as excited by the process of organizing my gear—or as meticulous. I'd been given a fresh start on climbing, and on the possibilities that lay ahead. No part of the task seemed tedious or too small. It was like reciting a poem that I was thrilled to remember after such a long year—though, as exciting as it was to imagine being exposed to the elements of a big wall, it was also terrifying. There were all the ropes, the hardware, the equipment that Vian and the production team and I needed, and the static and dynamic lines—two hundred pounds' worth. The portaledges weighed twelve pounds each.

They're bulky and tall, but they fit in a 140-liter "haul bag," a super-durable pack that I'd carry on my back.

I laid out my own climbing kit: climbing shoes specific to the terrain of Logical Progression—a stiffer rand (insole) for very technical climbing, a softer, more malleable shoe for steep climbing. My personal gear—sleeping bag, nail clippers, layering jackets, and face wipes (no change of clothes or showers on the wall), my "Shewee" (a female urination device so I can pee standing up), poop bags and bucket, freeze-dried food for all four of us for dinner, a Jetboil for cooking, nutrition bars for the day (no fresh vegetables, thus the need for my SEND Bars), a couple cans of Red Bull, individual packs of coffee (always coffee), and oatmeal.

And water, the most important survival ingredient. Three liters per person per day—approximately 220 pounds total. Every single day of water and meals was planned in order to bring the minimum supply for the maximum output (allowing for enough food in case weather conditions resulted in an additional day). We'd have enough for seven days on the wall, but we were planning on six—five days climbing, one rest day, one day rappelling. If we went past seven days, we would run out of food and supplies on the wall. *No pressure.*

By sunset the next day we had transported all our gear and supplies to the top of the wall. Tiny Almada had joined our crew to help guide Carina, Luc, and Erik to the vantage point where they would capture the climb—although Erik would have to leave in a day for his work back in the real world. That night we all camped out at the top so that Kevin, Pablo, Vian, and I could start rappelling the route first thing in the morning. At sunrise, I hugged Erik goodbye, trying not to let anyone else see how teary I was. I took a few seconds to gain my composure, and then I joined the others for our descent.

While on a wall, it's not possible to bivvy just anywhere. It's crucial to find a place with protection from rock fall, ideally on some form of natural ledge. There were two ledges on the three-thousand-foot wall, one at the eighteenth pitch and one at the top of the eighth. Before starting our rappel, we divided our gear and supplies into two haul bags to stash at each of the bivvy spots as we lowered. In doing that, we committed to reaching our first bivvy at the end of our first day climbing, which meant that we'd need to make it to our second bivvy, at pitch eighteen, by the end of day two.

We rappelled one after another, with Kevin leading. He would locate the anchor points at the top of each pitch and then tie off the rope at the anchor and set it as a static line for the rest of us to follow. Because a static line/rope has very little stretch, it is most efficient when hauling a load, rappelling, or filming; in contrast, a dynamic rope, designed to stretch to absorb the impact of a fall, is used for ascents. We set some of our static lines on the pitches we planned on filming. That way, when Vian and I were climbing, Pablo could ascend the static line with his camera and hang next to us.

We hadn't brought enough static line to fix the entire route, because that would have required three thousand feet of static—and an extra rigger—so as we rappelled we set the top with a portion of what we had. Ideally, an extra rigger would have been helpful, given how big the wall was, but it would have made for a crowd. Even if we did have another rigger to help Kevin, it would have been logistically challenging to try and capture every one of the twenty-eight pitches. Instead, we were selective in choosing which pitches to film. By 11 P.M. we made it down to the top of the eighth pitch and set up our initial portaledge. The next day we would continue our rappel to the base of the wall.

We were pretty wiped from that first day. Because the trip

had been twice delayed, we were headed into Mexico's summer months—the driest, balmiest weather is usually from November to March. Already, the sun felt blazingly hot on the wall, but what had really crushed me was the rappel. I'd been worried enough about the pressure of the harness against my hips, but the extra hundred-pound backpack tugging at my body increased the pressure twofold. The pain was so intensely familiar, I wondered if I had torn my labrum again, although that definitely wasn't information I needed to share with anyone else. Everyone was there because of me. I needed to stuff it and groan into my giant bottle of Advil.

On our first day of climbing, I led through the first four pitches. Only halfway through, we were already in direct sunlight, which made the technical, sharp edges on the climb even more challenging. Vian took the lead on five and six, and then I took over again on seven and eight while Luc shot us from across the valley. Pablo and Kevin had remained on the bivvy so that they could set up the static line on pitch nine, from which Pablo would film me as I finished those last two pitches. That way, he would also be in position to film the next pitch.

When we reached our bivvy at the top of pitch eight, I felt it would be best to knock out pitch nine as well, meaning that I would figure out the moves so that we'd be more likely to send it in one try. Pitch nine was one of the more challenging pitches, so I didn't want it to be the first thing I climbed the next morning after waking up stiff and sore.

I pulled on the wall, baked from my first full day of climbing. Halfway up on the onsight—my first try—I fell, but instead of checking out the rest of the climb, I lowered back down. I thought that maybe if I took a brief rest I'd have a better shot of succeeding, even if it meant waiting until sundown. With only a sliver of sun left on the horizon, and the sky deepening from blue to purple, I attached a headlamp to my helmet and pulled back on the wall. By the time I made my way up past where I'd fallen, I was surrounded by darkness. Three quarters of the way, my foot popped off a hold, and I fell.

The jolt of the rope on my already spent body intensified each ache and pain. I lowered, determined to give it one more try, even though it was midnight. Clawing and digging and grunting, I pulled from some hidden reserve of energy and sent the pitch. Not a second later, I lowered to our bivvy. We still had eight pitches to go the next day, but at least the first would be that much easier. We had to be up early to beat our uncompromising sun, at least until midday.

Vian and I woke with our sights on the tenth through eighteenth pitches, at which point we would reach our second bivvy. We worked through several pitches, but by afternoon we were scorched. It had taken me several tries to send one of the pitches, so at that point we decided to wait out the worst of the sun. For several hours, Vian and I hung in our harnesses, laughing at the ridiculousness of climbing a three-thousand-foot wall, in summertime, in Mexico. She admitted that she hadn't known all that much about the climb when she committed to coming with me. In fact, true to Vian's adventurous nature, she'd made her decision on a whim. "Would you have still come if you knew all this beforehand?" I asked her.

"Hmm. Eat freeze-dried food, be exhausted, pee all over each other, and deal with you stressing out about sending this climb? Maybe not?" she kidded, though the peeing part was no joke.

Because our climb was being filmed, we were acutely aware of both our cameramen—Pablo, who was on the wall with us, and Luc, situated across the valley with a long lens on us. When we needed to pee—which was fairly frequently—we would radio over to them, "Peeing." We'd move as far from the climb as we could manage, quickly drop our pants below our harnesses, stick our butts out into the open air, and urinate. Oftentimes, though, the wind would pick up and the urine would updraft. I was sprayed by Vian, and she was sprayed by me. As gross as it was, it was also one of those things we had to laugh about before moving on. What else could we do?

By day's end we were exhausted, and we'd only managed pitches ten through thirteen. Between 2 P.M. and 7 P.M. we'd been in the most direct rays of the sun, the rock like hot coal beneath us, searing our already raw skin. Those four pitches alone had totally destroyed us, and we still had four more to go to reach our second bivvy. Aside from the fact that it would be tremendously difficult to make our way back down to our first bivvy, none of our supplies were there anymore, and Pablo and Kevin had long gone ahead with gear to stash at the next bivvy. As darkness descended, we found ourselves at the base of pitch fourteen, the pitch that Nolan had fallen from.

There were few ways I could completely mitigate the risk on this wall, but I had assured my mom we would take every precaution to make our climb as safe as possible. One of those precautions was to climb only during daytime, especially since Nolan's accident had happened in the dark of night. Even though I'd already broken that promise, the last thing I wanted to do was to climb through the night on the pitch that had cost our team member his life, the same pitch I'd been haunted by for months—the scene of the crime.

I'd dreaded reaching it, but I also felt driven by it. I vowed going into Logical Progression that I would climb pitch fourteen in daylight so that I'd be aware of the integrity of every hold. In daylight, I'd be protected. In daylight, rock wouldn't peel off, cut my rope, and leave my body at the base of the mountain for my family to retrieve. But there were no deals to be made with the mountain, and no guarantee that daylight would triumph over darkness, especially if we were left to hang in our harnesses all night—which we would be forced to do if we didn't make it to our second bivvy.

I advanced slowly, sending my headlamp beam all around me, on everything in my path, on everything I touched, but it was still taking longer than I'd hoped to find the route. After about twenty minutes, I had climbed for fifty or sixty feet— about halfway up the pitch—when my headlamp started to flicker on the rock. But it wasn't just any random portion of rock. It was flickering, like a signal, right at a huge scar in the wall—a scar from a fairly new break where a massive chunk had dislodged.

My entire body tensed, as though every square inch of it was gripping the wall. For a moment, I dared not even move my head, but when I did, I saw the bolt that had clearly been struck by the fallen rock. It was intact but banged, hinting at what had unfolded a year earlier. I imagined Nolan standing on what had been a gigantic chunk of rock. Maybe he was about to clip his rope or rest when the rock dislodged. All I knew for sure was Aaron's account of seeing his best friend drop past him in the dark, the light from his headlamp disappearing into the abyss below.

I felt paralyzed with fear. *This is it. I don't know what to do.* It was the middle of the night, and my headlamp was dying. I had climbed too high above a steep section of wall to lower from my position and return to belay Vian. I took a deep breath. *I've done this before.* I exhaled and then breathed in and out a few more times. *You've got this,* I assured myself.

I switched my headlamp to its lowest mode to conserve the battery, and then I started to climb, this time more quickly than before, as I talked myself through the process: *Left hand. Move right foot. Right hand. Left hand up. Move left foot. Push. Okay, come on. Keep going.* I reached the anchor with enough light left to set up my belay for Vian. I nearly howled with relief as I belayed her. She pulled up beside me, with replacement batteries in our backpack. We were doing this. "Let's get to the bivvy."

The next day, our fourth on the wall, we had to rest. We did nothing except hang out on the portaledge, refueling and playing card games into the evening. From then on, we woke before sunrise to get the most climbing out of the day, navigating the difficult, dimly lit terrain as safely as possible. Of the twenty-eight pitches, over half were 5.12s and 5.13s on a mixture of solid and fragile rock—thin, chip-like rock that could easily pop off the wall, which is what made the route so challenging. We waited out the hottest hours, hanging in our harnesses until sunset. Afterward we climbed into the "headlamp hours"—when it was dark enough to warrant using headlamps.

On day five we completed pitches fifteen through eighteen, the ones we'd failed to send on day two. Day three of climbing—and our fifth on the wall—saw us through pitches nineteen through twenty-three. On the final day, the last we had scheduled for our attempt, we powered through twenty-three to twenty-seven. There was only one more to go.

At the bottom of the final pitch, my throat started to tighten, as though it was holding back a year's worth of emotions. A week prior, we'd all stood at the top of Logical Progression, humbled, excited, full of uncertainty, looking down over the three-thousand-foot drop. Now our journey was coming to an end. I thought back to the days in the hospital, to crying in my bed, missing my life, missing my normal routine, wondering what the future would hold. I thought about all the ways in which this climb had consumed me over the last year, and how it had compelled me to return.

I was past the point of fatigue—I could hardly stand—but it was time to go. I tightened the laces on my shoes. One more pitch. I climbed, hyperaware of the grit beneath my fingertips, feeling liberated, in control, and a little disbelieving. As I crested the top of the wall, I secured myself to the anchor and belayed Vian up.

We hugged and high-fived, nearly delirious in our joy. A surge of some other emotion coursed through my body like an electrical current. It wasn't unpleasant, but it took me by surprise. I covered my face with my hands and fell to my knees, and I did what I had never imagined doing at the top of a climb: I wept.

When I looked up and out at the valley below, I couldn't help but think of the climbers who had come before me, and how, in that moment, we were all connected. Nothing about the mountain or its capacity to connect generations of climbers had changed. Meanwhile, so much had changed. I thought about Nolan and the people I'd known who, despite their talent and heart, had succumbed on climbs. I felt connected to them as well. I felt a part of something so much bigger than anything I'd imagined.

20

Before the start of our climb, while hiking to the top of Logical Progression under a canopy of trees competing for the rays of early morning sunlight, I happened to fall in line with one of our crew members, Tiny Almada. Mostly we were silent, save for the crunching of brush under our boots and the sounds of the forest melding together in a reassuring drone. I couldn't say what came before or after, but I do remember at one point Tiny telling me, "Doing big walls reminds us that we are very small, but capable of doing big things."

I cannot articulate a simpler, more profound explanation of why I've spent nearly my entire life as a climber. There is nothing in the world as freeing as climbing up and away from the earth on a big wall. At times, on a climb, I have wondered: *How is it possible that I'm here, twenty feet . . . two hundred feet . . . two thousand feet off the ground?*

I know how fortunate I've been to have realized my passion and to have discovered this *place* where I've flourished and learned so many things about myself and about the world around me. I say "place" because climbing has been so much more than a sport for me, it has been a state of mind and my approach to life—a *place* where I have been able to express every part of me. One of my earliest memories is of that place.

I'm sitting in the paint bucket—my five-year-old, three-and-a-half-foot frame folded with my knees to my chin. My brother has rigged the bucket with a clothesline and tied it to the banister at the top of our staircase. Slowly, he lowers it—and me—over the banister. Peering over the lip, I can see the hardwood floor of our house way below. Suspended by a rope, high in the air, I feel weirdly calm and happy, bigger than myself and even a little invincible—until my mom walks into view, sees us, and screams.

Of course, I had no idea when I started climbing that I would still be at it twenty-five years later. I could never have imagined that my passion would become my purpose, but that's what this journey has amounted to. Climbing has been, and still is, my compass in life—it's like running toward a finish line that moves farther and farther away the closer I get to it. The challenge never ends. I have achieved small goals and huge objectives along the way, but this journey—this lifelong climbing expedition of mine—is ongoing.

Climbing has given me strength and confidence and a window into myself. It has required me to lay it all on the line to accomplish goals in every aspect of my life. It has provided me with a sense of who I am—from my awareness of my body and the way that each part of it moves to my relationship with nature. At the most basic level, it has required the best of me. It has served as my passport to see the world. It has led me to adventures in over fifty countries—in forests, jungles, and wide-open savannas, over lakes, rivers, and ocean waters.

Early on I realized that climbing outdoors was where I felt the most alive. Being in the outdoors—no matter where, no matter the climate or season—has not only given me an appreciation of this awe-inspiring natural world, it has also reminded me of my responsibilities as one of its residents.

At a party a few years back, I overheard a woman say to my mother, "Every time I hear about what Sasha does, I think, *I'm so glad that's not my daughter!*" To Mom's credit, she said that she didn't feel climbing was more dangerous than most contact sports, and that climbing had given me the focus to accomplish anything I set my mind to. But I understood that woman's fear. I also understood that it stemmed mostly from a fear of the unknown. We all have fears. The challenge in life is to understand the difference between rational and irrational fear—to harness one and conquer the other.

Through climbing, I have come to that understanding. Certainly, I was privileged to grow up in a household that respected me as a woman and saw me as an equal to my brother. I had parents who believed in me, supported my endeavors, and encouraged me to put my whole heart into whatever gave me joy. Still, despite that privilege, I struggled with disordered eating and feelings of inadequacy. I was dismissed for not looking like someone who could excel at my sport. I was underestimated, and my abilities and successes were questioned, but at the end of the day, those negatives propelled me in a positive direction.

My disordered eating drove me to learn everything I could about nutrition and to start a company dedicated to creating a product to nourish and replenish the body. The naysayers taught me that everyone has their own agenda—I can't change that. They will always be around, always coming from a place of fear or competition. Because of them, I have learned to surround myself with people who believe in the possibilities in life. I've also learned the importance of paying forward that belief.

For that reason, I continue to work with organizations that

provide opportunities to young people to take part in sports, to have an education, to travel the world and see beautiful places, and to push past pain and suffering. I encourage everyone to embrace their pain, acknowledge their strengths and weaknesses, and build their own personal team, whether in friendship, partnership, business, or sports. The teams I've been part of—as a young amateur athlete just starting out, as a professional climber, and as a businessperson—have enriched my life in ways I cannot even measure.

Who knows what would have transpired if I'd been a whiz at physics or math, or if I'd continued with my first loves of ice-skating or skiing? As it happened, climbing turned out to be the through line for nearly everything in my life, everything that I've become. Climbing has led me to live and see with an open heart, to feel empowered and confident in my own skin, to be appreciative and grateful for this body of mine, to have deep relationships with family and friends, and to be part of one of the greatest communities I know. It has allowed me to take the lead in my own life.

EPILOGUE

In the summer of 2022, after nearly a year of planning, I led fellow pro climbers Matilda Söderlund and Brette Harrington on a monthlong expedition in the Picos de Europa mountain range in Spain. Our trio made history as the first all-female team to successfully climb a 5.14b big wall.

I also realized a ten-year-long dream with the launch of my superfood energy-bar company, SEND Bars.

ACKNOWLEDGMENTS

When I began writing this book, I was at an inflection point in my life. With plenty of adventures ahead of me that I aspire to, I chose to write this book now because I have a story to tell that has brought me to my next chapter.

I could not have written this book without the help of my friends, my family, my team, and everyone who has supported me along the way. In the process of writing this book I was also reminded of the importance of cherishing the time with the ones we hold large spaces for in our hearts. Time is not guaranteed.

To my mom, for being my greatest fan. Who was never fazed by planes, trains, nor automobiles. For accompanying me around the world; from random warehouse gyms to beautiful places in the outdoors. You learned to belay so that you could further support me and my climbing. Thank you for always believing in me. For your love, your support, and your confidence. Thank you for being my inspiration to be independent, stalwart, and committed to following my passion. You have taught me to be inquisitive about the world and to keep an open mind. There are not enough words to describe the love that I have for you, and the love that I know you have for me.

Dad, I miss you every day. But I feel your presence above me. During my wildest, most weather-conditional climbs, when the sky opens, I feel your presence. When I reach the top of the mountain and a beam of light shines from the sky, I see you. While you may not physically be here, I know you are with me, still, looking over us. I love you, thank you for teaching me how to dream. And thank you for giving me my stubbornness to not give up.

To my brother, Charlie. For always pushing me, inspiring me, and for being the best big brother I could ever wish for. And thank you for having that birthday party! I love you and will always be your greatest fan. Now let's go ski in Japan!

My Erik. My rock. For always being there for me. For being the hardest-working human I know and for inspiring me. You are my home. To our fur family. To the adventures we have had and all that we will continue to see and become. I look forward to expanding our world together.

To Karen Rizzo. Who helped me find my words when I couldn't. Who took my, at times, incohesive thoughts and clarified them. Who understood me and my message, and helped me capture it and put it on these pages. This story would not have been possible without you.

To my editorial team. Joy Tutela, who met me as a second-year college student and waited until I was ready to tell my story, and for helping me make that a reality. Alice Pfeifer, Hannah Phillips, and everyone at St. Martin's Press: thank you for being an absolute joy to work with.

To my family. My cousins, namely Sadie, Jessie, and Saul, Katie, and Patrick. You are like my additional siblings. To all the memories and the love and support you have always shown me. To Aunty Deborah, Aunty Judy, Uncle Stephen, Aunt Missy, and my dad's younger twin, Uncle Lenny. And to Anne, Alan, Aletta, Ingrid, Rich, and my nieces, Finley and Adeline. I cannot wait to experience the world with you as you grow up!

While I have had the privilege to define my own path, Lynn Hill was the true pioneer who set this foundation before me. It is hard to believe that, after growing up with a poster of you on my wall, I now have the true honor of calling you my friend. Thank you for being my mentor and for setting the absolute standard for women and men in rock climbing. You are a true legend.

And to Conrad Anker. For being the steward of the outdoors; for opening the gates for everyone in this community to feel welcomed, valued, and a part of this global climbing family. You are a true mentor and friend, and I value everything that you continue to do for our sport and for our environment.

To my team at WME/IMG. Jeff, you're the greatest agent I could ask for. Thank you for always supporting me and believing in the dream.

To my best friend, Chelsea Balboni. To think, over a decade of friendship later, we would end up living on the same street, cofounding a business together. For dropping everything and going on whimsical adventures at an hour's notice. And to my godson, Giorgio. You are the brightest star!

To my fellow cofounders and business wives at SEND Bars, Alex Hanifin and Arianne Jones. I could not ask for a better team with whom to embark on this great journey!

To my coaches: Claudiu Vidulescu, Vadim Vinokur, Kevin Paretti, Brendan Killian, Alex Puccio, Robin O'Leary. For believing in me, pushing me, and being with me every step of the way.

To my sponsors. In particular, to my longest-standing

partners. Adidas, which signed me when I was a senior in high school and helped make my dream a reality, and Red Bull, which I have worked with since my first year in college. Thank you for putting climbing on the map, for the opportunities, and the incredible support. You have made me feel as if I am a part of a true family. Greg, Allison, Diane, Larry, Anton, and everyone at Agron; thank you for believing in me at such an early age and for quickly becoming my West Coast family!

To my teachers. My friends. My community. My colleagues.

To the Women's Sports Foundation, Right to Play, Up2Us Sports, Access Fund, American Alpine Club, and Ascend Athletics. For harnessing the power of sports and enriching the lives of young boys, girls, women, and men, around the world.

To the strong women who are proud to achieve greatness and inspire others to continue.

To all the adventurers in every field of endeavor, who push beyond the limits.

And, to those brave stewards of our planet who at this moment are fighting for its very life.

THE CLIMBS OF *TAKE THE LEAD*